ECONOMIC GROWTH AND RESOURCES
Volume 3: Natural Resources

INTERNATIONAL ECONOMIC ASSOCIATION PUBLICATIONS

Monopoly and Competition and their Regulation
The Economic Consequences of the Size of Nations
The Theory of Capital
Inflation
The Economics of Take-off into Sustained Growth
International Trade Theory in a Developing World
The Theory of Interest Rates
The Economics of Education
Problems in Economic Development
Price Formation in Various Economies
The Distribution of National Income
Risk and Uncertainty
Economic Problems of Agriculture in Industrial Societies
International Economic Relations
Backward Areas in Advanced Countries
Public Economics
Economic Development in South Asia
North American and Western European Economic Policies
Planning and Market Relations
The Gap Between Rich and Poor Nations
Latin America in the International Economy
Models of Economic Growth
Science and Technology in Economic Growth
Allocation under Uncertainty
Transport and the Urban Environment
The Economics of Health and Medical Care
The Management of Water Quality and the Environment
Agriculture Policy in Developing Countries
The Economic Development of Bangladesh
Economic Factors in Population Growth
Classics in the Theory of Public Finance
Methods of Long-term Planning and Forecasting
Economic Integration
The Economics of Public Services
The Organisation and Retrieval of Economic Knowledge
The Microeconomic Foundations of Macroeconomics
Economic Relations between East and West
Econometric Contributions to Public Policy
Appropriate Technologies for Third World Development
Economic Growth and Resources (5 volumes)

Economic Growth and Resources

Volume 3
Natural Resources

Proceedings of the Fifth World Congress of
the International Economic Association
held in Tokyo, Japan

**EDITED BY
CHRISTOPHER BLISS AND
M. BOSERUP**

First published 1980 by
THE MACMILLAN PRESS LTD
London and Basingstoke
Companies and representatives
throughout the world

Typeset in Great Britain by
PINTAIL STUDIOS LTD
Ringwood, Hampshire
and printed by
REDWOOD BURN LTD
Trowbridge and Esher

British Library Cataloguing in Publication Data

International Economic Association. *Congress, 5th,*
Tokyo, 1977
    Economic growth and resources.
    Vol. 3: Natural resources.
    1. Economic policy – Congresses
    I. Title
    II. Bliss, Christopher
    330.9   HD82

ISBN 0-333-27777-5

Mogens Boserup
1910–1978

Mogens Boserup's name appears on the title page as one of the two editors of this volume. He had played the major role in planning this part of the work of the Tokyo Congress, had contributed the very valuable paper which appears below as Chapter 4, and had been an active participant in the discussions of the other papers here printed. He had agreed to act as editor of this volume in collaboration with Christopher Bliss and had already started work on it before his sudden and unexpected death in the early days of 1978.

This book and his chapter in it represent, in effect, Mogens Boserup's last contribution to economics. A scholar of great distinction and learning, he had played an important part in several earlier conferences of the International Economic Association. The world, as well as Denmark, is much the poorer for his loss.

AUSTIN ROBINSON
(General Editor)

Contents

Introduction

Christopher Bliss
NUFFIELD COLLEGE, OXFORD

Economists have often been ridiculed for their failure to agree and nearly everyone has heard the joke about Keynes in the company of n economists (I have heard the story told for various values of n) giving rise to $n + 1$ inconsistent opinions. Sometimes it is argued that disagreement is not disreputable, rather the sign of a healthy and lively science, but this claim cannot be taken seriously with regard to the whole field. Ideally one would hope for a variety of views and beliefs at the margin of knowledge, in those areas in which the subject is currently being advanced, but founded in concord concerning the basics of the subject. Otherwise the situation would soon be reached, to which sociology has sometimes seemed uncomfortably close, in which the practitioners of the subject end up arguing about methodology and defending their academic credentials against outsiders and against themselves.

However the fact is that economists have a high propensity to agree, certainly when they are compared to other social scientists. The extent of agreement varies over time in different areas within the discipline, and notoriously it has declined in recent years in the crucial area of macroeconomics and monetary theory. But, speaking generally, for most economists most of the time, argument is more usually concerned with detail than with fundamentals. Of course this is not to say that economists of different views will not, as indeed they do, advertise their differences and play down their agreement.

This is nowhere more true than with regard to the economics of natural resources. At a time when the general public seem to be sharply divided, and when the pronouncements of prophets of 'Doomsday' are given a respectful hearing, economists seem to be united in what might appear to be an almost stultifying complacency. It is very difficult to persuade economists to take seriously the claim that the world has only a few years beyond the year 2000 before it must collapse, or grind to a halt or blow itself to pieces. Why is this?

First of all, on closer examination, the unity in the ranks of the economists is not quite so complete as the above description would imply. A few economists, notably Professor E. J. Mishan of the London School of Economics, have adopted a strongly 'anti-growth' point of view (see Mishan, 1977) but their arguments have usually been along different lines from those of the World Dynamics school (see Forrester, 1971 and Meadows *et al.*, 1972). Economists have been more ready to take seriously the social problems of economic growth and the issue of external diseconomies than they have been to accept the, literally, neo-Malthusian claim that the world will be run into an inexorable contradiction between finiteness and inevitably-exponential growth.

Secondly, the unity is to some extent a consequence of the Forrester–Meadows approach to prognosis and the influence which this approach has enjoyed. Economists may disagree about many things, but they unite in recognising slip-shod forecasting methods and 'measurement without theory'. After all, it was Malthus' views in particular that got economics the reputation of being the dismal science, so that it would be surprising if the failure of Malthus' predictions to stand up against experience had not taught economists to be careful about conclusions derived from arithmetic arguments unsupported by solid evidence.

Finally, it is natural to the economists to think about the effects of imbalances between supply and demand on prices and, in turn, the effect of prices on the demand for substitutes and, again, on the character of technical progress. It is almost a truism that eventually supply and demand for limited resources will be balanced. A possible mechanism is collapse of the world economy. But one needs to examine also the possibility of real prices for scarce resources increasing and that this will:

(1) increase the supply through new discoveries, the substitution of alternative inputs, recycling, and so on (substitution in supply);
(2) decrease demand through switching of expenditure to alternative products which make less intensive use of the inputs in short supply; and
(3) decrease demand through slowing down economic growth.

Broadly, the World Dynamics approach assumes that (1) and (2) will only happen to a limited extent and that (3) can come about only through a catastrophic collapse of the international economic system. It has often been said that this shows a failure to take account of economic theory, but one could equally well say that it shows a failure to learn the lessons that history has to teach us. Substitution in use and in final demand are phenomena that have been going on throughout the span of recorded history. A non-catastrophic slowing down of economic growth is something that has not been experienced frequently, if at all, but that is not to say that it is beyond our powers to achieve it if that is what is demanded.

OPTIMAL USE OF NON-RENEWABLE RESOURCES

Non-renewable resources pose a number of problems for the economist. Some of these problems are logical and theoretical, some are strictly empirical, and in both cases research to answer the main questions is still at an early stage.

The central question of a theoretical kind has to do with the optimal rate of depletion of a non-renewable resource. This apparently simple and basic question gives rise to some unexpected, even to paradoxical results. For this reason it merits the attention that it has received in the literature, even though some of the findings are not easy to apply. The paper by Koopmans in this volume takes a step towards bringing the theory into contact with the current questions of policy debate, by considering the transition from a scarce-resource-using technology to one which dispenses with that resource. This is of obvious importance in the light of current considerations of the long-term planning of energy where we have, presently, techniques which use non-renewable resources and, also, the prospect of techniques in the future which will use only exceedingly abundant resources. Nuclear fusion is the most exciting possibility under the latter heading.

To deal with this kind of question one needs both optimal rules for using up non-renewable resources and the data to apply those rules to the particular case to hand. At present we lack both rules that can be readily applied outside simple and stylised cases and, particularly, the information concerning stocks of resources and the future development of technology.

To introduce some purely theoretical questions, consider an exceedingly simplified model of an economy. We will assume that final output is produced from capital, K, and resources, R. Labour will not be taken into account explicitly, which would be appropriate if the growth of population were to be independent of consumption, the level of capital and the remaining supply of renewable resources. A long time ago, Frank Ramsey introduced a very simple rule for the optimal rate of saving (capital accumulation) in a growth model (see Ramsey, 1928). This rule, sometimes called the Keynes–Ramsey Rule after Keynes' elegant intuitive justification of it, has the interesting property that the rate of saving is shown to be independent of the production function, except in so far as the production function plays a role in determining 'Bliss', the point of maximal attainable utility. This result depends upon Ramsey's assumption that future utility is not discounted.

It is easy to show that (i) Ramsey's conclusion does not apply where there are exhaustible resources: the production function will play a role in determining the rate of saving; and (ii) the presence of exhaustible resources will lead to a higher optimal rate of saving than would be the case without exhaustible resources.

Ramsey supposed that the optimal saving plan is chosen so as to minimise the integral of 'Bliss' (the highest utility attainable) and the actual level of utility. Denote utility by U and consumption by C, then the criterion is:

$$\text{Minimise} \int_t^\infty [B - U(C)]\, dt \tag{1}$$

The lowest value that (1) can be made to take depends upon the quantity of capital available to the economy at time t and the level of exhaustible resources at t, denoted respectively K_t and R_t. We denote this minimised value $V(K_t, R_t)$. The interesting point is that we do not need to know very much about V, or about the production function that lies behind it. It would be plausible to assume that the level of output depends positively on K and on the rate at which resources are being depleted, $\dot{R}$ (a dot over a variable will denote the derivative of that variable with respect to time). Perhaps R itself will contribute to the current level of output because, where there is more of a resource left, less resources have to be allocated to 'mining' it. What we do need to assume is that V decreases (higher valuation) with an increase in K and with an increase in R. Then

$$V(K_t, R_t) = \int_t^\infty [B - U(C_t)]\, dt, \tag{2}$$

where C_t is the optimal function chosen to minimise (1) subject to constraints of feasibility.

Differentiating both sides of (2) with respect to time gives:

$$V_K \dot{K} + V_R \dot{R} = -[B - U(C_t)], \tag{3}$$

where

$$V_K = \frac{\partial V}{\partial K}, \quad \text{and} \quad V_R = \frac{\partial V}{\partial R}.$$

On an optimal path we must be indifferent at the margin between consuming and saving output. Hence V_K must equal $-u(C)$, where $u(C)$ is the marginal utility of consumption. Rearranging (3) and taking this result into account yields:

$$\dot{K} = \frac{B - U(C_t) + V_R \dot{R}}{u(C_t)}, \tag{4}$$

the generalised Keynes–Ramsey Rule. Where $V_K = 0$, as would be the case were the use of resources to make no difference to the integral of utility; or $\dot{R} = 0$, it is optimal not to use up the resource at all, then (4) reduces to the familiar Keynes–Ramsey Rule, and the production function plays no direct role in determining the rate of saving. But, typically, V_R and $\dot{R}$ will be negative, so that *the economy saves more for a given level of consumption when it is depleting resources than it would were no non-renewable resources present.*[1]

This result is not surprising, but it has to be considered in conjunction with the point that Ramsey's rule leads anyway to implausibly high rates of saving. Non-renewable resources only make the embarrassment of this type of conclusion more marked.

One argument which is often advanced to explain away the high rates of saving to which Ramsey's model can give rise is uncertainty about the future. The consequence of bringing in uncertainty is by no means unambiguous (see Foldes, 1978) and is anyway very complicated, but it is without doubt a very

---

[1] One cannot simply conclude that the scarcity of resources should lead to a higher rate of saving, because output will be different in the two cases.

crucial consideration where non-renewable resources are concerned. It would make a great contribution to the decisions concerning investment and the rate of depletion of resources if our knowledge about the availability of those resources and the future possibilities of substituting for them were better.

Most calculations concerning future critical shortages of resources have focused on energy and this is no doubt partly to be explained by the reaction to the OPEC cartel and the sharp increase in oil prices of 1973. If one makes some far-reaching but not implausible assumptions it is easy to show that the earth's energy resources are so enormous that it will take a very long time for them to be used up. But serious discussions of the issue, such as those that follow, note a number of important caveats. Sassin and Häfele make very clear the crucial point that it is not the quantity of energy but the 'negentropy' of the various energy sources that matters. If we could cool all the earth's oceans by 0.1°C and capture the energy released, the amount of energy generated would be enormous. But, in fact, one cannot use such a high entropy source.

This suggests, as Boserup argues, that 'resources' is a concept that needs to be refined if we are to arrive at something of economic relevance. One wants something closer to 'economically exploitable resources', but this defines a variable which will alter in value as prices and technology develop over time. Those who were unduly pessimistic about resources in the past usually erred in failing to predict how fast the proportion of resources that would in due course prove to be economically exploitable would increase relatively to the total supply. The economist would naturally think about diminishing returns in this context, but there is no law of diminishing returns where technical progress is concerned.

Food and population have figured less centrally in recent discussions than used to be the case. In this sense, Malthusianism has not enjoyed a revival. Probably the reason is that technical progress in food crops has been very marked and, also, that population growth rates, even in underdeveloped countries, have shown signs of slowing down.

However, these are problems which are not only, or even mainly, global problems. One of the things that is wrong with the 'Spaceship Earth' analogy, criticised by Boserup, is that it suggests a unity of purpose and an aggregation of supplies and needs which it would not be realistic to assume on experience to date. It has sometimes been claimed that the world could solve its food problems for some time if the resources put into trying to grow more food in Asia were put instead into increasing the output of North American farmers. Perhaps it is so, but consider the political implications of a world in which the political control of something as vital as food were to be localised in one country or region.

Parallel issues arise with regard to resources such as minerals, which Radetzki shows to be globally available in such abundance that we could think in terms of millions of years' supplies for most of them. If there are countries or regions which will turn out to be in resource deficit for economically exploitable resources, then there could be problems of transfer and adjustment, despite a globally adequate supply. How serious such problems will prove to be is, of course, a function of the cost of resources relative to labour. This has shown a secular downward trend in the past for most resources and the optimistic estimates of availability to which the authors of the following papers usually incline would lead one to expect a continuation of that trend.

The fact that, measured in labour time, the cost of resources has been going down, makes all the more impressive the continuing technical progress of a resource-saving character that we have witnessed. One might be tempted to infer that there is even more scope for this type of technical change, a scope which would have become apparent had relative prices developed according to a different pattern. The economic theory which would be most relevant to thinking about this question would be the theory of induced innovation, because it is the long-run substitutability between inputs, taking into account induced technical progress, which matters for the question, not the short-run elasticity of substitution. Rosenberg's paper argues, interestingly, that United States technical progress was influenced, relative to its European counterpart, by the abundance of resources in that country, but notes also the important point that changes in tastes may be resource-using as people, for example, grow to want open spaces and clean water.

Although technical progress has been a very popular subject for economists to study, there is still a great deal that we ought to know about it which is at present the subject for, at best, speculation. The gaps in our knowledge will need theory and econometric investigation if they are to be filled in. It is encouraging, however, to see that all the discussions of the issue included in this volume regard technical change as an economic activity which can be explained by the search for cost savings and economic improvements. Compared to the mindless exponential extrapolation of the World Dynamics school one feels that there is the possibility of some real insight here. But let no one think that extrapolation is ever easy. The excellent paper by Waelbroeck and his colleagues is infinitely more subtle, and less ambitious with it, than the overblown pretentiousness of the Doomwatchers. But, who could honestly say that the predictions inspire confidence? To say this is only to say that we have before us a need for endless and tireless improvement in our concepts and in our econometric techniques. The exercise does not depend for its justification on the immediate production of accurate forecasts.

If there is some complacency in the air, it is the fault as much of the Global Dynamics practitioners as of the escapist tendencies of humanity. By making the issue one of global availability of resources they have taken the attention away from problems of distribution and of social adjustment. If the world is to see rapid economic growth in the future, and even if per capita incomes stagnate, there will have to be growth in total output to avoid crisis, and there will have to be rapid change in ways of living, in consumption and work patterns, even in international relations. One would have to be extraordinarily complacent to assume that none of this will pose great problems. But the issues concern men, women and institutions and how they will adjust and change, not how exponentials will chase each other until a limit is hit.

REFERENCES

Foldes, L., 'Optimal saving and risk in continuous time', *Review of Economic Studies* (1978).
Forrester, J. W., *World Dynamics* (Cambridge, Mass., 1971).
Meadows, D. H. *et al.*, *The Limits to Growth* (New York, 1972).
Mirrlees, J. A., 'Optimal growth under uncertainty', *Allocation under Uncertainty* (Ed. V. H. Drèze) (London, 1974).
Mishan, E. J., *The Economic Growth Debate* (London, 1977).
Ramsey, F. P., 'A mathematical theory of saving', *Economic Journal* (1928).

Part One
Theories of Exhaustible Resource Use

1 The Transition from Exhaustible to Renewable or Inexhaustible Resources

Tjalling C. Koopmans
YALE UNIVERSITY

I. INTRODUCTION

Allow me to begin with some simple and rather obvious remarks on the nature of the transition problem from exhaustible to renewable or inexhaustible resource use. First, a shift in resource use means also a shift in technology, because in this age resources go together with technologies that process them and put them to use. Secondly, while I have used the word 'exhaustible', the term 'depletion' is a more suitable word, in that it suggests a more gradual process. The later stages of depletion will then whenever possible call forth a substitute resource that allows society to meet the same or a similar need to that met by the resource being depleted. Finally, I will follow the model of price as a regulator that will touch off the substitution, smoothly if the degree and rate of depletion are foreseen sufficiently in advance.

This means that the transition problem is one of phasing out the technology associated with the resource being depleted and phasing in one or more technologies associated with possible substitutes. This process requires research and development for the new technology, if not already known, and a turn-over of the capital stock and retraining of the labour force as needed. Therefore the transition problem is a long-run problem, involving, I would say, something of the nature of 50 to 100 years. Examples of this substitution process abound in the field of energy, and Chapter 2 by Sassin and Häfele in this volume contains several of these.

Another important characteristic of the transition problem is its interdisciplinary nature. It involves technology and engineering; it involves geology whenever resource availability estimates are important; it involves ecology and environmental science to assess and estimate adverse impacts on the environment; and it involves economics to face up to the problem of best use of resources, whether in a market or a planning context or in a mixture of the two regimes. Also, where uncertainty about resource availabilities or future technologies is important, decision theory under uncertainty has an important role. Last but not least, the problem of transition involves ethical considerations in regard to the balancing of the interests of present and future generations. Thus the problem is by its very nature interdisciplinary in character.

Moreover, with regard to the implementation of possible solutions, the problem has international as well as national aspects. As regards the possible effect of fossil fuel combustion on CO_2 in the atmosphere, which may in turn affect climates and crops in various regions – that is undoubtedly a world problem; as regards the transition from coal to nuclear energy (or conversely), that is in part national, in part international.

I tend to regard the communication difficulties arising from the interdisciplinary character of the problem as deserving as much attention as the international aspects. Between the disciplines involved, there is need for more exchange of information, translation of jargon, and debate, interdisciplinary as well as intradisciplinary, to remove the misunderstandings in one profession about the other's terminology and its choices of problems. This difficulty is not one-way, but mutual and universal.

As a modest preparation for these interactions and debates, I will describe and comment on three approaches to the transition problem that are professionally somewhat different, and cite some examples of each without intending this to be regarded as a survey. My examples are illustrations, rarely statements of results, but where they are the latter they are results reached by others.

II. THREE APPROACHES TO THE TRANSITION PROBLEM

What was to have been my *first example*, Hotelling's seminal article on the theory of depletion of resources through competitive markets, under monopoly, and in optimal planning, has already been fully covered elsewhere.

My *second example* is a landmark paper by Dasgupta and Heal, 'The Optimal Depletion of Exhaustible Resources'. I want to comment on some parts of that paper to add substance to the foregoing general observations. The paper has two sections. In each section an optimal allocation problem is considered. In the first one, there is just one resource which is gradually being depleted, and the optimality criterion (or 'objective function') is an integral of the utility of the flow of consumption of that resource over time, discounted with a fixed discount rate δ,

$$U = \int_0^\infty e^{-\delta t}\, U(C)dt, \quad \text{where } \delta > 0. \tag{1}$$

The consumption flow is

$$C_t = F(K_t, R_t) - \dot{K}_t; \tag{2}$$

that is, the output flow of the single finished good minus the flow allocated to capital formation, as in the Ramsey model. Next, the production function $F(K, R)$ is a function of the capital stock and of the resource flow, i.e., the rate of resource depletion. Finally, the latter flow integrated over time cannot exceed the total available, S,

$$\int_0^\infty R_t \, dt \leqq S, \quad \text{where } S > 0. \tag{3}$$

The problem thus is to maximise (1) subject to (2), (3), and given an initial capital stock K_0.

The first section of the paper describes the solution of this problem in rich detail. The second section constitutes, I presume, in the authors' intent the main purpose of the paper. It considers a case where an economy starts out in the circumstances of the first section, but in addition to that it may have the good luck of discovering and developing a substitute technology, to become available at some future date which is as yet uncertain. To my knowledge the second section contains the first theoretical model of this kind that expresses the idea of an uncertain ultimate transition to a durable solution. It assumes that at some moment in the future a constant resource flow becomes available. As an example, imagine that the solar flux can suddenly be tapped cheaply and on a large scale – the moment at which this happens being subject to a probability distribution.

I want to make two comments on the two parts of the paper. First, there is an interesting connection between the solution of the first problem and that of the second problem. To state that connection requires a long sentence: *If* the new technology in the second problem is so superior that, at the moment of its appearance it destroys the value of both the then existing capital stock and the then remaining resource stock, *then* the segment of the optimal path of the second problem, up to the appearance of the new technology, coincides with the corresponding segment in a suitably modified version of the first problem. The modification requires that the discount rate in the first problem vary over time in a particular way that depends on the probability distribution of the time of appearance of the new technology in the second problem. This is a case of a valid modification of a discount rate to allow for uncertainties – something that is often done with much less motivation.

My second remark concerns the first problem taken by itself. The tail-end of the optimal path in that problem should not be taken, I submit, too seriously. In the case of a Cobb–Douglas production function, as T goes to infinity the optimal path has consumption going to zero, the capital stock going to zero, the resource flow going to zero. All of that is to be expected. However, the ratio of the capital stock to the resource flow goes to infinity. I want to make two comments on that. *First*, as all these variables go to zero, one puts a great deal of strain on the assumption of constant returns to scale if one uses that same Cobb–Douglas function deeply into that corner. *Secondly*, even if one were to be adamant about that and say 'I believe that constant returns to scale holds at all scales', then one still has the difficulty that the ratio of capital to resource use goes to infinity. This places that ratio in an area in which we could not possibly have observations from which the validity of that Cobb–Douglas function in that area could have been tested econometrically. The authors point out that the difficulty I have referred to is even worse with the so-called CES (constant elasticity of substitution) function. For this type of production function, an inessential resource (i.e. a resource whose absence still allows positive production to take place) has, as T tends to infinity, a shadow price relative to capital that also becomes infinite. On the other hand an essential resource (one without which you cannot produce) has a shadow price that remains finite. As the authors point out, this is hard to accept as a trait of the real world.

I have mentioned both of these puzzles as examples of a difficulty that recurs in many modelling studies: on the basis of econometric practice one uses a constant elasticity of substitution, or a constant price elasticity of demand, or any other parameter of a behaviour relationship. Then somehow the optimising model carries you out of the area where the observations are found. I want to press a certain warning for the interpretation of these cases. They give theoretical insight, as long as they are not mistaken as being empirically validated by the econometric estimation of a function of that particular parametric form. Fortunately, in the case in hand, and due to the introduction of the second problem, the authors end up with the questionable tail-end of the optimal path in the first problem being amputated by the occurrence of the new technology.

My *third example* has to do with the young field of energy modelling. As far as participating professions are concerned, that field is still very much a concern of economists, but with equal participation by mathematical programmers, operations researchers and engineers. The professional basis widens as we proceed to this example. In particular, production possibilities are now best represented by the use of the process model and the techniques of mathematical programming. The empirical basis is the representation of production processes by fixed ratios of inputs to outputs for each process. That model is, I would say, squarely in the area of economic theory and of econometrics, but it has not penetrated as much as for instance the input–output model of Professor Leontief – which is that special case of the process model in which any one good can be produced only on its own, and that by only one process. In contrast, the energy sector has access to many alternative processes by which a given good or service can be produced, alone, or with one or more by-products. To generate electricity you can burn coal, burn oil, or have a nuclear plant, and it is hoped in due course you will be able to catch the solar flux – there are several alternatives. To my belief, a model consisting of a set of alternative processes is a more appropriate way of expressing production possibilities for the transition problem than either the input–output model or the smooth production function of longer standing in the economic textbooks and in the teaching of Econ 100. In this connection I would like to relate a conversation I had with a friend of mine who is working in this field. I expressed to him some puzzlement over the fact that I find it much easier to communicate with engineers about the process model of production than with economists. He said 'That is simple: engineers have never heard of a production function'.

The basic idea is that you have the individual processes represented. Any production function should be constructable from these processes if there is a need to. The programming model allows several resources and technologies to compete side by side. The optimisation suggests the best technology mix and its change over time. In a planning context, the planners would be customers for that type of analysis. In a market context, to the extent that the market process approximates a situation that in economic theory we label as perfect foresight and perfect competition, the model would simulate the market outcomes.

III. THREE MODELS OF THE UNITED STATES ENERGY SECTOR

I will refer to three long-term models of the US energy sector that apply optimisation in this role of a simulation device. One is essentially a supply model, developed in stages at Brookhaven National Laboratory by Kenneth Hoffman, William Marcuse and their associates. Now called 'DESOM', it treats final demand for energy services as an exogenously given vector path, and solves for the vector path of primary extraction, conversion and utilisation of energy by minimisation of the sum of discounted costs over time.

Two other models, 'ETA' by Alan Manne and what I will call 'Nordhaus' by William Nordhaus, while also treating the supply side by a process model, represent consumers' demand by utility maximisation. Here the utility function is derived by integration from an estimated demand function.[1] The optimisation then maximises the discounted sum of future utilities derived from consumption of energy services minus the cost of supplying them.

I will give one example of the application of these procedures to a much debated problem in which different professions have had quite different expectations about the answer. This is the question of the feedback from constraints on the growth of energy use to the growth of GNP over a particular future period in the United States. Since I cannot take time to describe the models more fully, it is more the nature of the problem that I want to place before you rather than to claim that the information supplied here is sufficient to present the conclusion as fully established – although I, myself, think it is a significant finding.

Table 1.1 summarises two sets of projections, in which the role of cause (shown in square brackets) and of effect (no brackets) is interchanged between the principal variables. Rows (0) and (1) report on 'base case' projections in which the growth rate of GNP is assumed to be a driving variable (exogenous), that of energy use a dependent variable. The principal finding is that if GNP grows at an average of 3.2 per cent p.a. over the period 1975–2010, then, depending on the model used, the energy use would grow somewhere between 1.7 and 2.9 per cent. Here capital and operating cost and resource availability parameters are the same for the various models, but inter model differences in price and income elasticities of demand could not be removed.

[1]An econometric basis of these estimates is provided in one case (WN) and claimed in another (AM).

TABLE 1.1   FEEDBACK FROM CURTAILED GROWTH OF ENERGY USE
TO GNP, 1975–2010, US

	(0)	(1)	(2)
(0)	[Driving]^a and effect variables	[GNP ≡ G_t]	Energy use ≡ E_t
(1)	Growth rates in base case	[3.2% p.a.]	1.7 to 2.9% p.a.
(2)	Gauge of effect and [policy] variable	$G \equiv \sum\limits_{t=0}^{35} \dfrac{G_{1975+t}}{1.06^t}$	[E_{2010}]
(3)	Curtailment fraction [specific policies]	1 to 2%	[up to 20%]
(4)	Curtailment fraction [zero-energy-growth through conservation tax]	$\begin{cases} 1 \text{ to } \ 2\% \text{ if}^b \ \eta = -0.5 \\ \text{up to } 30\% \text{ if} \ \ \eta = -0.25 \end{cases}$	[about 50%]

^{a}In each set of projections causal or 'driving' variables and their values are marked by square
brackets. Effect variables are without marking.
$^b\eta$ = constant price elasticity of demand for energy.

SOURCE *Energy Modeling for an Uncertain Future*: Report of the 'Modeling Resource
Group' of the Committee on Nuclear and Alternative Energy Systems, Tables III.0, III.22,
Charts III.11, III.12, National Academy of Sciences, 1978.

Rows (2), (3) and (4) summarise a policy analysis in which policies
constraining energy use are assumed to be imposed. In Row (3), various
policies curtailing the growth rate of specific forms of energy supply are
assumed to be imposed for reasons of environmental protection (coal, shale
oil), or from a concern with the risks of various nuclear technologies. The cause
of the departure from the base case now lies in the constraint on energy use
over a 35-year period (represented in the table only by the percentage
curtailment of the use figure for the year 2010). Note that now the percentage
figure does not stand for per cent per annum, but for the fraction of curtailment
out of the base case, in column (2) of the energy use in 2010 (representing the
cause), in column (1) of the sum of discounted GNP over the 35-year period (a
gauge for measuring the effect).

I want to emphasise the implicit assumptions that (a) the way in which the
constraining policies are imposed is gradual as well as foreseeable, and that (b)
there is a reasonably full employment policy consistently and successfully
applied. Therefore we do not in this discussion deal with such matters as the
effect of a sudden OPEC type embargo and the shooting up of the price of oil
that might be connected with that. If such events occur, they are not covered or
foreseen by this analysis. Then the up-to-20 per cent curtailment of energy use

imposed by these particular policies or combinations thereof still affects aggregated discounted GNP by a moderate 1 or 2 per cent. The basic reason for this outcome is that in time the technology mix can be shifted. If coal is curtailed because of the environmental effect of the dust and the sulphur it releases or because of the risk or damage from the mining, then, the constraint being foreseen and carried out gradually, nuclear fission can be called into a higher growth rate, and in that way the effect on GNP growth can be diminished. Actually, the feedback effect is due to the fact that the constraint of one technology (that is deemed harmful) to a value below the *strictly economic* 'optimum' will be not quite compensated by the gain from shifting to another technology (that is deemed less objectionable), just because you are moving away from the economic 'optimum', for non-economic reasons.

In Row (4) a much more drastic curtailment is imposed on *all* energy use, merely for analytical purposes, and in no way implying that sensible policies might lead to such a measure. This is the imposition of a low or a zero energy use growth rate brought about by an imagined conservation tax on all primary energy, where the tax rate grows fast enough to hold the energy use down to a low or zero growth rate – still making the same assumption about gradualness of the imposition. Then two new things happen – the effect turns out to be more than proportional to the curtailment, and also depends strongly on the price-elasticity of demand for energy. If that price elasticity (the parameter η) is one-half in absolute value then even the no-growth energy use policy still leaves GNP under these assumptions affected by not more than 1 or 2 per cent. But if the price elasticity of demand is only one-fourth, then, in the ETA model in which this assumption is used, the GNP is curtailed very remarkably by up to 30 per cent. So we also have a non-linearity here in the dependence of the effect of a severe policy on the price elasticity of demand for energy – assuming that elasticity to be a constant all along the demand curve.

Here is another case where our econometric practice leads us to work with a constant parameter, because we have not yet refined econometric methods to face up to a situation away from what the available data represent. However, on reflection, the price elasticity of demand cannot be a constant in the whole space. In fact, there is a theorem that has been in the folklore for some time, and of which the best proof known to me was given by Professor Hirofumi Uzawa in 1974 while at IIASA. I do not know whether he has published it, but I have a copy of his notes. Again, the theorem requires a long sentence. It says that if you consider the demand for a number of commodities as a vector function of the prices of all these commodities, and if for all prices the budget constraint is satisfied – total consumers' income is spent – and finally if you assume that all the cross- and own-price elasticities are constant, even only in a small neighbourhood of a point in the price space, then the only possible constant values of these elasticities are -1 for all own-price elasticities, and zero for all cross-elasticities. Any other set of values cannot stay constant. This theorem is rather upsetting for our econometric practice, but perhaps it does help us in further exploration of a situation in which a constant price elasticity is found to have so large an effect.

The findings summarised in Table1.1 are the work of a modelling group that forms one of many parts of a joint study committee of the two US National Academies, of Sciences and of Engineering, that is still continuing its work. I have been involved in the work of the modelling group as its chairman, but the work that has been drawn on in Table 1.1, while leaning mostly on DESOM, ETA and Nordhaus, cannot be attributed in detail because the specific findings have been combined in the aggregation and compression into one brief table.

IV. A FOURTH SUBSTITUTABILITY MODEL

My *fourth* and last *example* contemplates a still longer time horizon. It describes a contribution from the physical sciences, by Harold E. Goeller and Alvin M. Weinberg in an article entitled *The Age of Substitutability*. The approach is still more explicitly empirical than that in the previous models I have just discussed. This is not my field. I am impressed by the work the authors have done but I cannot claim that I can evaluate it. They have gone through the entire periodic system examining all the elements plus some important compounds, to determine the flow of their extraction in 1968, and estimate for each the total resources potentially available according to a rather generous definition of potential sources – the atmosphere, the ocean and a mile-thick crust of the earth. That may be a little more justified if one takes a very long-run view, but I would have liked to see a discussion also of costs of extraction and processing, and of how these costs would evolve in the race between depletion and technical advances. In any case, the ratio of total resources to demand in that year is expressed in years to go until exhaustion at the constant 1968 rate of extraction – a simple signal of relative abundance or scarcity. In that list the most serious case, to worry about in the very long run, appears to be phosphate – 1300 years supply at the 1968 rate of use. Next come coal, oil and gas, taken together in the symbol CH_x, where x is zero for coal and positive for oil and gas. Because of the coal component this aggregate would still have 2500 years at constant use. Then manganese (13,000 years) and everything else comes out at more than a million years.

Through the entire list and in the cases where there is a clear indication of a finite life time, the authors trace the important uses and possible substitutes in these uses. Their proposal is akin to building up, for the entire list of resources, the type of process model that I have spoken of previously.

On the basis of their scrutiny of these geological and technological data, Goeller and Weinberg pronounce the principle of infinite substitutability: with the exception of phosphorus and some trace elements for agriculture, mainly cobalt, copper and zinc, and finally the CH_x (coal, oil and gas), society can exist on near-inexhaustible resources for an indefinite period. This extends into the future the thesis of Barnet and Morse that in the past a new substitute for a dwindling resource was always found. They do not say much more about the case of phosphorus except that at some point that element may have to be recycled, and emphasise its essentiality to sustaining life. Similarly with the trace elements, but on the hydrocarbons they have a very interesting observation. It is related to the doctrine of energy as the crucial resource, with which Weinberg has been strongly associated. The remark is that carbon and hydrogen are abundant, that both are tied to oxygen in nature, that it takes energy to detach the oxygen, and that there are a number of technical processes that do just that, putting in energy and obtaining the various hydrocarbons needed by industry or transport. For this to work, of course, the energy source has to be non-fossil and abundant. Among the various possibilities are solar, geothermal, the nuclear breeder reactor, and nuclear fusion. Each of those has difficulties associated with it. Solar on a central power station basis is expensive by present projections. Geothermal is still very much untried except in special situations. Perhaps the principal problem with the various nuclear breeder reactors is the difficulty that the by-products can, if so desired, be processed and diverted to become nuclear weapons-grade materials. And I understand that the technical feasibility and commercial viability of nuclear fusion reactors is still an open question. At least one of these options would have to work to make the doctrine of energy as the crucial resource a reality.

I have already said that I cannot evaluate these ideas, but I wanted you to be acquainted with this line of thought and be aware that when you look very far into the future quite a different type of information becomes important. Traditional econometrics doesn't help us here. There is a type of thinking here that draws on basic scientific notions and knowledge, and that economists should take note of.

REFERENCES

Barnett, H. J. and C. Morse, *Scarcity and Growth* (Johns Hopkins Press, 1963).
Dasgupta, P. and G. Heal, 'The Optimal Depletion of Exhaustible Resources', *Rev. of Econ. Stud., Symposium* (1974), 3–28.
Goeller, H. E. and A. M. Weinberg, 'The Age of Substitutability,' *Science* (20 Feb 1976), 683–9.
Hoffman, K. and E. Cherniavsky, 'A Model for Interfuel Substitution and Technological Change', (Brookhaven Nat. Lab., June 1974).
Hotelling, H., 'The Economics of Exhaustible Resources', *Jn. of Pol. Econ.* 39 (April 1931), 137–75.
Manne, A. S., 'Waiting for the Breeder', *Rev. Econ. Stud., Symposium* (1974), 47–66.
———, 'ETA: A Model for Technology Assessment', *Bell Jn. of Econ.* (Autumn, 1976), 379–406.
Marcuse, W. *et al.*, 'A Dynamic Time Dependent Model for the Analysis of Alternative Energy Policies', BNL-19406 (Brookhaven Nat. Lab., July 1975).
Nordhaus, W. D., 'The Allocation of Energy Resources', *Brookings Papers*, (1973), 4, 429–570.
———, 'The Demand for Energy: An International Perspective', in Nordhaus (Ed.), *Proceedings of the Workshop on Energy Demand*, CP-76-1, Int'1 Inst. for Appl. Syst. An., Austria (1976), 511–87.
Ramsey, F. R., 'A Mathematical Theory of Savings', *Econ. Jn.* (Dec. 1928), 543–59.

2 Energy and Future Economic Growth

W. Sassin and W. Häfele

INTERNATIONAL INSTITUTE FOR APPLIED SYSTEMS ANALYSIS
LAXENBURG, AUSTRIA

I. THE PRESENT ENERGY PROBLEM

The difficulties of energy supply are growing, and the outlook for the decades ahead is dim. There is little doubt that energy-related problems will have their bearing on future economic growth. We still have an economic recession, to which the oil embargo of 1973 and the sudden fourfold price increase of crude oil have been contributing factors. Medium-term economic and energy growth projections have continually been revised downward since 1974. Yet the expert community still expects a possible major energy supply shortage around 1985 that would further aggravate the economic situation [1, 2, 3]. So the question is not whether energy prospects will affect the economic situation but rather: For how long will the energy problem be a major problem for economic development? and more so, which strategies could lead away from the foreseeable dilemma?

It is the merit of the Club of Rome and especially of Dennis and Donella Meadows [4] that they drew public attention to the finiteness of our natural resources, even though there are many uncertainties and inaccuracies in details of their work. Their projections of population growth and extrapolations of technological capabilities are based on the period of 1950 to 1970. They arrive at a catastrophic breakdown of their model system around 2050.

Many reactions could have resulted from this new awareness of the shortcomings of our present technoeconomic system, so far poorly captured in 'holistic' models. Out of the many, only this reaction seems to have gained large momentum with the public: that which centres around the concept of conservation. The growing perception of environmental pollution and the 1973–74 oil crisis have obviously favoured it; events were too readily understood as giving credit to the notion of a deteriorating carrying capacity of the globe. 'Limits to Growth' transformed from a constraint to be observed over the long run into an immediate tactical objective. And here the public discussion is stuck. Unfortunately Dennis Meadows and, more recently and emphatically, A. Lovins now assume that the only realistic road to be taken is to adapt to 'an unavoidable worldwide crisis' instead of exploring ways to alleviate such constraints. They state in [5]

> The global population will not rise above eight billion people, perhaps not above six billion. War, pestilence, and famine will continue in cycles more or less as they have over the millennia. The conflicting trends of consolidation

12

of political blocks on one hand and increasing breakup of others will persist. Under these circumstances one does not count on the adoption of global energy strategies, or even on programs that require massive shipments of energy across national boundaries.

Meadows' and Lovins' scenario may be taken as a working hypothesis but certainly it is not fate.

Strangely enough, most of the arguments generally used to demonstrate the limitations of technology or the – equivalent – limitedness of natural resources including the ability of the environment to absorb and neutralise pollutants, are borrowed from the area of energy supply and consumption. Energy resources are certainly not severely limited, not in physical terms at least. Taking this example is therefore not only inappropriate but also misleading. We will try to demonstrate that for the energy system more than one long-term option exists to circumvent the most serious, if not virtually all, constraints upon future economic development and growth. This neither means that we are not in a critical situation with respect to the energy supply problems of the next decades, nor does it imply that a successful energy strategy will be an easy and simple achievement.

II. FUTURE ENERGY DEMAND AND FOSSIL RESOURCES

For the sake of orientation, let us first look at the development of energy consumption before going into the resource question. The perspective chosen is global and long-term. Figure 2.1 summarises the history of primary energy consumption over the past 100 years [6]. Total consumption has grown at an average rate of 5 per cent per year, except in periods of worldwide crises: the two world wars, the economic recession of the thirties, and the post-oil embargo phase. The first period of major growth was supported by coal, and the second was based on oil and natural gas. Oil and gas together now account for slightly more than 70 per cent of (global) primary energy consumption.

Economic and, along with it, energy growth have been and will further be stimulated by three independent causes: world population growth, the development of less developed countries, and continued industrialisation in developed countries, each of them having different weight and changing their relative influence on future energy demand over time.

Making a judgement concerning the role of energy resources in future economic development presupposes projections of future energy consumption. While many different assumptions can reasonably enter such projections, we will pick out a few very simple scenarios in order not to cloud the essence of our global energy problem.

Figure 2.2 is based on past population figures and a UN projection published at the 1974 World Population Conference in Bucharest [7]. On that basis, the global population will continue to grow fairly rapidly from 4.10^9 at present with a continual reduction of net reproduction rates (i.e. the number of

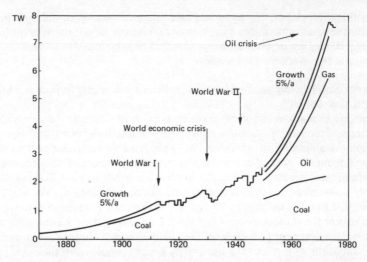

Fig. 2.1 Primary energy consumption: world. Source of data [6]

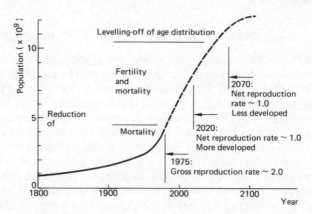

Fig. 2.2 World population growth

children born to one individual who live up to their age of reproduction) and, around the end of the next century, level off at 12.10^9. Other models project both higher and lower asymptotic population levels. However, what is important for analysing our energy problem is not really the equilibrium level but the development of the next 50 to 70 years. Within this time period population projections do not vary too much, since the demographic growth process for the next two to three generations is predetermined: the babies are already born who will have babies themselves.

With the UN population projection as a basis, three alternative scenarios for global energy demand are given in Figure 2.3. They differ in the final energy consumption level of the average global citizen. The lowest curve, only introduced to demonstrate the extreme, assumes that the present level of 2 kW/cap is to be frozen immediately. The solid line and the dashed line assume that the process of economic development of the LDCs requires 70 or 100 years, respectively, resulting in an average energy consumption of 5 kW per capita. This level corresponds to the present central European average and that of the USSR; the USA is at 11 kW per capita. Such a scenario implies that the LDCs undergo the same transitional process from an essentially rural and agricultural to an industrialised society, as was started 100 years ago by the developed countries; it also implies a successful energy conservation by the developed countries [8]. The intermediate curve essentially extrapolates the growth rate of the global per-capita consumption prevailing between 1914 and 1950. This was a period of growth under crisis conditions with an annual growth of 1.3 per cent. If this rate were resumed from now on it would lead to approximately 3 kW per capita around 2020 and would then be cut off.

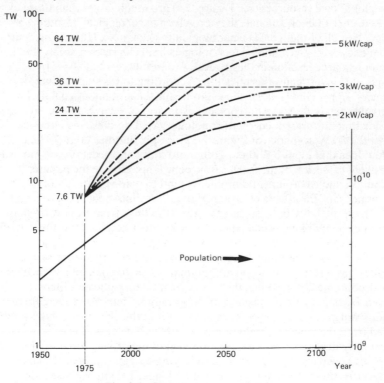

Fig. 2.3 Global energy scenarios

A side remark is necessary here. Energy consumption is, for good reasons, a suitable indicator of economic performance [9]. Thus the scenarios in Figure 2.3 essentially refer to three different economic development paths, assuming that the relationship between energy input to an economy and economic output will not change. With possibly deteriorating energy supply conditions, economists strongly hope for a lowering of the energy elasticity, the coefficient which describes that ratio. However, we will assume an essentially constant coefficient and return to this critical point after a brief discussion of resources and supply.

Figure 2.4 shows the cumulative consumption resulting from the scenarios of Figure 2.3 as well as oil, gas and coal resources given at the 1974 World Energy Conference [10]. Irrespective of the scenario chosen, oil and gas will be exhausted within 30 to 40 years from now if one assumes no change in the present total share in the consumption balance of approximately 70 per cent. As much or as little as 15 to 25 years would be added with even a doubling of the estimates for ultimately recoverable oil and gas resources: this includes non-conventional deposits of hydrocarbons and improvements of the recovery factor, both contributing to substantially higher production costs [11].

The global coal resources (see Figure 2.4) are much larger than those of oil and gas. Other than oil and gas, they are given as 'geological' resources in practice. Not all of that coal is technologically accessible. Harvesting coal economically with given mining technologies limits its recoverability and leaves a certain resource fraction in the ground. A careful recent analysis by Fettweis [12] investigates this question. According to his study, a world average of 15 per cent is a realistic estimate for the amount of coal that might conceivably be used. Adding up present estimates of recoverable fossil energy one finds that our present energy technology based on these resources can support the 5 kW scenario (of Figure 2.3) for only another 60 to 70 years.

What does that imply? Without going into much more detail, one may say that a likely extension of the fossil resource will not change the picture. Distribution and environmental problems tend to compensate, if not overcompensate, the effects of exploration and technological progress and will reduce the availability of fossil energy [13]. It follows from Figure 2.4 that, without doubt, mankind is compelled to make the fundamental transition of changing the global energy system to one of non-fossil energy resources.

This change is comparable to the one which, starting 100 years ago, led the developed nations from firewood and animal power to coal, oil and mechanical power. Economically speaking, there is at least one significant difference, however. During the first transition of the energy system, the driving force in the industrial production process was innovation: the changing energy pattern resulted from the changing technological pattern. The cost of energy continuously declined. For the transition ahead, the driving force will be scarcity of cheap energy. The cost of supplying energy is expected to rise continuously, and the energy system will no longer be only a consequence of, but a constraint for, future technological evolution.

Another fundamental observation can be derived from Figure 2.4. Even the lowest hypothetical scenario, which assumed an immediate switch to zero energy growth for the average individual, will not avoid the exhaustion of the given fossil resource base. It would certainly extend the time horizon for a

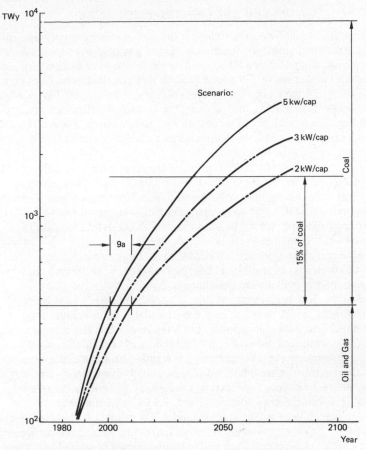

Fig. 2.4 Fossil energy reserves and cumulated energy consumption

transition away from fossil energy, but at the price of drastically limiting economic progress. The *nine*-year difference in the exhaustion of oil and gas resources between the highest and lowest scenarios (Figure 2.4) quantifies the small degree of flexibility of long-term energy conservation. We stress long-term because conservation measures in a short-term context demand a different evaluation. The deeper reason for our general resource dilemma – for fossil energy exemplified by Figure 2.4 – is definitely not future economic growth. Instead it is the quantum jump mankind has taken during the past 100 years. We only have to remember that between 1880 and today energy consumption has grown by a factor of 30 (Figure 2.1) to the present level of 7.5 TW. At the same time population has grown by a factor of 3 (Figure 2.2). The idea of low or zero growth is dangerous because it distracts from this fact. It is our present achievements and not an affluent future that are at stake in the long run.

III. RENEWABLE ENERGY SOURCES

With this danger in mind we have to assess the global energy supply options
that should gradually substitute for scarce oil and gas resources within a
transition period of some 50 to 70 years. The yardstick to be applied is a global
energy demand of dozens of TW (see Figure 2.3). Even the lowest hypothetical
scenario leads to 24 TW. The highest scenario totalling some 60 TW is still a
conservative estimate. Taking into account the technical difficulties which put
an extra burden on harvesting of almost all alternative energy forms, 100 TW
is not out of range for a possible global energy demand beyond the mid-twenty-
first century.

It is useful to note that the 5 kW scenario compares with the results of
Leontief's study on *The Future of the World Economy* [14]. According to
Leontief, both the old economic system and a New Economic Order favouring
the development of LDCs lead to an identical global energy demand of 20 TW
in 2000. In the following, the 5 kW scenario will be our reference case of
50 TW in 60 years from now.

Renewable energy sources are advocated these days as a solution with
respect to the finiteness of traditional energy resources [15]. Indeed, they help
adjust our economic activities to the changed conditions on the globe
introduced by modern man in his billions. Wherever there is a possibility of
using hydropower, wind, biomass, or locally available solar energy, they
should be developed with high priority. On a regional basis this can turn out to
be very significant indeed. Sørensen, for instance, has studied the use of
windmills for Denmark [16]. Wind energy is steadier and more intensive in
Denmark than in most other inhabited places, and so this development might
make sense there. In a global context, it is necessary to analyse the overall
potential of renewable energy sources (Table 2.1). Let us start with
hydropower. A technical potential of around 3 TW already includes projects
such as the use of glacier power in Greenland. Melting water from an area of
more than 150,000 km² is collected and used by a series of dams [18]. The
technical potential of hydropower by far exceeds its economic potential which
is on the order of 1.1 TW out of which 13 per cent is harvested today. It is
difficult to quantify wind power. The unconstrained technical and economic
potential of windmills – whose rated mechanical power is between 1 and
3 MW – is of the order of 30 TW. Taking into account settlement patterns and
discarding transcontinental power transmission, one arrives at a rough estimate
of 3 TW for their technical potential (compare also reference [8]). A detailed
study would most probably yield a significantly lower figure for wind power.
The technological potentials of wet geothermal energy and tidal power rank
much lower. Wave power appears more attractive but linear installation of
almost the perimeter of the earth would be needed to obtain one terawatt. The
only source in Table 2.1 comparable to long-term global energy demand is the
ocean thermal gradient for power production. To produce 70 TW, practically
all of the tropical and subtropical ocean currents would have to be utilised. The

TABLE 2.1   LOCALISED RENEWABLE ENERGY SOURCES

	Technical potential TW[a]	Technological maturity	Ecological problems and safety
Hydropower (Glacier Greenland)	2.9 0.1	Mature Economic potential 1.1 TW presently utilised 13%	
Wet geothermal	0.1	Installed 1350 MW	Salinity of water
Wind	3		Regional planning storage
Tidal power	0.04	Installed 240 MW	–
Wave power	1 TW/35,000 km	To be developed	?
Ocean thermal gradient	70? 0.35[b]	To be developed	Climatological effects?

[a]Note 1 TW = 1 TW · a/a.
[b]Within 10 km distance from coastline.

SOURCE Basic data from [17].

production of one-tenth (7 TW) would imply displacements of a body of water roughly equal to that of the Gulf Stream. Major ecological and climatological impacts would occur. Under realistic conditions the ocean thermal gradient could certainly not contribute more than a few TW. Solar energy, which is not included in Table 2.1, will be considered among the long-term options. From the studies existing so far, one may safely conclude that renewable energy sources, apart from solar power, can, for technical reasons, contribute a few TW at best. Economic viability, local environmental limitations, and competing land use requirements will further reduce their contributions to the global supply balance. There is a fundamental gap of the order of 50 TW between the capacity of these sources and an anticipated demand. This gap illustrates the real danger in committing large societies to head for soft options [15].

IV. LONG-TERM ENERGY SUPPLY OPTIONS

Let us now turn to the three options capable of supplying energy in the 50 TW range beyond the turn of the century: solar, nuclear, and – in a different function than considered above – coal.

Solar energy in this context is a hard technology. It is certainly not characterised by a few solar panels operating in the backyard. These figures should help characterise a global solar option: The average insolation at the surface of the earth is the key parameter. In mid-latitudes, such as central Europe or northern USA, one square metre receives roughly 100 W (yearly average). This is much more than in the case of wind power. For comparison, present energy consumption densities in highly populated areas, such as in greater Calcutta or in the Rhine-Rhur area, FRG, are 10 W/m^2. In rural areas energy consumption densities are one to two orders of magnitude smaller (see also reference [8]). Despite this favourable ratio solar energy is a dilute source requiring immense areas of land. One reason is the generally low efficiency of converting sunlight into a convenient form of secondary energy. For electricity production estimates range from 10 to 20 per cent, depending on the technology used [19]. Other reasons are the variations of the daily, but mainly of the seasonal, cycle.

The maximum to minimum ratio of the seasonal cycle in mid-latitudes is close to 7:1, while in southern desert regions it is nearly 2:1. These ratios point to the fundamental problem of energy storage. If solar energy is to be more than an auxiliary source it must supply base load energy. This most probably will require the production of hydrogen which at the same time would alleviate the problem of long-distance energy transport [20]. Assuming a most favourable siting in desert areas, where insolation is around 200 W/m^2, which enjoy a low seasonal variability, it is optimistic to estimate an overall efficiency of 10 per cent of producing, storing and transporting hydrogen from sunlight. With this figure energy requirements of 50 TW translate into a requirement of 2.5 million km^2 of land. 2.5 million km^2 of land covered with solar installations then compares with 13 million km^2, which are currently used for agricultural

TABLE 2.2   OPTIONS FOR A NON-RESOURCE CONSTRAINT ENERGY SUPPLY

	Potential[a] TWa	Technological maturity	Side-effects
Fission (breeder)	10^8	Sufficient for power plants Not yet sufficient for large-scale fuel cycle	Storage of fission products Emission of radio nuclides
Fusion (D–T)	10^8	To be developed	Storage of activated material Emission of radio nuclides
Solar	(∞)	To be developed for large scale	Land and materials requirements Climatic disturbance? Storage and transportation
Coal	$7 \cdot 10^3$	Mature at present scale To be developed for large scale and combination with nuclear and solar	Unfavourable working conditions Land requirements CO_2 waste and other pollution

[a]TWa compared to present primary energy input spectrum.

purpose, and 0.4 million km^2, which is the built-up area of human settlements. Soft solar devices on the other hand, such as harvesting sunlight on the roof or in the backyard, can therefore supply only a few per cent of our future energy demand.

Thus solar energy (in Table 2.2) is clearly understood as a hard, large-scale, and remote technology, to be viewed perhaps as a new kind of agriculture. There will be supply and deficit regions, and – in the best tradition of the oil system – a world market for energy carriers that are derived from solar energy. We are certainly not accustomed to this dimension of solar technology, but it is this global context in which it is to be compared with its main alternative, nuclear power.

The nuclear option in Table 2.2 comprises both fission and fusion. While fusion still awaits demonstration of its technological and commercial feasibility, fission is already a commercial energy source today. Light-water reactors (LWRs) which on a net basis use only 1 per cent of the atoms of natural uranium, would suffer from limited uranium resources, however, if they were to supply a substantial share of the world's energy consumption. Because of the economics of nuclear power production in LWRs, the energy yield of uranium resources is just about the same order of magnitude as that of our oil resources, or even less. The real potential of nuclear fission is the breeder, which increases the use of uranium by a factor of 60 to 80. Therefore, the production cost margin of uranium resources is higher by a similar factor, and even the uranium content of the oceans becomes economically accessible. *De facto*, 10^7 to 10^8 TW years of energy are available through breeder reactors, enough for millions of years and all conceivable energy needs. Fusion, the nuclear twin of fission, seems to have only one type of reactor with a realistic chance of success shortly after the year 2000. It is the deuterium-tritium reactor. Tritium, which is not a natural resource, must be derived from lithium. The resource base for the fusion breeder is not defined by the abundant deuterium but by lithium which would yield an energy equivalent of the order of 10^8 TW years. Waste disposal, containment of radioactivity, the use of liquid metals and other features of the two breeder types are similar in most respects [21]. Therefore speaking of the nuclear option in the following refers to either of the two breeder technologies.

Nuclear energy suffers from the same setback as solar energy in that it cannot by itself provide an energy carrier to suit consumer needs. So far the development of nuclear power has concentrated on electricity generation. While electricity has been gradually extending its market share, it will most probably not be able to achieve more than 25 per cent of the final energy demand [22]. The remainder must be provided as a gaseous or liquid secondary energy carrier. One candidate is hydrogen, the other is methanol. Their transportation properties together with the need to integrate energy production and the nuclear fuel cycle for various economic, ecological and safety reasons stimulate the concept of nuclear centres [8]. Their natural size is at the one-terawatt level, which is not unusual for a system with an overall capacity of 50 TW.

A few words on coal must be added. As we have seen, coal resources are large but perhaps not more than 15 per cent can possibly be used as an energy resource. The future development of coal very much depends on the transitional strategy resulting from local and regional decisions in the next one or two decades. One could assume that evolving emergency conditions would force mankind to recover more coal than is considered feasible today. In view of the long-term potential of solar and nuclear power it seems more realistic to assume that coal would be used where hydrocarbons are genuinely needed: in the transportation sector and for part of the low-density energy consumption with a genuinely low load factor. Methanol (CH_3OH) would be a good candidate to substitute for liquid fuels, at present derived from crude oil [20]. Since the energy content of methanol containing 1 kg of carbon atoms is twice as much as that of one kg of pure carbon, the energy supplied via methanol would virtually double coal resources, assuming that the process heat for methanol synthesis is taken from a solar or nuclear source. If a substantially higher coal production cost were acceptable for such a combined process, recoverability of coal would be increased and submarginal coal resources could be mined to provide carbon in the form of lost storage material rather than as traditional primary energy. Since no detailed studies are available we assume a possible overall recovery factor of 40 per cent, which permits an 'oil equivalent' energy supply of 7000 TW a. Even for a 50 TW society, this use of coal would satisfy all genuine demands for liquid energy carriers for a few hundred years.

This short analysis, touching just some of the main, well-established facts of our present and future energy system, clearly reveals that energy sources in the long run need not pose a major problem for economic development and growth. Nuclear and solar energy, and coal in its double role are not resource-constrained. The term 'resource' is used here in its rather narrow, traditional sense. Side-effects of the use of energy resources even at the present 7.5 TW level have come to the forefront, which restricts the use of many resources long before they are physically exhausted. High-sulphur coal is a case in point. From our present experience it is legitimate to ask whether our global environment is not bound to deteriorate as a consequence of producing 50 TW, be it from nuclear or solar resources.

Environmental movements that generally focus on nuclear energy have been gaining some political influence. They must be given credit for raising concern about some severe symptoms of our technoeconomic system. But, as in the case of general growth, it is vital not to misinterpret these symptoms as characteristics of modern technology; characteristics which would safely permit discrimination between coal and nuclear energy, for example, and to discard one option in favour of the other.

An example will illustrate the interdependence of energy resources, environmental constraints and general material resources, where attempts at curing some environmental symptoms might adversely affect the global ecological system. To simplify matters, we will again refer to the 50 TW scenario. Providing 50 TW by fission breeders for example, would force mankind to handle and dispose of some 10^4 tons of fission products per year.

An overwhelming degree of meticulousness is required to keep such a flow of potentially dangerous material separated from the environment. According to present maximum permissible dose rates, not more than some ten grams of fission products per year would be allowed to leak to the environment [23].

Harvesting 50 TW from solar energy on 2.5 million km² of land would lead to a similarly staggering effort. Many features, such as apparent waste heat as a consequence of albedo changes or interference with natural vegetation make it a new kind of agriculture. But there is at least one fundamental difference in that 'solar-culture' cannot rely on natural recycling of its structural materials. With the solar tower concept as a reference technology and a lifetime of 50 years per installation, an annual flow of waste materials of the order of 2.10^{10} t would result. This is equal to the present overall consumption of 'demandite', the feed material of industry [24]. Apart from the environmental side-effects, which we experience today as a result of handling and processing nearly 20 billion tons of demandite, this illustrates another dilemma: by switching from fossil resources, i.e. stored energy in deposits, to a practically unlimited energy flux from the sun, we would only shift the energy-resource problem to a materials-resource problem. A similar shift would occur with environmental problems. The investigation of this interplay is very recent [24], and no final results can yet be presented. Still, it is clear that energy strategies which serve to solve the resource dilemma must cover this dimension.

V. NEGENTROPY AND ECONOMY

It is important to realise that the fundamental differences with respect to the environment between a nuclear and a solar option are of a quantitative rather than qualitative nature. The former requires strict containment of very little matter, and the latter causes movements and processing of very large amounts of materials, interfering permanently with nature in a soft way density-wise but involving a significant portion of the earth's surface. Both options invite criticism and appear hardly attractive; they even seem to open a new, somehow perplexing, perspective. There is no easy way around this. If we neither want to believe that a technological miracle may eventually save us, as some do, nor that we have to adapt to an unavoidable crisis, we must go back and check our basic economic mechanisms. While we have so far operated on firm and well-known ground, we must now enter largely unknown scientific territory. In view of what is at stake the authors feel committed to that road, even if the analytical tools at hand might turn out not to fully match those problems.

Let us start by considering – as a mental block breaker rather than realistic suggestion – a concept which sounds like such a technological miracle: the negentropy city by C. Marchetti [26]. It in fact provides all the services, mechanical power, heating and cooling, and the like of our present energy system without consuming energy. There is no trick, and everything can, at least in principle, be done with today's technical components. In explaining the different steps, in Figure 2.5, let us start with the use of the temperature

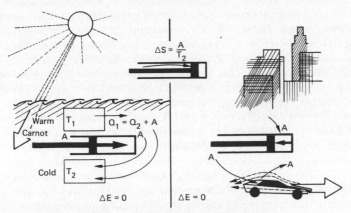

$$\Delta S = \frac{A}{T_2}$$

Warm Carnot T_1 $Q_1 = Q_2 + A$

Cold T_2

$\Delta E = 0$ $\Delta E = 0$

(A:Work, E:Energy, Q:Heat, S:Entropy, T:Temperature)

Fig. 2.5 Negentropy City. SOURCE After C. Marchetti, IIASA

differences in tropical oceans. A kind of steam engine produces mechanical power A by extracting heat Q_1 from the surface layer at temperature T_1, discharging a smaller amount of heat Q_2 to deeper ocean layers at temperature T_2. Instead of using the mechanical power to drive a generator and to transport electricity to the consumer, compressed air is produced. The compression heat, which equals A, is discharged to the deeper ocean layer at temperature T_2.

On balance, no energy has been taken from the ocean. The net result is a simple mixing: the oceanic temperature difference has been reduced or, scientifically speaking, the entropy of the ocean has been increased. In turn we have obtained a certain amount of compressed air at ambient temperature which does not contain more energy than before compression. It might be helpful to recall that no energy was taken from the ocean so that the energy of the compressed air cannot have increased. What has changed instead is the capability of the compressed air to produce work, and this is expressed quantitatively by the reduced entropy content of the compressed air ΔS. As it is easier to operate with a quantity that is used up instead of being increased in a process yielding a useful output, we will henceforth deal with the negative complement of entropy, simply called negentropy. Compressed air carrying negentropy can be stored and transported to the place where it is to be used, for instance to propel a car. There the process is reversed: expanding in a cylinder, the air tends to cool off. The amount of energy which is extracted as heat from the ambient air to maintain the temperature of the expansion cylinder, is delivered as mechanical power. When driving the car it is again quantitatively transformed into heat by friction, and the energy balance is closed. Using this principle it is possible to heat homes (for example, by combining a compressed air expansion engine and a heat pump) or perform all the other services delivered by today's energy technology.

What can we learn from this *Gedankenexperiment*? First, it helps us better to understand our basic economic processes: What we actually consume is not energy but negentropy. In fact, all energy we produce is finally rejected as waste heat to the environment. While we have a law of conservation for energy, there is no such law for negentropy. Second, the hypothetical negentropy city of Figure 2.5 does not suffer from the classical environmental problems of our present-day energy system. There is no waste heat, and there are no chemical pollutants, irrespective of the negentropy consumption density assumed. So there is hope that the side-effects of a 50 TW society considered above can be controlled if the right technologies are chosen or those available modified.

The negentropy city concept has only been used to demonstrate the principle. In reality, the technologies described (Figure 2.5) have two severe drawbacks: the low density of the oceanic negentropy source, and the low negentropy-carrying capacity of compressed air. Both features translate into enormous material requirements leading to even greater problems than those related to the solar option.

By way of analogy one may similarly conclude for the materials problem that materials are not consumed in the economic process; rather specifications and tolerances are used and destroyed – or, in other words – the information content carried by materials. There have been several efforts to quantify this observation [27]. Recycling of worn material is the key example here, since it requires additional negentropy. It turns out that energy and raw materials problems are two sides of one and the same coin.

Our set of problems thus reduces to essentially one question: can mankind dispose of a rich negentropy source that itself is not initially tied to material carriers? As such a tie is established both by the material forms of primary energy and the structural devices necessary for handling negentropy the principal answer is *no*. For all practical levels of human activities, a practical answer is *yes*, however [28]. In this context the general tendency towards centralisation, increased densities and efficiencies appears in a new light. There are at least some obvious possibilities to combine the use of various negentropy sources in such a way as to reduce the requirements for resources with tight natural limitations. A combination of nuclear power plants and very simple solar reflectors that compensate for their waste heat release is one example; another is the location of energy parks at sites where a negative feedback to stable meteorologic and hydrologic cycles can be achieved [29].

How do these different observations fit into one simple scheme? Figure 2.6 displays different ways of organising the energy or, more precisely, negentropy supply. Figure 2.6 is meant to provide a basis for relating these alternatives to economic strategies, which in the long run must clearly be adapted to the diminishing flexibility of technology with respect to nature. Let us go through the figure by following the alternative flows of energy, negentropy and entropy through various strata. Entropy flows indicate losses of negentropy which could be at least partly avoided or, whenever they occur in nature, could be used by man. The *stratum of nature*, comprising resources as well as our

Standard of living, economic development, technology and environment

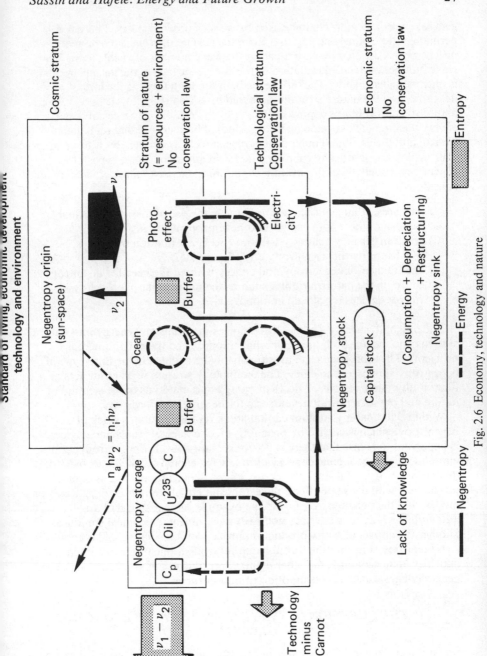

Fig. 2.6 Economy, technology and nature

general environment, is characterised by a set of ordered states. There is a
permanent flow of negentropy to it from the *cosmic stratum*. This flow of
negentropy is denoted by v_1, indicating the wave number of visible light. The
wave number of the backradiation of the earth's surface in the far infrared, v_2,
is much smaller than v_1. The difference between both flows is the loss of
negentropy in the nature stratum indicated by the entropy flow $(v_1 - v_2)$. The
nature stratum contains deposits of negentropy, e.g. the resources of fossil
energy accumulated in geologic time periods. The energy radiation balance of
the sun and the earth and outer space, respectively, is denoted by $n_a h v_2$ and
$n_i h v_i$, which are practically equal in a quasi-steady state. Three types of
negentropy supply from the stratum of nature to the *technological stratum* are
considered:

(1) our present mode of operation, namely the use of fossil and nuclear
    deposits, where both energy and negentropy are transferred;
(2) the transfer of negentropy without energy, a situation which was
    illustrated by the negentropy city (Figure 2.5);
(3) the transfer of negentropy and energy without the need for an entropy
    buffer in the nature stratum, such as the use of solar photocells with
    mirror devices for albedo compensation.

Entropy buffers represent the dispersion of materials and energy into natural
systems and include both the traditional resource and the environmental
problems. These problems can most probably be avoided in the third type of
negentropy supply technologies. The technology stratum in all cases acts as a
filter: it ultimately returns all flows of energy and materials to the stratum of
nature and passes a flow of negentropy to the *stratum of economy*.

Within the economy stratum capital stock represents man's stock of
negentropy, which is carried by productive technological plants and devices. It
is important to realise that there is no conservation law for negentropy, and
consequently no economic conservation law for capital stock. Apart from the
deterioration of capital stock by its use, called depreciation, there is another
mechanism with the same effect: the establishment of standards, regulations or
modes, and their change over time. One example is the disposal of an
automobile which runs but does not meet governmental technical standards,
another the impact of a new production process on the value of old plants.

Negentropy consumption through capital stock is one of the two main
activities in an economy, the other is the immediate use of goods and services,
generally aggregated as consumption of non-durables.

VI. THE QUESTION OF CAPITAL AND FUTURE ECONOMIC GROWTH

So far it is not possible to quantify rigorously the scheme of Figure 2.6 without
running into problems of inconsistency. The key with which to solve the

TABLE 2.3   CAPITAL REQUIREMENTS FOR ALTERNATIVE ENERGY SUPPLY SYSTEMS

		Oil, gas, coal 25% to electricity	Nuclear LWR + FBR + electrolysis	Solar photovolt. + electrolysis	thermoelectr.
Specific investment[a] costs	[US\$/kW]	200	1500	3000	5000
Energy related capital stock for 5 kW/cap	[US\$/cap]	1000	7500	15000	25000
Total capital stock[b] for present economies consuming 5 kW/cap	[US\$/cap]	~5000			
Non-productive/productive capital stock		0 : 1	1.3 : 1	2.8 : 1	4.8 : 1

[a]Costs are estimated for a split electric/non-electric secondary energy supply as of today.
[b]Mean value Western Europe, based on [30]; as large discrepancies exist between different sources, this figure is more an indicator than a weighted average.

problem of metrics is obviously different in the various strata. It appears to us that this has to do with the various mechanisms that lead to an 'unnecessary' loss of negentropy introduced by lack of information. Much effort is certainly needed to operationalise the concept of interaction between resources, environment, technology and economy. None the less, even in its present simple and crude form, our scheme leads to two important observations: first, as said earlier in different words, the earth is not a closed spaceship. By a proper choice of technologies that are well within our capabilities, human activities are limited neither by resources nor by environmental mechanisms. Neither technology nor nature provides an upper ceiling for our economic activities, if technological changes are initiated in time. Second, the central problem in adapting our economy to the quantum jump of mankind is to replace within only a few decades dwindling negentropy stocks, (e.g. oil or gas deposits) by stocks of capital which require costly investments. As this type of investment would only substitute for goods which so far nature has essentially offered for free, the related capital investments can no longer be considered productive in the classical economic sense. There has been a similar experience with environmental protection. The production of abatement devices adds to the GNP. They do not produce a real output but only maintain a given environmental quality. This observation of non-productive capital in future energy systems is important because of the huge quantitative differences between old and new energy technologies. (Including all side-effects, it would be more appropriate to call them negentropy technologies.) Table 2.3 puts some figures into perspective. Compared to the present economies based on oil, gas and coal a hypothetical economy operating today with the same input of secondary energy derived solely from nuclear energy, for example, would have to more than double its total capital stock. The ratio of non-productive additional capital stock to the original total capital stock would be on the order of 1:1. For solar power this ratio is even more dramatic, if not prohibitive (see Table 2.3). If a distinction is made between non-productive and reference capital stock, a quasi-constant monetary metric can be maintained which simplifies the discussion of long-term development problems. The question of energy elasticities can be split into two parts: one concerns the extent to which energy productivity in the reference economy of today can be improved. The other question is completely different: how much effort must be allocated to the build-up of a new energy system during the transition period, which would do nothing but secure the availability of the same production factor, secondary energy?

The formation of this 'non-productive' capital must be seen as the main process drawing upon the capabilities of national economies to invest in traditional growth processes. Its impact will depend on the time horizon set for a transition of the energy system with a longer transition period being less demanding than a shorter one. A constant allocation of 5 per cent of the GNP for a gradual transition from oil to nuclear energy over 50 years indicates the dimension of our problem. It compares to existing armament efforts, and – as we might conclude from this experience — would not necessarily interfere with long-term economic growth. A substantially shorter transition period or a transition into solar technologies visible today appear impossible. It is this quantitative situation which has led us not to change the energy elasticities for our energy demand scenarios in Figure 2.3. It might well appear necessary over time to increase rather than decrease these elasticities.

Our initial question as to the time for which the energy problem will impede our economic development and growth can now be answered at least in part. The development of appropriate economic strategies to clarify actual requirements for capital formation in the energy sector must be considered a key element. Genuine economic growth can certainly be organised on a slightly less rewarding but nearly infinite resource basis, and we have seen that technological options exist. If the economic decision on substantial capital allocation for a transition is delayed because these resources do not appear productive in the short run, the price for an unavoidable transition will continue to grow. The sooner economic science can spell out which roads to take the higher are the chances for successfully managing the energy problem.

REFERENCES

[1] Exxon; *World Energy Outlook* (Exxon Corp. New York, March 1977).
[2] OECD, *World Energy Outlook* (OECD, Paris 1977), ISBN 92-64–11595-1.
[3] Wilson, C. L., *Energy: Global Prospects 1985–2000, Report of the Workshop on Alternative Energy Strategies* (McGraw-Hill, New York, 1977).
[4] Meadows, D. L. *et al.*, *The Limit to Growth* (Universe Books, New York, 1972).
[5] Sassin, W., A. Lovins, D. L. Meadows and P. Penczynski, 'Which Way to Go?', OPTIONS 77, No. 1 (International Institute for Applied Systems Analysis, Laxenburg, Austria).
[6] Hildebrandt, R., H.-D. Schilling and W. Peters, 'Consumption of Primary Energy Carriers in the World, the USA and the Federal Republic of Germany' (Reihe Rohstoffwirtschaft International, Verlag Glückauf Essen, FRG), (in German).
[7] United Nations Recent Population Trends and Future Prospects, Report of the Secretary-General. Proc. UN World Population Conf. UNE/Conf. 60/3 (United Nations, New York).
[8] Häfele, W. and W. Sassin, 'The Global Energy System', *Ann. Rev. of Energy*, Vol. 2 (1977), (Annual Review Inc., Palo Alto, Calif., in press).
[9] Charpentier, J.-P. and J.-M. Beaujean, 'Toward a Better Understanding of Energy Consumption', *Energy*, Vol. 1, pp. 413–28 (1976).
[10] Goeller, H. E. *et al.* (Eds.), *Survey of Energy Resources 1974*. 9th World Energy Conference, Detroit, 22–7 September, 1974. (World Energy Conference, London).
[11] Barnea, J., Special Issue on UNITAR-IIASA Conference on the Future Supply of Nature-Made Oil and Gas, Important For the Future, Vol. 1, No. 5, 1977. United Nations Institute for Training and Research, New York, N.Y.
[12] Fettweis, G. B., 'Global Coal Resources', *Reihe Bergbau Rohstoffe Energie*, Vol. 12 (Verlag Glückauf GmbH Essen, FRG, 1976).

[13] Häfele, W., 'Possible Impacts of Waste Heat on Global Climate Patterns', in W. Häfele *et al.*: *Second Status Report of the IIASA Project on Energy Systems 1975* (International Institute for Applied Systems Analysis, Laxenburg, Austria, IIASA RR-76-1, 1976).

[14] Leontief, W. *et al.*, *The Future of the World Economy* (United Nations, New York, 1976), UNO Scales Nr. E.76.II.A6.

[15] Lovins, A., 'Energy Strategy: The Road Not Taken', *Foreign Affairs*, 55, 1, 65–96, 1976.

[16] Sørensen, B., 'Energy and Resources', *Science*, 189, 4199 (1975), 225–60.

[17] Matthöfer, H., 'Energy Sources for Tomorrow? Non-nuclear, non-fossil sources of primary energy', *Reihe Forschung Aktuell* (Umschauverlag Frankfurt, FRG, 1976), (in German).

[18] Partl, R., *Glacier Power from Greenland* (International Institute for Applied Systems Analysis, Laxenburg, Austria, IIASA RR (in print).

[19] Weingart, J. M., *Systems Aspects of Large-Scale Solar Energy Conversion* (International Institute for Applied Systems Analysis, Laxenburg, Austria, IIASA RM-77-23, 1977).

[20] Sassin, W., 'Secondary Energy – Today and Tomorrow', in *Large-Scale Energy Deployment and Human Environment*. Proc. Joint Seminar Techn. University Vienna/IIASA Laxenburg, Austria (in German, in print).

[21] Häfele, W., J. P. Holdren, G. Kessler and G. L. Kulcinski, *Fusion and Fission Breeder Reactors*. (International Institute for Applied Systems Analysis, Laxenburg, Austria), (in press).

[22] Häfele, W. and W. Sassin, 'Applications of Nuclear Power Other Than for Electricity Generation, Nuclear Energy Maturity. Progress in Nuclear Energy Series'. Proc. of the European Nuclear Conference Paris 1975. Plenary Sessions. (Pergamon Press, Oxford, 1976).

[23] Avenhaus, R., W. Häfele and P. E. McGrath, *Considerations on the Large-Scale Deployment of the Nuclear Fuel Cycle*. (International Institute for Applied Systems Analysis, Laxenburg, Austria, IIASA RR-75-36, 1975).

[24] Goeller, H. E. and A. M. Weinberg, 'The Age of Substitutability'. Proc of the 5th Int. Symposium of the UK Science Foundation: A Strategy for Resources. Eindhoven, 18 September 1975.

[25] Grenon, M. and B. Lapillonne, *The WELMM Approach to Energy Strategies and Options* (International Institute for Applied Systems Analysis, Laxenburg, Austria, IIASA RR-76-19, 1976).

[26] Marchetti, C., *Transport and Storage of Energy* (International Institute for Applied Systems Analysis, Laxenburg, Austria, IIASA-RR-75-38, 1975).

[27] Thoma, J., *Energy, Entropy and Information* (International Institute for Applied Systems Analysis, Laxenburg, Austria, IIASA-RM-77-32, 1977).

[28] Marchetti, C., *On 10^{12}: A Check on Earth Carrying Capacity for Man* (International Institute for Applied Systems Analysis, Laxenburg, Austria (in print)).

[29] Marchetti, C., 'Geoengineering and the Energy Island', in W. Häfele *et al.*, op. cit. [13].

[30] Doblin, C. P, *Capital Formation, Capital Stock and Capital/Output Ratios – Concepts, Definitions, Data, 1850–1975* (International Institute for Applied Systems Analysis, Laxenburg, Austria, IIASA WP-77-5, 1977).

3 Future Capital Requirements of Alternative Energy Strategies: Global Perspectives

Bruno Fritsch[1]
TECHNISCHE HOCHSCHULE, ZURICH

I. INTRODUCTION

While concern about the global energy situation does not date from the quadrupling of oil prices beginning in 1973, this event certainly accelerated the number of investigations into the problems associated with long-range energy planning. Studies have focused on three major problem areas:

(1) Are there limits to available energy resources?
(2) Are there climatic constraints on our use of energy due to the adverse side-effects from the use of fossil fuels (emission of carbon dioxide) or from the transformation of high-grade energy into low-grade energy (waste heat emission)?
(3) Will we be able to change the composition of our present energy source, now overly dependent on the fossil fuels, so that we have sufficient alternative energy sources available to compensate for the gradual exhaustion of fossil fuel resources?

II. ARE THERE LIMITS?

The first two questions do not seem to pose critical problems for the time being. As for the first, it can be easily demonstrated that the total amount of available energy is virtually unlimited, assuming that the various forms of nuclear energy are also taken into account.

Häfele and Sassin[2] give the following estimate of the total reserves theoretically available to mankind:

Coal	200 Q
Fission (breeder)	$\approx 5 \cdot 10^6$ Q
Solar	∞
Fusion	$10 \cdot 10^6$ Q

[1]The author of this paper is one of a staff of seven economists, engineers, systems analysts and mathematicians who contribute to the work of the Zencap Project here reported.

[2]See W. Häfele and W. Sassin, *Energy Strategies*, Plenary Lecture, European Physical Society, Third General Conference 'Energy and Physics', Bucharest, Romania, 9–12 September 1975. See also the previous chapter, by the same authors.

$1Q = 10^{18}$ BTU $= 2.52 \cdot 10^{17}$ kcal

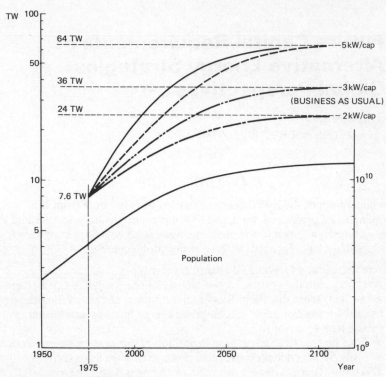

Fig. 3.1 Global energy scenarios
SOURCE   W. Häfele, *Energy Systems: Global Options and Strategies* in IIASA
Conference, Vol. 1, 10–13 May 1976, p. 59

At present man's energy consumption represents only 1/23, 026'th of the
energy provided to the earth by solar radiation. Studies have indicated that
climatic factors become critical only after man's energy consumption,
measured in watts, reaches a level equivalent to 1 per cent of the total energy
provided by the sun.[1]

Considering that the total solar energy flow to the earth's system, expressed
in watts, is 175,000 TW and that man's present energy consumption stands at
7.6 TW, the 1 per cent level mentioned above theoretically will be reached in
approximately 109 years given a 5 per cent annual increase in energy
consumption.[2]

[1]Simulations with a heat release equivalent to 150 TW, i.e. 0.08 per cent of the solar input
were conducted by IIASA researchers. See: J. Williams, G. Krömer and A. Gilchrist, *Further
Studies of the Impact of Waste Heat Release on Simulated Global Climate* (IIASA, RM-77-15,
April 1977).

[2]This follows from the following growth formula: $E_t = E_0 \cdot e^{rt}$ where r = growth rate p.a.,
t = time in years, and E_t, E_0 = energy consumption in TW in the year t or at initial time period
respectively. Taking the above relation, and solving for t, it follows $t = 1/r \cdot \ln(Y_t/Y_0)$, i.e. for
$Y_0 = 7.6$ TW and $Y_t = 1750$ TW, t = 109 years.

However, because we can justifiably expect that the total world population will level off at 10–11 billion people by 2025, man's total energy consumption will probably also stabilise well below the critical ratio of 1 per cent of total solar energy inflow, even if we assume an overall increase in the present average energy consumption of 2 kW per capita to 5 or more kW per capita. For example, scenarios suggested by IIASA indicate the ranges of magnitudes shown in Figure 3.1. These figures imply that man's total energy consumption will eventually stabilise between 20 to 100 TW.

III. CAN THE COMPOSITION OF ENERGY SOURCES BE CHANGED AS SOON AS NECESSARY?

Therefore it seems that for the present and the near future it is the third question which calls for closer investigation: that is to say, technical, economic and political factors will be crucial in determining the actual composition of energy resources available within the energy system.

While the substitution of coal for wood and oil and gas for coal occurred in earlier decades without serious economic disturbances as a combined result of the price mechanism and technical progress, any future substitutions are going to be increasingly subject to political, economic and technological uncertainties. The historical path of substitutions expressed in terms of market penetration is depicted in Figure 3.2.

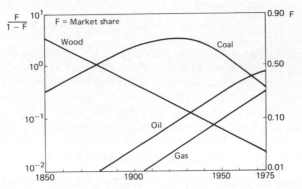

Fig. 3.2 Energy market penetrations: world
SOURCE   IIASA Conference, Vol. 1, 10–13 May 1976, p. 74

Many scenarios of future energy systems have been suggested in the last few years. They centre around three basic options, which are, to some degree, mutually exclusive:

(1) Using up the oil reserves in approximately 25–30 years, followed by the exhaustion of all gas reserves some decades later; then activating the coal reserves via large-scale transformation into liquid fuel, followed by the increased use of nuclear energy based on conventional reactors and, later on, on fast breeder technology. The phase portrait of such an option can be visualised as shown in Figure 3.3.

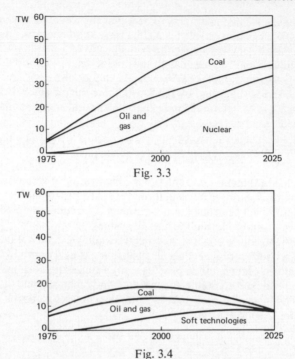

Fig. 3.3

Fig. 3.4

(2) The non-fossil, non-nuclear, soft technology future: the utilisation of oil, gas and coal will phase out in the next 50 years or so, and decentralised solar energy systems combined with other 'unconventional' energy sources such as tides, geothermic energy, wind etc. will take over (this is the Lovins' 'soft technology' scenario) (see Figure 3.4).
(3) Exhausting fossil resources, gradual extension of nuclear energy use supported by 'big' solar technologies (hybrid solar power plants), both used as the prime sources for hydrogen production.

The first option is more or less 'conventional'; it reflects the main stream of thinking behind most of the strategies currently being considered by government policy-makers. The second option – or strategy – is vigorously advocated by Lovins,[1] whereas the 'hydrogen future' is the option explained and espoused by C. Marchetti.[2]

It is evident that the 'conventional strategy' and the 'Lovins strategy' are mutually exclusive in relation to the implied or intended future growth rates of GNP and of energy consumption. It is obvious that levels of energy consumption in the 20 to 100 TW range cannot be sustained under the 'Lovins

[1] Amory B. Lovins, 'Energy Strategy: The Road not Taken?' in *Foreign Affairs*, October 1976, 65–96.
[2] C. Marchetti, *On Hydrogen and Energy Systems* (IIASA, RR-76-7, March 1976).

Strategy'. Lovins himself makes this point very clear in his article. In his opinion, it is not a question of where the upper level of energy consumption *ought* to be stabilised, but where it *must* be stabilised, taking environmental and capital requirement constraints into account. Citing his calculations presented at the Future Strategies of Energy Development Symposium, Oak Ridge Associated Universities (October 20–21 1976), Lovins concludes that '... the capital cost per delivered kilowatt of electrical energy emerges as roughly 100 times that of the traditional direct-fuel technologies on which our society has been built.'[1] Lovins' argument can be summarised as follows: since the capital costs of conventional growth-oriented energy strategies (strategies numbers 1 and 3 above) far exceed the capital formation capacity of the economic system even of the United States, and since the environmental and health hazards of these strategies are unbearable, the only viable option available to us in the future is one which involves a curtailment of the growth in energy consumption with an eventual stabilisation at a level not significantly higher than our present one. At such a level the amount of energy required can eventually be supplied by a number of soft technologies using non-fossil and non-nuclear energy sources. These technologies and systems have the advantage of being environmentally neutral, decentralised, safe, labour-intensive and 'eternal'. They thus appeal to a number of otherwise antagonistic political groups such as environmentalists, military people concerned about security, economists concerned about employment, and 'eternalists' who worry about the exhaustion of our resources. All that is required to get this strategy underway is the decision to stop the growth of energy consumption as soon as possible.[2]

The big technology, nuclear and/or hydrogen, scenarios assume, contrary to Lovins, that both the environmental as well as the capital formation problems can be solved. However, most of the advocates of this strategy recognise the importance of political and institutional factors: 'The problems here (in the TW domain) are not so much technological hardware elements; we have learned to master these. Instead, they concern institutions and the soft aspects of complex management and decision making, licensing, regulations, standard setting. Our limited capability to deal with these questions, including that of a global political order, will establish the real limits.'[3]

As to the official energy policy statements, most of the industrial countries, both in the West and in the Soviet bloc, can be considered as variations on the first option: the USSR has announced that it is aiming for a plutonium future, i.e. for the further development of fast breeders which, in the coming decades, will gradually replace the diminishing fossil sources. The US has opted for the continuation of nuclear development; however – for the time being – without

---

[1]*Foreign Affairs*, op. cit., p. 69.

[2]Although this argument is sustained by a certain logic, it amounts to a statement analogous to the following: smoking will not be hazardous to health if men can reduce their breathing needs.

[3]W. Häfele, *Energy Systems*, op. cit., p. 90.

the fast breeder component and with a more substantial exploitation of her own coal resources. Europe, with few oil and gas resources, with virtually no uranium reserves[1] and with coal deposits which are unsuitable for large-scale scraping, is in the most disadvantageous position. France seems to be pushing the fast breeder programme. The Federal Republic of Germany is relying heavily on research while trying to continue the already delayed nuclear programme in spite of all the political difficulties caused by new forms of citizen protests.

Reviewing the three strategy areas mentioned above, we can observe that each of them is subject to either political, economic and/or technological constraints. In the following section we will first take a closer look at the economic constraints, particularly at the capital requirements of alternative energy strategies. Then at a later stage we will also investigate, at least in part, some of the political factors involved in the decisions related to alternative energy strategies.

IV. CAPITAL REQUIREMENTS OF ALTERNATIVE SYSTEMS

Let us now consider the capital requirements for alternative energy systems. It is important to note that, given today's technologies, any energy-generating and transforming system, even in a stationary state, will itself use up energy in two ways. First, energy is directly absorbed in the transformation of one form of energy into another. Secondly, energy is indirectly absorbed by the system through the energy required to produce materials needed for reinvestment. In a growing economy with an increasing total consumption of primary energy, the long lead times of investment make the energy-generating and transforming systems absorb even more energy. Thus, even with physically unlimited energy resources, the growth rates of the two systems, the energy-generating/transforming system and the non-energy production system of the economy are mutually interdependent: one system cannot 'outflow' the other. This situation can be visualised as shown in Figure 3.5.

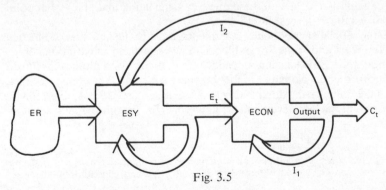

Fig. 3.5

Given the following variables: Y_0 = initial income, Y_t = income at time t, r = growth rate of GNP, r' = rate of technical progress, C_t = consumption at time t, I_1 = investment in the energy system, I_2 = investment in the non-energy system, I = total investment ($= I_1 + I_2$), E_t = energy production in time t, ($= \sigma I_2$), K = lead time of investment, α = fraction of income used for consumption, λ = fraction of unconsumed income going into the energy system, σ = productivity of investments in the energy system, we can determine the ratio

$$\frac{E_t}{C_t}$$

by using the following definitions and relationships

$$C_t = \alpha Y_0 \cdot e^{rt}$$

$$C_{t-K} = \alpha Y_0 e^{r(t-K)}$$

$$I_2 = \lambda(1-\alpha)Y_0 e^{r(t-K)}$$

$$E_t = \alpha_t I_2$$

$$\sigma_t = \sigma_0 e^{r't}$$

$$\frac{E_t}{C_t} = \frac{\sigma_0 e^{r't}\lambda(1-\alpha)Y_0 e^{r(t-K)}}{\alpha Y_0 e^{rt}} = \frac{\sigma_0 e^{r't} \cdot \lambda(1-\alpha)}{\alpha e^{rk}}$$

Thus the fraction of production going into the energy system, together with σ, the growth rate of the economy, and the lead time of investment, determines the ratio E_t/C_t. Since both λ as well as σ depend, among other factors, upon the technology available, the most important parameters influencing the ratio E_t/C_t are the rate of technical progress and the growth rate of the economy. Assuming that the growth rate of the economy and technical progress are positively related, and assuming that λ is a decreasing, and σ an increasing function of technical progress, one could envisage an equilibrium position between the growing demand for energy in a growing economy and the increased efficiency of the energy generation and transformation processes, thus keeping the net share of investment going into the expansion of the energy system as a percentage of total investment constant. For the time being, we are still far from achieving such a dynamic equilibrium. In fact, the world energy production and consumption patterns reflect three types of fundamental disequilibria, two of which are shown in Figure 3.6.

(1) In consumption as well as in production we depend heavily upon a 'spot source' of energy, i.e. oil and gas. Roughly 7.0 TW out of the total 7.5 TW world primary energy use is still based on fossil sources (5.5 TW gas and oil), and these are in turn heavily centred in one region of the world.

(2) We have an extremely unequal distribution among states and regions in the consumption of energy. Consumption ranges from 12 kW/cap for the US to 0.3 kW/cap for certain Asian countries.

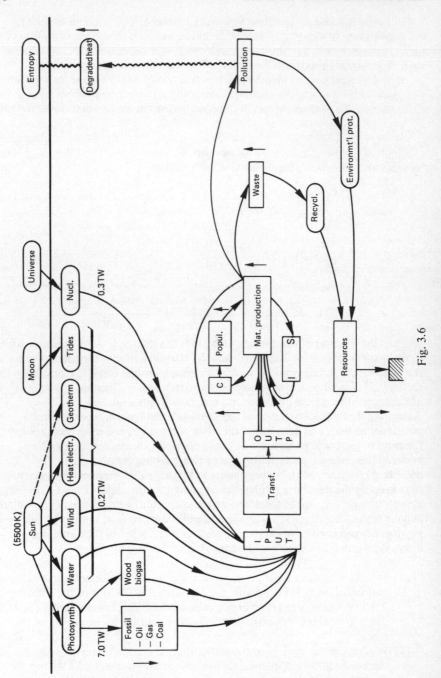

Fig. 3.6

(3) The third disequilibrium is the most fundamental one: we receive high-grade energy from the sun (5500 K) i.e. energy in the form of high negentropy, and we 'use up' this high level of negentropy by 'producing' entropy. Using negentropy for the transformation of matter in producing material goods, we form new structures and hence new 'orders' which can be considered as a form of negentropy. However, in the course of this production we also generate new entropy in the form of waste, pollution, and, finally, in the form of degraded (waste) heat released into the atmosphere. As can be seen from Figure 3.6 our present production system, through its high dependence upon fossil resources, is exacerbating rather than ameliorating this kind of disequilibrium: while rapidly using up the negentropy (accumulated over many millions of years) in the form of fossil sources, we build up waste, pollution and waste heat which is partly 'accumulated' or 'locked' into the atmosphere by the release of CO_2 due to the burning of fossil fuels.

There is little hope that these three disequilibria will be corrected by the usual economic adjustments via the price mechanism or other semi-automatic adjustments such as classical stabilisation policy measures. This is even more unlikely under the concrete conditions of the international system which are characterised by a still-growing population and the necessity to expand production for the growing population in the Third World.

As can be seen from Table 3.1, the various regions of the world differ substantially both in the magnitude of GDP, their investment potential, and in the average annual increase in total energy consumption. We will use this table as a reference for the estimate of the cost — expressed as a percentage of the investment potential — involved in the various energy strategies.

Table 3.2 shows the structure of the present primary energy use, including regional differences. As can be seen from the regional distributions, 85 per cent of total primary energy is consumed by the industrial nations and only 15 per cent by the LDCs.[1] The respective TW-values as well as the shares of the four basic energy carrier systems (solid, liquid, natural gas and hydro-nuclear) in their regional distribution are given in this table.

In estimating the cost of additional energy production we assumed that at present prices, the following costs would apply:

$ 588 per installed kW for coal
$ 390 per installed kW for liquid fuels and natural gas
$1000 per installed kW hydro-nuclear.

We are aware that these figures represent approximate values and that costs for distribution networks are usually estimated to be at least as high as costs for the installation of the respective production facilities.

Taking these tentative figures and the approximate levels of primary energy

[1] But it has to be considered that the industrial nations produce the bulk of the materials needed for reinvestment in 'low energy consumption' countries.

TABLE 3.1   1973, GDP, GROSS DOMESTIC INVESTMENT IN BILL. US$ AT CURRENT MARKET PRICES, AND ANNUAL INCREASE OF ENERGY CONSUMPTION IN % P.A.

Item \ Regions	North America[a]	Western Europe[b]	Japan	Southern hemisphere[c]	Centrally planned economies[d]	Developing countries Total	OPEC[e]	Other	World total
GDP	1422.6	1298.2	413.3	85.2	724.3	869.6	126.0	743.6	4813.2
Gross Domestic Investment 1965–73 as % of GDP	18.4[f]	25.0[f]	37.4	26.7[f]	34.0[g]	18.6	24.3[f]	17.6[g]	24.6[f]
Investment potential[h]	261.8	324.6	154.6	22.7	246.3	162.0	30.6	131.4	1172.0
Average annual increase in total energy consumption 1970–73 in %[i]	3.6	4.4	7.5	5.3	5.0	7.4	12.2	6.3	–

[a] United States and Canada

[b] Austria, Belgium, Cyprus, Denmark, Finland, France, FR Germany, Greece, Iceland, Italy, Luxembourg, Malta, Netherlands, Norway, Portugal, Spain, Sweden, Switzerland, Turkey, United Kingdom and Yugoslavia

[c] Australia, New Zealand, South Africa

[d] Albania, Bulgaria, Czechoslovakia, German Democratic Republic, Hungary, Poland, Romania and USSR

[e] Algeria, Ecuador, Gabon, Indonesia, Iran, Iraq, Kuwait, Libyan Arab Republic, Nigeria, Qatar, Saudi Arabia, United Arab Emirates and Venezuela

[f] Weighted average

[g] Estimate

[h] Defined on the basis of the weighted average percentages of GDP for 1965–73

[i] World Economic Survey Table 18, p. 60

SOURCE *World Tables 1976* (IBRD, Washington D.C. 1976); *World Economic Survey* (United Nations, New York, 1976).

TABLE 3.2   STRUCTURE AND REGIONAL DISTRIBUTION OF THE PRIMARY ENERGY USE IN PER CENT AND IN TW, 1973

Regions countries — Structure of primary energy use	North America	Western Europe	Japan	Southern hemisphere	Centrally planned economies	Developing countries			Total
						Total	*OPEC*	*Other*	
Solid in TW	19.7% 0.517	25.1% 0.376	18.9% 0.07086	60.0% 0.09	55.0% 0.94875	6.7% 0.07537	1.5% 0.01237	21% 0.063	27.7 2.07798
Liquid in TW	44.7% 1.173	58.7% 0.881	76.7% 0.28763	34.3% 0.05145	26.9% 0.46403	54.52% 0.61335	50.2% 0.41415	66.4% 0.1992	46.3 3.47046
Natural gas in TW	33.0% 0.866	12.7% 0.191	1.8% 0.00675	3.6% 0.00540	17.0% 0.29325	36.71% 0.41303	46.9% 0.38693	8.7% 0.0261	23.7 1.77543
Hydro-nuclear in TW	2.6% 0.068	3.5% 0.053	2.6% 0.00975	2.1% 0.00315	1.1% 0.01898	2.0% 0.02325	1.4% 0.01155	3.9% 0.0117	2.3 0.17613
As % of total world consumption	35% = 2.625TW	20% = 1.5TW	5% = 0.375TW	2% = 0.15TW	23% = 1.725TW	15% = 1.125TW	11% = 0.825TW	4% = 0.3TW	100% = 7.5TW
Percentage ratio of production to consump. Total	89.8	39.7	9.0	102.7	106.4	394	1655	75	
Petrol	74.8	3.7	0.4	54.4	120.0	562	3169	62	

SOURCE Calculated from *World Economics Survey 1975, Changing Structure of Energy Production and Consumption 1961–1973*, Table 18, p. 60.

consumption in the various regions of the world, we will estimate the cost of the following four alternative energy 'strategies':

(a)   Continuation of the energy demand at historical growth rates (1970–73) within the traditional structure of energy carriers. This is the short-term status quo scenario.
(b)   Switching over to nuclear supplies in order to satisfy the projected increase at the historical growth rates of 1970 to 1973. This scenario may be called the 'nuclear switch' scenario.
(c)   Remaining within the historical energy resources structure but at only a 2 per cent p.a. growth rate of primary energy consumption.
(d)   Going nuclear only to provide the projected increments (as with (b)) but at a growth rate of only 2 per cent p.a.

The results of these four different 'strategies' are expressed in Table 3.3 in terms both of absolute amounts in billion dollars at current prices as well as in percentages of the investment potential of the various regions.

If our figures are approximately correct, we can draw from our findings the following conclusions:

(1)   For scenario (a) which is politically the easiest but at the same time the shortest term in view of the gradual exhaustion of fossil resources, the net investment costs of expansion can easily be met following certain economic adjustments. As percentage of the investment potential, these additional costs vary from 8.1 per cent (for Japan) to 18.1 per cent (for the Southern hemisphere).
(2)   In order to cover the incremental increase in primary energy consumption (at historical growth rates) using nuclear energy only, (scenario (b)), the energy investment 'burden' would increase to 36 per cent of the investment potential of North America and 35 per cent for the centrally planned economies. This is the most expensive scenario of the four. If one takes into account that, as mentioned above, the installation of distribution networks requires the same amount of investment as the setting up of new additional production facilities – in this case conventional nuclear reactors – the share of investment going into energy generation and distribution systems may well exceed 50 per cent of total available investment potential. This may cause certain adjustment problems in terms of increased capital costs and hence decreased growth rates of the respective economies accompanied by rising prices and the possibility of declining overall employment (stagflation). However this is only one possible – and by no means certain – outcome of such a scenario. Whether or not such a development would take place depends on the constellation of many technical and economic parameters which can be dealt with only within the framework of a complex model such as the one developed by the research team on the ZENCAP-Project.

TABLE 3.3 COST OF ADDITIONAL ENERGY PRODUCTION, IN BILLION US$, ASSUMING ALL INCREASED ENERGY CONSUMPTION REQUIRES NEW INVESTMENT

Scenarios	North America	Western Europe	Japan	Southern hemisphere	Centrally planned economies	Developing countries OPEC	Other
(a) Within the historical pattern at historical growth rates of consumption	42.0	30.5	12.5	4.1	43.6	40.4	8.6
As % of investment potential	16.0%	9.4%	8.1%	18.1%	17.7%	137.9%	6.5%
(b) Nuclear only at historical growth rates of consumption	94.5	66.0	28.1	7.9	86.2	100.6	18.9
As % of investment potential	36%	20.3%	18.2%	34.8%	35.0%	343.3%	14.2%
(c) In the historical pattern but at 2% p.a. increase in total energy consumption	23.3	13.8	3.3	1.6	17.4	6.6	2.7
As % of investment potential	8.9%	4.2%	2.1%	7.0%	7.0%	22.5%	2.0%
(d) Nuclear only at 2% p.a. increase in total energy consumption	52.5	30.0	7.5	3.0	34.5	16.5	6.0
As % of investment potential	20%	9.2%	4.8%	13.2%	14.0%	56.3%	4.5%

(3) Slowing down the growth rate to 2 per cent p.a. and continuing to rely on relatively inexpensive (fossil) sources is the 'cheapest' alternative. This scenario shows the importance of conserving energy by decreasing the growth rate of consumption. However, it is in the very nature of conservation that the 'potential to conserve' itself is subject to early exhaustion.

(4) Scenario (d) represents, in a way, a reasonable alternative. It is based on the assumption that the growth rate of primary energy consumption can be reduced to 2 per cent p.a. (this corresponds for example to the present policy targets of the US) and that the supply of this additional energy requirement will be covered by nuclear energy. The 'burdens' involved in this scenario are economically acceptable and probably even lower than stated in Table 3.3 (last line), if one assumes a gradual replacement (rather than sudden, as assumed in our scenario) of the energy supply by nuclear energy.

One remark has to be made in reference to the apparently 'impossible' consequences for the OPEC countries of scenarios (a) and (b). We have relied on the official statistics. According to the data made available through the World Bank's World Tables, the total GDP of all OPEC countries at market prices (as listed in Table 3.1) in 1973 was 133.2 billion US $. Taking the estimated investment ratio of 0.22 (average of 1965–73), the 'investment potential' yields only 29.3 billion $ for all OPEC countries. In view of the developments of the years 1974 to 1976 this figure represents a great underestimate as to the present potential of these countries. In the year 1973–74 alone the net increase in GDP for all these countries was 28 per cent. On the other hand – and this seems to be equally important – these countries obviously cannot sustain a 12 per cent annual increase in energy consumption for long even if they were to derive all of their energy supply from their own oil and gas sources. Thus the results of our investigation concerning the energy strategies open to the OPEC countries should be viewed with caution.

V. CONCLUSIONS

The future capital requirements of alternative energy strategies are influenced by technological, political and economic factors. Our findings suggest that, although the total burden involved in the development of additional and new energy-generating systems will substantially increase, the overall economic stress with respect to the capital formation ability of the various regions of the world will not be excessive and lies well within the adjustment capacity of the developed economies. With the increasing level of total energy consumption, the LDCs will have to allocate a higher percentage of their investment potential into the further development of their own energy resources. The importance of (and sensitivity of the various models we have worked with to) technical change is obvious. It can therefore be concluded that, at the present time, it may be a wise decision for a highly developed country such as Germany, to invest a considerable amount of money in energy research.[1] Buying time through conservation is a necessary but only temporarily effective policy. If exaggerated it may even jeopardise further technical progress required to solve the long-range energy problem.

This long-range and in a sense 'ultimate' solution of the energy problem consists in the restoration of the fundamental equilibrium between the use of negentropy and the 'generation' of various forms of entropy. For the time being, mankind, with its present methods of exploitation of the various energy resources, still tends to increase rather than to decrease this fundamental disequilibrium.

Without doubt, further intensive research in this highly complex matter is required. The work of the research group which in a joint effort under my responsibility developed the attached models (to be validated within the next few months) may be considered as a modest contribution to the solution of these problems which are also the subject of intensive research in many other places in the world, such as the International Institute of Applied Systems Analysis (IIASA) in Laxenburg, the Brookhaven National Laboratory, and ERDA or the MIT-Workshop on Alternative Energy Strategies, to name only a few.

REFERENCES

Bell, Charles R., *Solar Energy Options* (IIASA, RM-77-20, May 1977).
Choucri, Nazli *et al.*, *A Forecasting Model of Energy Politics: International Perspectives*. Paper prepared for the Annual Meetings of the International Studies Association, Toronto, February 1976.
Doblin, Claire P., *Data Provided for W. D. Nordhaus Study: the Demand for Energy: an International Perspective* (IIASA, RM-76-18, March 1976).
Häfele, W., *Energy Systems: Global Options and Strategies*, in IIASA Conference 1976, op. cit.
Häfele, W. *et al.*, *Second Status Report of the IIASA Project on Energy Systems*, RR-76-1.
Häfele, W. and A. Makarov, *Modeling of Medium and Long-Range Energy Strategies*, IIASA Workshop on Energy Strategies, Conception and Embedding. May 17–18 1977.
Häfele, W. and W. Sassin, *Energy Strategies*, Plenary lecture, European Physical Society, Third General Conference 'Energy and Physics', Bucharest, Romania, 9–12 September 1975.
IIASA *Conference 1976*, 10–13 May 1976, Vols. 1 and 2, 1976.
Lovins, Amory B., 'Energy Strategy: The Road not Taken?', *Foreign Affairs* (October 1976), pp. 65–96.

---

[1]According to the latest data, the Government of the Federal Republic of Germany has allocated more than 600 million $ for energy research.

Marchetti, C., *On Hydrogen and Energy Systems* (IIASA, RR-76-7, March 1976).
OECD, *Energy Conservation in the International Energy Agency* (Paris 1976).
OECD, *World Energy Outlook* (Paris 1977).
Williams, J., G. Krömer and A. Gilchrist, *Further Studies of the Impact of Waste Heat Release on Simulated Global Climate:* Part 1. (IIASA, RM-77-15, April 1977).
Workshop on Alternative Energy Strategies (WAES): *Energy Demand and Projections of 1985 Demand* (MIT Press, 1977). Analysis of 1972.

4 Are there really Depletable Resources?

Mogens Boserup
INSTITUTE OF ECONOMICS, UNIVERSITY OF COPENHAGEN

I. NO SPACESHIP

Among the least helpful slogans coined in the resources and environment debate was that of 'Spaceship Earth'.

The comparison of the earth with a spaceship is misleading in at least two important ways. First, it conveys the idea of our planet as a fully independent and closed system. In such a system, with no possibility of input from the outside, the law of entropy (the second thermodynamic law) works inexorably, as is well known. But the 'spaceship' metaphor makes people forget that the planet earth is only part of a larger system which includes the sun from whose reservoir of low entropy life is kept going on the earth. That reservoir is by no means undepletable but I am told that it is huge enough to last for a few billion years which is far beyond the conceivable duration of the species *homo sapiens*. Therefore, the entropy story, entertaining or thrilling as it may be, is irrelevant, in the precise sense that nothing follows from it for human action and policy, today or in any future about which we can sensibly talk and plan.

The second and quite different way in which the 'spaceship' metaphor is misleading is the implied idea of cessation, once and for all, of technological progress. To be in a spaceship means, if it means anything, to be in a fully and fatally programmed world, where the supply of resources, including of course natural resources, is rigidly fixed in quantity and cannot be put to use in new and better ways. In short, a world without substitution and without bright new ideas.

Suppose for a moment – and only for the sake of the argument – that the Doomsayers are right. If there really were the likelihood of depletion of one or more resources which are essential for human survival and for which no replacement could be imagined, then it would be insufficient, and indeed unethical, just to slow down the growth of consumption of such resources or even to stop all further increase of their consumption since this, under the given assumption, would be at the cost of coming generations. The only ethically defensible policy, if the welfare of the following generations is deemed to be as important as that of the present one, would be to reduce *per capita* consumption of the resource or resources in question to survival levels. To use more would be to murder coming generations, and to consume less would be to starve present generations to death and thus indirectly a kind of genocide of future generations.

49

The fact that this conclusion is rarely, if ever, drawn by those who worry about depletion suggests that in the end they are perhaps not quite convinced about the truth of their main contention: that use of natural resources today goes at the expense of such use tomorrow.

II. KINDS OF NATURAL RESOURCES

The fear of depletion of natural resources is only one element in a triple 'syndrome' including problems of environment in a large sense, population growth, and insufficiency of natural resources. The present chapter is almost exclusively concerned with the last-named problem, and even within this limited field – that of natural resources – the scope of the chapter had to be restricted in two ways.

First, only the so-called depletable resources are to be considered at some length. Little will be said about the renewable or regenerating natural resources, which may be limited in quantity – for instance agricultural land – but cannot be depleted, although they may be diminished or destroyed by overtaxing their productive capacity. Secondly, apart from some incidental remarks we shall consider only those kinds of depletable natural resources which deliver raw or auxiliary materials for manufacturing or energy production. This excludes the important problems of natural resources which enter directly into consumption, e.g. recreative resources, access to solitude in natural surroundings, and similar amenities.

Thus what remains for consideration is mineral deposits of all sorts, including fossil fuels; and the purpose is to consider critically the very concept of 'depletability', so as to see whether, in our time, it can be given an interpretation which makes it useful for economists.

For further clarification, the distinctions just made are set out in Table 4.1, with a classification of physical resources along two dimensions: permanent/non-permanent and producible/non-producible.[1]

In box A are resources which are both permanent and producible, the main example being those kinds of soil improvement which are so durable that they may be regarded as produced once and for all.[2] In group B, permanent but non-reproducible resources, are, of course, agricultural land and also some sources of energy, e.g. waterfalls, which are permanent *sub specie humana*, and

---

[1] This classification was borrowed, with minor changes, from Hayek, *The Pure Theory of Capital* (1941), p. 58. For Hayek, the classification was intended, of course, to throw light on the relationship between different possibilities of defining the concept of capital.

[2] This closely corresponds to Quesnay's *avances foncières*, i.e. clearing work which makes potentially cultivable land cultivable for good. Cfr. Ricardo, *Principles*, Ch. 18 *in fine*, where the concept of 'original and indestructible powers of the soil' is extended to include capital which 'once expended in the improvement of a farm, is inseparably amalgamated with the land ... [so that] ... the return obtained will ever after be wholly of the nature of rent'. At the other extreme, Kaldor maintains that 'no type of natural resources truly possesses "indestructible powers"', since, for instance, land can be kept permanently in good condition only by continued maintenance. (See N. Kaldor, 'The Controversy on the Theory of Capital', in *Essays on Value and Distribution*, 1960, vol. I, Ch. 9; first printed 1937, and cfr. Hayek's objections, *op. cit.* pp. 54 and 58.)

TABLE 4.1   CLASSIFICATION OF PHYSICAL RESOURCES

Permanent? \ Producible?	Yes	No
Yes	**A** e.g. soil improvements	**B** e.g. agricultural land, waterfalls, wind, sun, tidal water
No	**C** produced means of production	**D** e.g. fossil fuels, ores and other minerals, landscape for recreation

wind, sunshine and tidal water which are permanent *sub specie Telluris*.
Likewise, water may be classified in this category.

The group of producible and non-permanent resources (C) includes physical capital in the usual sense of produced means of production. We are left, then, with category D, resources which are neither regenerating nor producible: mineral deposits and fossil fuels, together with the 'natural amenities' already mentioned. Category D can be taken to include also the 'capacity of the environment to absorb waste', which is indeed a natural resource necessary for sustained production.

Naturally, there are some borderline problems in such a discrete yes–no classification, but for our purpose these four boxes will do.

A more fundamental objection to this schematic presentation is to ask whether the two distinctions producible/non-producible and permanent/non-permanent are perhaps misleading under modern scientific and technological conditions. This question of whether the very idea of 'existing quantities' of the non-producible resources, and hence the concept of depletability, is useful for the economist, or for anybody else, is the main theme of this paper. To approach that question in an orderly way, we begin with a brief account of the treatment of 'depletion' in modern economic theory.

III. THEORIES OF 'DEPLETION'

As often mentioned, a crucial distinction must be made between the economic and the physical availability of a resource.[1]

To make this difference quite clear, it is sufficient to list the rigorous conditions which would have to be fulfilled if physical and economic depletion of a given resource were to occur simultaneously: The necessary (though often insufficient) conditions would be that the resource in question consist of a completely homogeneous, and, consequently, sharply delimited deposit which

---

[1]See, for instance, Paul G. Bradley, 'Increasing Scarcity: The Case of Energy Resources', *American Economic Review* (May 1973), p. 124, and Robert Solow, 'The Economics of Resources and the Resources of Economics', *American Economic Review* (May 1974), p. 3.

can be extracted under conditions of constant cost. Such deposits, if they exist, must be extremely rare. In the normal case, 'economic exhaustion' of a deposit occurs when further extraction becomes unprofitable owing to higher cost per unit output of given quality and/or to changes on the side of demand. Needless to say, this point of economic exhaustion is usually reached long before the deposit is depleted in any physical sense. This is confirmed by everyday observation: it frequently happens that the exploitation of a mine which had been abandoned is later resumed under changed conditions of demand or technology.

The economic 'theory of the mine' can be traced back at least to Ricardo,[1] and it is clearly, though briefly, set out by Marshall: The marginal supply price must cover not only the marginal cost of extraction, as in the case of true Ricardian rent, but also a royalty per ton of ore produced equalling the diminution of the value of the mine caused by the removal of 'the ton from nature's storehouse'.[2]

With due acknowledgement of a pioneering article by L. C. Gray,[3] the first major treatment of this problem area came in 1931 with a magisterial analysis by the late Harold Hotelling.

Hotelling's motivation for examining the depletion problem in depth came from contemporary concern about excessive use of natural resources, loudly voiced by the American conservation movement. It can be seen in the introduction to his article that Hotelling shared this anxiety, at least to some extent:

> Contemplation of the world's disappearing supplies of minerals, forests and other exhaustible assets has led to demands for regulation of their exploitation. The feeling that these products are now too cheap for the good of future generations, that they are being selfishly exploited at too rapid a rate, and that in consequence of their excessive cheapness they are being produced and consumed wastefully has given rise to the conservation movement...
>
> In contrast to the conservationist belief that too rapid exploitation of natural resources is taking place, we have the retarding influence of monopolies and combinations, whose growth in industries directly concerned with the exploitation of irreplaceable resources has been striking. If 'combinations in restraint of trade' extort high prices from consumers and restrict production, can it be said that their products are too cheap and are being sold too rapidly?[4]

Already these first sentences show that Hotelling's concept of depletion was more hard and fast than most economists would now, 45 years later, be

[1]Ricardo. *Principles*. Chs. 2, 3 and 24.
[2]Marshall. *Principles*. V. x. 6.
[3]L. C. Gray. 'Rent under the Assumption of Exhaustibility', *Quarterly Journal of Economics* (1914). 466–89.
[4]Harold Hotelling. 'The Economics of Exhaustible Resources', *Journal of Political Economy*. vol. 39 (April 1931). p. 137ff. Cfr. Robert Solow's comment on this same passage. *op. cit*., p. 1.

prepared to accept. As mentioned further below, this half-century brought an important change in the perception of the physical meaning of 'resource quantities' and of their 'consumption' and 'depletion'. Corresponding changes have occurred in economists' attitude to Hotelling's approach.

A present-day reader of Hotelling's article may wonder why he emphasises the danger of increasing monopolistic control of the extraction of irreplaceable resources. The explanation is probably to be found in Hotelling's American background and we would now be more inclined to think (*pace* OPEC) that the world markets for metals and other minerals are examples of relatively effective competitive price formation.

Be that as it may. Hotelling's search for a criterion for the optimal rate of extraction was carried out within a field delimited by two opposite possibilities: the Scylla of *too low* prices at the expense of future generations, and the Charybdis of *too high* prices, at the expense of today's consumers. Hotelling's analysis takes him through what he describes as 'a whole forest of intriguing problems', but we must here be content with a short and highly simplified sketch of just those features of Hotelling's theory which are necessary for a comparison with the answers now given to the same questions.

The analysis is explicitly concerned with 'absolutely irreplaceable resources', which is broadly coterminous with mineral deposits and fossil fuels.

Hotelling's firm assumption is that the owner will wish to maximise the present value of all future profit. Under full competition among the mining firms the time profile of production is then determined by the condition that marginal profit per physical unit extracted and sold in the current year must equal the discounted value of expected profits from an additional unit extracted in any future year. The fulfilment of this condition would normally imply that the producer, even under full competition, holds his scale of production down to a level where marginal cost is lower than the market price. The point is that each single mining firm is assumed to think that the deposit it owns is of inexorably given size, so that one extra ton of ore extracted this year involves a corresponding reduction of the amount available for future extraction, under different conditions of cost and demand.

In other words, the optimal extraction plan for a mining firm intent on maximum profits under competition must be such that it is impossible, by a change of the time-shape of production, to increase the present value of expected profits over the mine's lifetime. This implies that the present value of the difference between expected price and expected marginal cost must be the same for all periods with production. Or, to put it another way, the spread of extraction over future years must be such that the joint net advantage of expected lower cost (owing to smaller scale of delayed extraction) and/or expected increase of the market price per unit equals the loss of interest which is caused by the postponement of extraction and is measured by the discounting to present value.[1]

[1]See also the recently published book by Orris C. Herfindahl and Allen V. Kneese, *Economic Theory of Natural Resources* (Columbus, Ohio, 1974), Ch. 4, esp. pp. 116–19.

Very briefly, this is the 'theory of the mine' under competition, which has been the normal, almost traditional doctrine since Hotelling's article of 1931. It is hardly necessary to add that there is a wide distance between reality and the assumptions made, *inter alia* that of full knowledge and anticipation of all relevant circumstances. Hotelling was himself the first to warn against *laissez-faire* conclusions from his exposition of the solution in an ideal situation of perfect competition.[1]

As already mentioned, Hotelling thought that monopoly was widespread in mining and other extractive industries. Not unexpectedly, his thorough discussion of monopoly concludes that

> monopolistic exploitation of an exhaustible asset is likely to be protracted immensely longer than competition would bring about or a maximising of social value would require.[2]

In our time, however, Hotelling's fear of widespread restriction of output owing to monopolisation in the mining industry does sound somewhat exaggerated: the possibilities of substitution among different metals, and between these and other natural materials, are now so great that an effective and somewhat durable monopoly of supply *ad modum* OPEC seems unlikely for raw produce other than oil.

Let us therefore return to the case of competition. The question is this: is it realistic to expect that the passage of time will raise the net price per unit (i.e. market price less unit cost) and thereby raise royalties, actually paid or imputed? If yes, there must be (as already hinted) a motivation for limitation of current production, by accepting a lower current profit than could have been achieved, in the hope of future compensation through a higher net price under increasing scarcity. In Hotelling's words:

> The growth of population and the rising prices to consumers of competing exhaustible goods would lead to a positive value of g.* On the other hand, the progress of science might lead to the gradual introduction of new substitutes for the commodity in question, *tending to make g negative*.[3] (Italics added).

*In Hotelling's notation, g is a coefficient indicating the effect of the passage of time on profits per unit.

And in another connection Hotelling mentions as a possible assumption that

> ... the sign of g is reversed, owing to the progressive discovery of substitutes, the direct effect of the passage of time being then to decrease instead of increase the price.[4]

[1] *Op. cit.*, p. 144ff.
[2] *Op. cit.*, p. 152. Hotelling was fully aware not only of the possibility of monopoly (as mentioned in the text) but also of non-monopolistic deviations from the solution of full competition such as the effects of fear of nationalisation. This and other deviations (in contrast with that of monopoly) tend, according to Hotelling, towards an excessively rapid rate of extraction.
[3] *Op. cit.*, p. 153.
[4] *Ibid*, p. 159.

Thus, Hotelling did hint at the possibility that the passage of time, far from leading to increased scarcity, might lower the profitability of extraction. But it is highly interesting, I think, that this possibility is mentioned only *en passant*, as a conceivable case which must be noted for the sake of completeness. In this special, but crucial point Hotelling's 1931 article now seems to have dated.

IV. A MORE RECENT CONCEPTION

Hotelling's approach – let us call it the traditional view – is now to be compared with modern reality, and with more recent theoretical literature on depletion problems.

As mentioned, a main point in the traditional theory is that under certain assumptions the owner of a 'depletable' resource – a 'mine', taken in a wide sense – will limit current production in such a way that current profits are held below their possible level for the sake of higher profits in the future. But, as stressed in a seminal article by Richard L. Gordon, published in 1967,[1] this reasoning can be pertinent to the realities of our time only on one further condition: not only must the mine be depletable in the purely physical sense in which any particular mine is depletable. It is further required that the owner considers it as certain, or at least highly probable, that the mine will actually be emptied within a future near enough to influence current decisions about the rate of extraction. *Only under that assumption is it true that the extraction of an additional ton of ore this year means that one ton less can be extracted in the future.* If that assumption is shown to be unwarranted, the traditional theory of depletable resources falls like a house of cards. And the question then immediately presents itself whether the very concept of 'depletability' is economically meaningful in connection with natural resources for production.

One way to pursue this question is to ask: is there empirical evidence of that abstention from profit maximisation in the current period which is postulated by the Hotelling theory? Richard L. Gordon's answer is candid:

Since mineral industries generally do maximize current profits, the theory actually seems to suggest that exhaustion of minerals is unlikely. Thus, instead of providing rules of conservation policy, the theory *suggests* that conservationists are concerned about a non-existent problem.[2]

In this connection, Gordon also refers to a remark by the late Orris Herfindahl which says almost the same thing, but in a slightly different way, so that the word 'exhaustion' is saved:

... the future may exert so little pressure on present decisions that the effects of exhaustion are too small to measure (that is, user costs ... are nearly

[1] Richard L. Gordon, 'A Reinterpretation of the Pure Theory of Exhaustion', *Journal of Political Economy* (1967).
[2] *Op. cit.*, p. 276. Gordon's italics.

zero). Exhaustion will occur, but present generations may wisely ignore it.[1]

Even more recently, in 1974, J. A. Kay and J. A. Mirrlees arrived at what is in practical terms the same conclusion, although by a different route: they asked the question about the relative size of the gap between the price per unit of output and the marginal cost of extraction which is postulated by the Hotelling theory, as already mentioned. They found that under reasonable assumptions about the size of the resource still in the ground (measured as a multiple of current annual extraction) and on the assumption that the rate of interest is not exceedingly low, this gap is extremely small, indeed negligible, except in the very last 2–4 decades before exhaustion. Thus, the market would be 'pretty much like a rather competitive market for a *non*-exhaustible commodity.[2]

The preceding paragraphs are not meant to imply that the market behaviour of private resource owners is necessarily optimal. In a way, Kaldor is right to say that 'it is notorious that … the price mechanism fails completely in making any allowance for the probable higher scarcity of *exhaustible* natural resources in the future.[3] It is of course true that the market mechanism has no clairvoyant power. At best, it can register the weighted average of the market agents' visions of the future. It is pertinent, nevertheless, to ask why Kaldor is here speaking about a *higher* scarcity of natural resources in the future as being *probable*. Might not the market mechanism just as well fail by *overrating* future scarcity?

We cannot here go far into this question of whether a kind of socialist planning of the use of so-called depletable resources for production would be more restrictive than the market mechanism. It may well be that a social (or socialist) evaluation would try to take care of a more distant future, i.e. use a lower rate of discount to establish the present value of future utility, implying a relatively slow rate of extraction.[4] But it remains an open question whether such more conservationist policies would turn out, in retrospect, to have been well-advised: future events may well vindicate the defiant statement by Kay and Mirrlees (in the article just mentioned) that 'in the currently topical case of oil, the arguments that the world is using too little rather than too much seem irresistible'. (p. 171f.)

[1]This is Gordon's rendering of a text by Herfindahl, 'Depletion and Economic Theory' presented at the annual meeting, March 1965, in the *American Institute of Mining, Metallurgical and Petroleum Engineers*. The text itself was not available to the present author.

[2]John A. Kay and James A. Mirrlees, 'The Desirability of Natural Resource Depletion', in D. W. Pearce and J. Rose (*ed.*), *The Economics of Natural Resource Depletion* (London 1975), p. 160ff. The authors show that if, for instance, the resource stock is 250 times current consumption, and the rate of interest is even as low as 5 per cent, the gap between price and marginal extraction cost would stay below one per cent for the first 130 years.

[3]N. Kaldor, 'The Irrelevance of Equilibrium', *Economic Journal* (December 1972), 1246. Kaldor's italics.

[4]A dissenting voice should be noted, however. Robert Solow questions the assumption that public authorities have a far-reaching time horizon: 'The next election is not so far away'. (*Ekonomisk Debatt* (Stockholm) no. 8, 1974).

V. TECHNOLOGICAL MUTATION SINCE HOTELLING

As was shown, there is a sharp contrast between the modern approach, as represented by Gordon and others, and the more traditional view found in Hotelling's article. But it is important to note that the contrast does not lie in different theoretical arrangements but rather in a shift in the conception of empirical facts about depletion.

It is not difficult to suggest an explanation for this shift: the half-century since Hotelling wrote his article has brought a radical change in the rate of technological progress, in the mining industries as in most other fields. It has become economical to extract far deeper lying and less concentrated ores and other minerals than was previously considered possible. Thereby, the quantities of economically interesting reserves of metals and fossil fuels have increased immensely, and experts seem generally to agree that they will most probably continue to grow for that future about which we can speak sensibly at all.

Indeed, we seem to be faced with a wholly new view of the meaning (if any) that can be attached to expressions such as the 'existing' or 'remaining' quantities of natural resources. And once this idea of existing 'funds' of the various minerals vanishes, so does the concept of depletion. It is now widely agreed that statistics of 'known reserves' of metals and other minerals are almost completely irrelevant for judgements about future depletion.[1]

The new approach to the question of quantities of resources has much to do with some special features of scientific discovery in recent decades. This was concisely described in the important study by Harold J. Barnett and Chandler Morse on *Scarcity and Growth*.[2]

The authors mention the traditional conception, taken over from the nineteenth century, of a kind of dualistic economy, where industry, itself working under increasing returns, owing to technical progress in the industrial processes, at the same time makes ever more voracious claims on limited quantities of fossil fuels and metals, etc., the production of which is subject to the law of diminishing returns. The two authors continue:

> These earlier, simplistic views of a world divided into two economic sectors – one progressive, but recessive, the other regressive and dominant – have continued to govern economic thinking down to the present time. Yet they, and the analogies by which the classical law of diminishing returns is 'demonstrated' to be approximately descriptive of today's long-term growth potentiality, border on the archaic. The transformation of materials into final

obvious reasons, such figures have a pronounced tendency to be consistently equal to 2–4 decades of consumption at the current rate. The last time this kind of information was misused in a major way was the publication in early 1972 of the scientist manifesto *Blueprint for Survival*. It was followed on the heels by the too well-known book on *Limits to Growth*, the reasoning of which is largely based upon the idea of a fixed stock of natural resources being diminished year by year.

[2] Harold H. Barnett and Chandler Morse, *Scarcity and Growth* (Baltimore 1963). (Published by Resources for the Future Inc.).

goods has become increasingly a matter of chemical processing. It is more
and more rare for materials to be transformed into final products solely by
mechanical means. The natural resource building blocks are now to a large
extent atoms and molecules. Nature's input should now be conceived as
units of mass and energy, not acres and tons. Now the problem is more one
of manipulating the available store of iron, magnesium, aluminium, carbon,
hydrogen, and oxygen atoms, even electrons. This has major economic
significance. It changes radically the natural resources factor of production
for societies that have access to modern technology and capital.[1]

This text, written in 1962, is an early and clear recognition of a new trend in
scientific and technological progress, and the following fifteen years have given
further confirmation, for instance with the possibilities now in the horizon of
producing metals, other minerals and energy from materials – granite, the
ocean floor, ocean water — are available in huge quantities, even when
measured in terms of useful content.

VI. SPECIFIC BUT DECISIVE CASES?

Thus far we may conclude that the fears of depletion of metals and other
minerals are vastly exaggerated, and that, barring monopolistic supply, a
general and considerable increase of scarcity of such materials, and hence a
general increase of their real prices, is unlikely for that future which present-
day political decisions can seek to influence.

But even if it were admitted that this is quite true *in general*, it might still be
rejoined that there are some specific cases of threatening depletion, sooner or
later, of something essential, perhaps just one resource item which is
indispensable for human survival.

To deal with this postulate, specific empirical evidence must be considered.
In the following, I shall refer to some such evidence, hoping that my selection
of reported facts will be found to be fair.

The requirements for a clear-cut case of dangerous depletion to exist can be
specified in the form of three questions:

(a) Does the resource considered exist in rigidly fixed amount; and is
recycling an unpromising solution?
(b) Is it impossible to point to any actually or potentially available
substitute?
(c) Is it true to say that the immediate product of the resource considered is
both irreplaceable and indispensable in its role as raw or auxiliary
material for the manufacturing of final products? And are these final
products, in their turn, indispensable, in the sense that no acceptable
substitute can be envisaged?

[1]*Op. cit.*, p. 238.

Clearly, it would be difficult to find convincing examples of metals, minerals and other resources of the kind usually described as 'depletable' for which all three questions could be confidently answered in the affirmative. At one stage, at the Stockholm Environment Conference, *helium* was mentioned as being 'both without good substitutes and in threateningly short supply',[1] but this evaluation, presented in 1972, was firmly denied in 1973,[2] and to my knowledge it has not since been resuscitated.

In the same year of doom-saying, 1972, a group of ecologists at the University of Michigan announced that reserves of *phosphorus*, an indispensable catalyst for the metabolism of living organisms, would be depleted towards the end of the twenty-first century, after which time only a world population of 1 –2 billion people could be sustained. This announcement was widely publicised all over the world, and it was, for instance, swallowed uncritically by the biologist Paul Ehrlich in his much-read book on *Population, Resources and Environment*. Meanwhile, the Michigan prophecy had been promptly and emphatically gainsaid by leading phosphate experts.[3] Needless to add, the refutation, being a piece of good news, was less widely publicised than the assertion had been.

So much for metal ores and other specific minerals. The conclusion would seem to be that it is hard to name any such material which is not either in ample supply for even a distant future, or else is substitutive, even though it may be at a price.

VII. PERVASIVE NATURAL BARRIERS?

But we are not quite at the end of our problem. For it is often contended that some major and more pervasive limitations are lurking. In considering these, we must go beyond the strict category of 'depletable' natural resources (box D in the schema above) and consider also some natural resources which are regenerating but of limited quantity (box B). For these resources, e.g. agricultural land, the danger would be that of reaching a state of full utilisation rather than of reaching the bottom of a 'fund'.

At least six overall limiting factors of this kind have been proposed in the resources debate of recent years. They are listed below, and, to anticipate, I tend to think that in the final analysis only the last-named – the space constraint – is a compelling and effective limitation calling for some political action now. My own space constraint forbids me to give more than the briefest

---

[1] Preston Cloud, 'Resource Use and Population Pressure'. Paper presented to the U.N. Conference on Development and the Environment, 1972, p. 11f.

[2] See David B. Brooks, 'Minerals: an Expanding or a Dwindling Resource?', *Mineral Bulletin* (Department of Energy, Mines and Resources) (Ottawa, 1973), p. 11.

[3] G. Donald Emigh, 'World phosfate reserves – are there really enough?', *Engineering and Mining Journal* (New York, April 1972), 90ff., and an unsigned article 'Phosfate reserves and the ecologist. Mountain or Molehill?', in *Phosforus and Potassium*, March–April 1972. See also *The Population Debate: Dimensions and Perspectives* (United Nations, 1975), vol. I, p. 86.

comment on each of the six items, together with a few references to the literature.

(1) Total supply of energy

In the long run, the extraction of ores, etc. can be increased or even maintained only at the cost of increasing input of energy. Opinions on future energy supplies and prices tend to be rather confused because the monopolistic price increase of oil – to levels some 50–100 times marginal cost of extraction – has fostered a widespread belief that exhaustion of oil resources is already on the horizon, or, at any rate, that the elasticity of oil supply is low. The truth is that in recent years the discovery of oil resources has tended to run ahead of consumption, so that known and probable reserves have been steadily increasing, and it would be hazardous to make real (i.e. dated) predictions about depletion – economic or physical – of world oil resources.[1]

But far more important is the availability of new sources of energy. It is a curious fact of social psychology that fears of long-term energy shortage, or even 'depletion' of energy sources, should be fashionable precisely at a time when no less than three quite different kinds of practically inexhaustible sources of energy have come into view as more or less certain possibilities for the not-so-distant future: breeder reactors, nuclear fusion and the tapping of solar energy. Surely, the long-term prospect for mankind's energy supplies has never before been as bright as it is now.

(2) Agricultural land

We are here concerned with long-term potentialities, and to cut it short I mention only major conclusions from a study by Roger Revelle, recently published by the United Nations.[2] On the exceedingly conservative assumption that no new discovery or invention in agricultural science and technology will from now on become available, the amount of potentially arable land would suffice, in the long run, for the provision of an adequate diet, including sufficient high-quality protein, for a world population of some 40–50 billion. This is on the assumption, of course, that the necessary amount of investment can be financed, and that needed changes in the social structure of agriculture will occur, so that presently known technology can be universally applied.

---

[1]According to a leading expert on the economics of the world oil market, the 'official truth' in America, that prices have risen because of a surge of demand against inelastic supply is 'in utter conflict with the fact of enormous supply elasticity at a cost of at most one-fortieth of the current price'. (M. A. Adelman, 'Politics, Economics, and World Oil', *American Economic Review*, May 1974).

[2]*The Population Debate, op. cit.*, vol. II, pp. 3–14.

(3) Fresh water for agriculture

Water, of course, is an indispensable natural resource for agriculture, and it has sometimes been mentioned as the decisively limiting factor for food production. The author just quoted gives detailed information about the amount of water in the hydrological circular flow. Owing to a highly uneven geographical distribution of river systems and rainfall, some stretches of land, which could become cultivable only under irrigation, must remain uncultivated, under the chosen assumption that no new technologies come to the rescue. However, this limitation has been taken into account in the estimates of cultivable land mentioned under point (2), and, therefore, the conclusion reached under that point cannot be invalidated by reference to the problem of water supply.

(4) The long-term climatic effect of increasing energy production[1]

The existence of this long-term barrier to increasing energy production is denied by nobody. But, given the fact that the science of 'global climate' is still in its infancy, there is controversy and uncertainty about the level of energy production that could eventually be sustained without unacceptable heat effect. An often-quoted estimate is that made in 1970 by Weinberg and Hammond.[2] Its conclusion is as follows: If the acceptable once-and-for-all average increase of the temperature on this planet is put at 0.2 degree Celsius – again an utterly conservative assumption – then a world population of 20 billion people could be supplied on a continuing basis with a per capita amount of energy about 20 times the present world average.[3]

(5) The environment's capacity to absorb waste

Under this head are a number of effects for which no long-term estimates exist, comparable to those for agricultural land or global climatic effects of the use of energy. It is clear enough, however, that the absorptive capacity will depend, to a large extent, on such factors as, for instance, the rate of technological progress with regard to waste disposal (including recycling), and the location of industrial and other economic activity. Such variables would probably be quite responsive to price signals.

(6) Living space for man in society

Long-term estimates of future 'optimum' size or 'optimum' growth rate of population with respect to income *per capita* are hardly meaningful. Nor is it

[1] The so-called 'hothouse effect' is quite another story and need not detain us. It arises from the emission of carbon dioxide from the burning of fossil fuels. That danger can be circumvented by the transition to other sources of energy, including nuclear reactors.

[2] A. M. Weinberg and R. P. Hammond, in *American Scientist*, vol. 58, 412.

[3] These computations are meaningful only under the assumption that one of the inexhaustible forms of energy (cfr. point 1) will eventually become available. It is also assumed that the location of energy production will not be so highly concentrated that unacceptable effects arise in 'hot spots'.

possible (or, indeed, necessary for present political decisions) to quantify now with any confidence the limit for the territorial density of population above which civilised and peaceful human society cannot endure, quite regardless of the capacity to produce food, energy and anything else. The size of world population at which that limit is reached must depend upon technological, economic, demographic and not least sociological factors which determine *inter alia* the evenness of future distribution of world population over the inhabitable territories.

Also, the history of economics is there to warn against hasty statements about the final carrying capacity of the world or any of its major parts. John Stuart Mill was worried about impending overcrowding in a 'world from which solitude is extirpated' and 'with every rood of land brought into cultivation which is capable of growing food for human beings'.[1] At that time the population of Great Britain was less than two-fifths and that of the world about one-quarter of what they are now. Half a century later, Alfred Marshall[2] suggested that the potential increase of food production might eventually support a world population of six billion people, i.e. fourfold the $1\frac{1}{2}$ billion of 1890, and about one-eighth the figure of final carrying capacity with respect to food which is now suggested by some knowledgeable persons, as mentioned above.

What figures would sensible people suggest today if pressed to guess at the maximum 'carrying capacity' of the planet, purely from the point of view of living space? Perhaps the answers would typically lie somewhere between 15 and 30 billion.[3] But even such vague and impressionistic guesses are of interest for the purpose of this paper: It appeared from the above comments on the five possible limiting factors suggested in the resources debate that they could become effective barriers only at a world population well beyond the size which most people would suggest as the maximum imposed by considerations of sheer space.

In particular, this seems to be true of those two barriers which *prima facie* appeared to be the most fearful among the five: the global heat effect of energy production, and the amount of land for agricultural production.

It is simple logic that for any kind of supply only one bottleneck can be effective at a time. And if one particular bottleneck (here: the factor of living space) is taken to be absolutely unbreakable, even in the long run, then it is unnecessary to worry about potential bottlenecks lying behind that one 'master bottleneck' or final barrier.

[1]Mill, *Principles*, IV, vi, section 2.
[2]Marshall, *Principles*, IV, iv, section 3.
[3]A world population of 30 billion would be tantamount to a density of some 175 persons per km² as an average for the whole land area of the Earth. The present population densities of Italy and India are 185 and 180, respectively.

VIII. THE UPSHOT FOR RESOURCE AND GROWTH POLICY

The necessary vagueness of ideas about final 'social carrying capacity' of the planet is no valid argument against vigorous *population policies* aimed at reducing rates of human fertility in countries where they are high, not excluding the countries of presently low territorial density. The essential reason for this is the long 'braking distance' for population growth, given present age distributions.[1]

By contrast, if the reasoning of this paper is at all sound, it seems that no good case can be made for *conservationist policies* to restrain effective demand for natural resources of the 'depletable' kind, including metals and raw materials for the production of energy, be it by raising their prices through national or international taxes on amounts extracted, or by various kinds of rationing of production or consumption.

To end with a quite subjective reflection, I would add that Doomsday worrying about depletion of natural resources seems to me to be not only pointless but also harmful, because it serves to divert the attention of concerned and well-intentioned people from the really valid grounds for worrying. These are of a political and sociological, rather than physical nature: How to use rapid technological change for a radical reduction of the appalling differences in levels of income and culture. And how to avoid nuclear bombs, rather than nuclear reactors.

[1]This is further discussed in the author's contribution to *The Population Debate, op. cit.*, vol. II, pp. 192–200, 'Resources, Environment and the Rationale of Population Policy'.

Part Two
Population Growth and Resource
Supplies

5 Are we at a Turning Point in the World Demographic Situation?[1]

Léon Tabah
UNITED NATIONS

I. HOPE, DISILLUSIONMENT OR RESIGNATION?

Are we, in the matter of world population, about to pass from a period of rank pessimism into a period of wait-and-see, resting upon a doubtful mixture of hope and disillusionment, not to say resignation, without profound misgivings about the final result? There is hope in so far as birth rates recently seem to have begun to decline, especially in the Third World. But there is also disillusionment, because, contrary to all the predictions of experts, mortality rates look like rising, so much so that by the joint operation of these two factors the rate of population increase may be about to fall quickly. Malthusians may find their long-cherished hope fulfilled.

What are we to think of all this? At first sight it seems somewhat surprising, given that demographers have ceaselessly propounded the view that so much inertia has built up in demographic structures for decades that no change can be expected for a very long time. Furthermore, history tells us that prolonged periods of falling fertility have never been associated with sustained mortality rises. However, obsession with the past should perhaps not lead us to rule out in advance the possibility that something new may happen.

I propose to take a brief look at some recent important developments in order to see how much truth there may be in these assertions.

II. THE END OF POPULATION GROWTH POTENTIAL

In Europe, to begin with, a simultaneous and so far unexplained downward trend of fertility has been apparent since 1964, which has brought the number of surviving descendants down to around two per woman. In 1975 twelve European countries, as well as the United States, Canada and Japan, had negative rates of increase, which means that if the trend were to continue for ten or twenty years, these countries would fail to replace their generations. Admittedly, in some countries of Eastern Europe there has been a reaction in response to policies designed to raise the birth rate, but is is hard to predict the future of this reaction, which seems to be losing its impetus. Of the thirty countries classified as 'developed', only half a dozen now have a fertility rate

[1]Translation by Elizabeth Henderson.

67

high enough for generation replacement. However that may be, it would seem that fertility in Europe is indifferent to economic, social, religious and even political conditions; the trend is towards homogeneity in time, in space and in the social hierarchy, as though the modern family were moulding itself to a common pattern dictated by circumstances beyond any one individual or couple. In these countries the population seems to fluctuate around a precarious equilibrium such that any swing of more than a certain amplitude inexorably calls forth a readjustment towards a stationary state. It seems vain to try and explain present differences among countries otherwise than by byzantine discussions.

Those whose business it is to work out projections no longer have any grounds for predicting population growth of any size. On the other hand, it is highly unlikely that negative growth rates will persist for any length of time, given that the serious consequences of ageing in the population structure would inevitably lead to 'natural' corrections on the part of society. We are approaching the moment when the growth potential due to demographic inertia will be reduced to virtually nil in all industrial countries, with the possible exception of Japan, the United States and the Soviet Union, where growth still owes everything to the strength of the past. It is also certain, today, that the prospect of zero growth is no longer viewed with dismay by demographers, economists and sociologists. They regard it with equanimity and what they all care most about nowadays is what influence fluctuations around a stationary trend may have on such things as public investment and national expenditure on education and housing, the life cycle of which differs from the family cycle.

III. THE THIRD WORLD'S FALLING BIRTH RATE

Natality trends in the Third World are much more difficult to analyse, given the great diversity of situations not only from the demographic point of view, but also as regards economic, social, cultural and political background. Contrary to Europe, no convergent trend can be discerned here. In broad outline, it can be said that what is new in the Third World is that the decline in the birth rate, which some ten years ago had no more than token significance, in so far as it applied only to small nations where those with power to conduct a population policy can easily communicate with parents, has by now spread to many more countries and is beginning to affect even large ones. This new trend responds to the now virtually universal desire of men and women to possess an active form of freedom, the freedom, that is, to influence the conditions of their own life, and first and foremost the shape of their own family.

In most cases this movement is still in its beginnings. It has not taken the experts unawares, though it often started later than expected, except in China, which is a special case. Of the seven countries other than China which have more than 50 million inhabitants and together account for two thirds of the total population of developing countries and for half the world population, one

(India) is experiencing a fertility decline slower than the government wishes to see, four (Brazil, Indonesia, Mexico and Pakistan) are cases of a recent decline which still leaves the birth rate close to, or even well above, 40 per thousand (which is more than $2\frac{1}{2}$ times the European rate), and two (Bangladesh and Nigeria) remain at their traditional levels. There are indeed signs which suggest that in Africa as a whole fertility has been rising slightly rather than declining, which would be in line with what has always happened where death rates dropped sharply, as in Europe during the nineteenth century or recently in the Third World. In any event, the dispersion of the birth rate about the mean must be expected to increase in developing countries. Taking the Third World as a whole, psychosociological investigations have shown that the 'expected' number of children is higher than their 'ideal' number, and that the 'ideal' number in its turn is higher than the 'desired' number of children; clearly, traditional norms still have greater force than individual choices.

   Overall, the difference between birth rates in the Third World and in the industrial countries is wider now than ever before in recorded history, to wit, more than three births per woman on the average. The fact remains that a decline definitely has set in, that it affects a large part of the Third World, that it was expected and that indeed it was allowed for in the 'medium' variant of United Nations projections; the one thing that we do not know as yet is how fast the decline will be.

IV. MORTALITY DECLINING MORE SLOWLY THAN PREDICTED

As regards mortality, there is nothing to suggest, for the time being, that death rates in the Third World as a whole have been increasing in recent years, notably as a result of the 1973–74 famine which might be interpreted as the first sign that we are approaching the limits of the earth's 'carrying capacity'. The spokesmen of this view invariably point to the case of the arid zones of Africa which suffered disastrously from the drought, or to Bangladesh, which, according to United Nations estimates, indeed went through a severe mortality crisis in the years 1970–74; this crisis, however, may well have owed as much, if not more, to the war at that time as to famine. Other examples adduced are some of the Indian states. But the truth is that none of these cases can legitimately be extrapolated to the whole of Africa or Asia, and even less to the entire Third World.

   On the other hand, what does seem to be happening is that while death rates have fallen for several decades, they are falling less fast than expected. Take the case of India. In 1964 the Indian Planning Commission based its projections on an increase in the expectation of life at birth to 57.3 years for men and to 56.9 years for women during the period 1971–76. The 1971 census disappointed these hopes, and the figures had to be sharply revised downwards, to 50.7 and 49.3 years respectively. It seems that almost everywhere in the Third World the experts were overhasty in proclaiming an illusory victory over death towards the end of the sixties and that, if new successes were to be shown, more reasonable estimates would have to be substituted sooner or later. Progress has been slow but not nil, and the prospect of an increase in the rate of population growth by virtue of a fall in the death rate persists for 29 developing countries where the expectation of life at birth does not exceed 40 years.[1]

In a country like Mexico the fall in the death rate during the last ten years was almost entirely offset by a concurrent fall in the birth rate, so that the rate of population growth is peaking out, but at so high a level as to be unsustainable if it should last for many years.

Actually, what is happening in Mexico is fairly characteristic of many other countries as well: the natality curve has a much longer downward trajectory to traverse than the mortality curve, and a reversal in the trend of the growth rate will lead to the latter's progressive deceleration which, however, must be expected to be slow because at least one third of population growth is due to demographic inertia, and that inertia will not weaken for at least 40 or 50 years. The deceleration will be slow and when it comes to an end it will leave national populations twice as high as now, or sometimes even more. Ineluctably, the world's population will double between now and the first quarter of the coming century.

V. THE PUZZLE OF CHINA

The case of China is of exceptional importance because of the sheer size of the country's population – as much as one third of all the inhabitants of the Third World. In the absence of nationwide population statistics, speculation is rife. There is good reason to think that the authorities in fact know the situation very well, and that indeed they are conducting psychosociological surveys similar to those carried out elsewhere. But the figures do not cross the Great Wall of China, and the experts have to labour patiently in an attempt to interpret every least indication, even if it often is purely qualitative in nature. United Nations estimates suggest that the birth rate may have fallen from 37–40 per thousand around 1957 to 27 in the years 1970–75. The death rate is estimated to have dropped sharply, during the same period, from 17–19 per thousand to less than 10. Consequently the demographic growth rate, which twenty years ago was estimated to be a little over 2 per cent, has probably declined by no more than a few tenths of points. The definite success of the policy to reduce the birth rate seems to have been largely offset by the equally spectacular success of China's health policy. According to our estimates the population of China this year is not far short of 900 million, and will almost certainly reach 1200 million by the year 2000, a sizeable part of the increase being attributable to inertia. I do not go along with those who are led by a mixture of scientific curiosity and political wishful thinking to estimate the birth

[1]United Nations' document prepared for the 19th session of the Population Commission (E/CN.9/323).

rate at well below 20 per thousand and the growth rate at 1 per cent or less. To announce such figures in elaborate detail, down to decimal points, and year after year, testifies to ignorance of the difficulties of this kind of research. But where such grave issues are at stake, scientific rigour and objectivity are imperative.

VI. GOVERNMENT ATTITUDES

It is only recently that much interest has been shown in government attitudes. However, a United Nations survey of 156 countries in 1976,[1] shows that 81 per cent of the Third World's population are resident in countries whose governments declare a lower rate of population growth to be desirable, 16 per cent live in countries whose governments are satisfied with the growth rate, and only 3 per cent in countries whose governments say they want higher rates of population growth. It has been worked out that if all these governments' wishes and targets were to be achieved in the year 2000, population size at that date would barely exceed the so-called 'low' variant of the United Nations projections. Although comparison with the past is not possible, there can be no doubt that in the last few years there has been a distinct change in governmental attitudes to the population problem. The nineteen-seventies may well go down in the history of ideas as the decade when politicians began to realise that the demographic situation called for action without the sort of ulterior motives which only a few years ago befogged the political atmosphere and inhibited decisions.

VII. RANGE OF UNCERTAINTY OF 420 MILLION PEOPLE

We have the problem that we cannot change demographic projections every year, depending on whether harvests happen to be good or bad. Agronomists have a more volatile spirit than demographers. There is no point in watching population like a saucepan of milk on the gas ring, nor in setting up Earthwatch Systems all over the place, as is the fashion. Let us beware of the blasts of irrationality to which worldwide models expose us. With a year's better harvest and with the prophets of doom having had nothing to show for some time, they try to scare us in other ways. Regrettably, public opinion can be aroused more easily by bad projections than by good ones.

There is no reason for any fundamental revision of the United Nations demographic projections which, for the 'medium' variant, assume the world's population to number 6200 million in the year 2000, or half as much again as now. The margin of uncertainty is 7 per cent either way, which corresponds fairly accurately with the 'low' and the 'high' variants. Much of the uncertainty is due to doubts about the slow-down of population growth in Asia. The

---

[1] United Nations' document prepared for the 19th session of the Population Commission (E/CN.9/324).

margin is narrow and shows what can be expected, at best, of the population policies which governments have freely adopted, especially since the 1974 World Population Conference in Bucarest.

There seems to be little room for manoeuvre. Yet it does make a big difference whether there will be 420 million people more or less by the end of the century.

Take the food situation first, according to figures calculated by the Food and Agriculture Organisation of the United Nations (FAO). Of 86 developing countries for which statistics are available, 39 countries accounting for 24 per cent of the Third World's population, during the period 1961–74 experienced population growth in excess of food supplies. What is equally important is that, for 80 per cent of the Third World's population, food requirements were in excess of food supply. The energy crisis, with its crucial impact of fertilisers, has further widened the gap. Merely to maintain the present, desperately low, levels of *per caput* consumption, cereal output would have to increase by something like 30 million tonnes a year, which amounts to two-thirds of the Third World's average imports during the years 1970–75. By the year 2000, with a population of about 6200 million and annual population growth of 110 million, the shortfall will, *ceteris paribus*, have increased by 70 per cent. If there is one thing that is certain, it is that agriculture cannot be transformed from one day to the next, just as little as demographic attitudes can be so changed.

As regards education, calculations have been made of the likely incidence of the combination of schooling rates and fertility rates, both in terms of a comparison of the 'low' variant with the 'high' one. The calculations were made for the period up to the year 2000, and they show that in each case the variation was likely to have considerable repercussions, in so far as the number of additional schoolchildren between 6 and 11 would range from 100 million for the low hypothesis to 450 million for the high one.

But the more important point is that whatever will be done, or not done, in the course of the next few decades will leave its indelible mark on future generations, so that a policy of wait-and-see may have irreversible consequences. Take the problem of employment. In the Third World the number of people classified as 'working' – a euphemism which, according to the documentation prepared for the World Employment Conference last June, includes 40 per cent of unemployed and partially employed workers – amounts to 1100 million. By the year 2000 potential workers will number some 1900 million. In actual fact, the world has to be prepared to accommodate and train roughly 1000 million newcomers to the labour market in the next 25 years, which is very nearly as much as the present labour force. This, at any rate, is so for the 'medium' variant, which assumes a 20 per cent fall in fertility; with the 'low' variant and its assumed 30 per cent fall in fertility, the labour force will be about 8 per cent smaller. This is far from negligible in a general context of underemployment, at a time when tolerance limits will already be transgressed. But if we take the trouble to look beyond the year 2000, the differences become really considerable. The same United Nations calculations suggest that by the year 2050 the labour force should number 3900 million in the 'medium' projection, and 3000 million in the 'low' one. In the particular case of Mexico the labour force would settle down at 66 million in mid-century, instead of 84 million.

All this shows that the future is already predetermined by the present, and that the results of what is done today must be evaluated in the very long period rather than in the short or medium term. The effects of population policies applied between 1975 and 2000 will become apparent only after the year 2000. We should therefore not think in terms solely of measures due to show their effect before the end of the century. In any case, the year 2000 is almost tomorrow – closer to us than the end of the Second World War.

6 Resources for Increasing World Food Production[1]

Joseph Klatzmann
INSTITUT NATIONAL AGRONOMIQUE, PARIS

I. INTRODUCTION

(1) The problem

Regardless of the uncertainties to be discussed later in this paper, it is quite certain that we must greatly increase world food production, and more especially agricultural production, since, as we shall see, it is no use counting on food of non-agricultural origin. The problem of hunger is one of extreme urgency in the world today, yet it would be wrong to try and solve it without reference to the long term. Mankind's distant future must not be compromised by destruction of natural resources now, or by growing pollution due to efforts to increase agricultural production.

(2) How to attack the problem

(a) Psychological difficulties. Most of the literature devoted to the problem of hunger in the world and to ecological problems shows how difficult it is, in practice, to preserve an attitude of scientific objectivity. There are the prophets of doom who predict an almost inevitable world catastrophe, and underpin their arguments with carefully selected facts. Others work on the principle that science has so far always solved all problems, and will continue to do so in the future. Yet others are ready to believe that the food problem is solved each time some new discovery is announced. This last attitude is fairly common among economists, who know nothing, or wish to know nothing, about the innumerable technical problems involved in applying any new discovery.

(b) Uncertainties. Evaluation of resources is beset with a great many difficulties, which will be discussed further. But, in any case, there is no point in evaluating food resources without knowledge of food needs, as compared both with present nutrition patterns and with future prospects.

There are far more uncertainties in this field than is generally realised. The very question of what constitutes food needs is debatable, and published data

---

[1]Translation by Elizabeth Henderson.

74

are contradictory – often considerably so. Some estimates of protein requirements, for example, are twice as high as others. As regards calories, it is often overlooked that there is a difference between available calories and those consumed, after allowing for losses at every stage, for waste in cooking and for leftovers.

The world's future food needs, moreover, obviously depend on population growth. Not long ago population estimates for the year 2000 ranged from 6 to 7 thousand million; today, some forecasters have pared this figure down to $5\frac{1}{2}$ thousand million.

And when it comes to the present food situation itself, what do we really know, to give just one example, about what happens in countries with traditional subsistence agriculture, which unavoidably lack reliable statistics?

Other difficulties arise from the fact that so many assumptions have to be made in estimating by how much food production needs to be increased. Is it enough, for instance, to increase world output (and put one's trust in satisfactory distribution), or must absolute priority be given to raising food production in the countries afflicted by malnutrition? Is there, or is there not, any hope of reducing inequalities within countries? Should the aim be to cover minimum needs, or should we set our sights higher on 'satisfactory nutrition' for all?

Finally, the measurement of food production involves all but insoluble difficulties. Just to calculate calories is obviously not good enough, but neither is the mere distinction between calories of vegetable and of animal origin. One calorie in the form of refined sugar is not equivalent to one calorie in the form of vegetables or fruit, because the latter contain in addition other valuable nutrients, such as mineral salts and vitamins.[1]

(c) Extra-economic aspects of the problem. The world food problem is a political as much as an economic one. In some countries agricultural progress is virtually impossible without land reform. The world as a whole will never have the resources required for indispensable investment in agriculture so long as the arms race goes on. We must bear in mind that any analysis of the mere economic aspects of the problem covers only part of it.

II. RESOURCES AND THEIR USE

(1) The concept of resources

Resources available for increasing agricultural production include land, water, fertilisers, technical experts, etc. None of them is available in determinate quantities. To be sure, there are some absolute limits, such as the total land

---

[1]Calculation in terms of money values does not help, either. Vegetables out of season are more expensive to produce and command a higher price, but they contribute far less to the solution of the problem than does a quantity of cereals of the same value.

surface of all continents, the whole earth's content of phosphorus, and so on. But, generally speaking, the effective supply of any resource depends on the price people are prepared to pay for it. One of the most telling examples is that of phosphates; depending on whether only easily accessible deposits are mined or whether people are prepared to pay the higher price of extracting phosphates from the continental shelf, mankind's supply of phosphate fertilisers will last for a century or for three thousand years.

In some cases even a slightly higher price will greatly augment available supplies. In others much more effort, and hence a much higher price, is needed for only a slight increase in available supplies. To take the example of arable land, it will no doubt soon cost a great deal to bring into cultivation additional land of progressively less and less fertility.

(2) Competition for the use of resources

There is a problem of competition even at the stage of allocating mankind's overall resources (say, investment for the production of wheat or of airplanes). But the more immediate problem in our context is that of competition between agricultural and non-agricultural uses of certain specific resources.

More and more land is needed for all sorts of non-agricultural uses. Often the same land is best both for food production and for non-agricultural uses; e.g. an airport can be built only on flat land, not on a rocky hill. The agronomist's view that the best land must in all cases be reserved for farming is not really tenable. But market prices do not automatically guarantee optimal use of resources. Market prices take no account of the long term, nor of the irreversible nature of certain transformations. If, some day, demographic pressure becomes so strong that it will be more important to grow wheat than to build airports, it will be too late, for the land now withdrawn from farming will never be fertile again.

Competition also exists in the use of water, including questions of quality differences; the purest water, which contains least salts, is generally most in demand by all users.

Then there is competition within agriculture itself. Who should have priority in the distribution of limited water resources? In the short term, the biggest increase in global output can be secured by giving additional water supplies to the best farmers, who are already the richest. The long-term view must be different. World agricultural production can be expected to expand very strongly only if technical progress is brought to the great mass of small, traditional farmers. To teach these small farmers to use water now, even if immediate results are far from spectacular, means to build for the future.

(3) The general problem of resource allocation

Some aspects of the optimal use of scarce resources are common to all of them. So-called political choices have to be made, in which to all intents and purposes economic rationality has no say; a choice has to be made between the short term, the long term and the very long term; and there are problems of co-ordinating the use of resources throughout the world. But other aspects of resource allocation are peculiar to agriculture, or at any rate more acute in this sector.

First of all, economic calculation requires precise knowledge about a large number of resources. Detailed information is needed about the capability of all the land that is already cultivated or can be taken into cultivation, suitably broken down into units as homogeneous as possible. This is the only way to determine, for example, whether it is better to increase the cultivated area or to raise the yield of land already under cultivation by improved fertiliser applications.

A second special difficulty is that economic problems overlap with political and social ones more widely in agriculture perhaps than in any other field. The land tenure system is often an obstacle to progress. So how can the results that might be achieved in a given region at the end of the century be predicted without making assumptions about the political, economic and social order in force at that date?

The choice between the short and the long term likewise has aspects peculiar to agriculture. If it is intended to step up agricultural output quickly, it is no doubt best to help the most advanced farmers. But the very object of increased output is to improve the nutrition of the poorest. Allowing for imperfections in distribution, would it not in the end be better to aim at a moderate increase in the output of the small traditional farmers?

Another very important problem is that of the cost and efficiency of agricultural extension work. National accounts for agriculture usually allow for fertilisers, fuels, expenses for veterinary services, but hardly ever for the cost of extension work, since this is borne by the state. Yet intensive and high-quality extension work is often a necessary condition of progress in agriculture. If water is counted among production costs, why not the wage of the man who teaches the farmer how to use water? More generally, the problem is not to omit any item in the list of expenses necessary for improving and augmenting food production.

III. ANALYSIS OF SELECTED RESOURCES

(1) Optimal use of existing food resources

Before talking of any increase in agricultural production, there is the prior question of making better use of existing food resources. Several possibilities come to mind:

(a) reduction of losses (in harvesting, in storage, etc.) – but this would soon reach its limits;

(b) reduction of inequalities in food consumption, which would be of benefit

both to those who eat too much and to those who are undernourished.
If the inhabitants of rich countries each ate a few kilogrammes of meat
less a year, this would save enough grains to supply several hundred
calories a day to 500 million of the hungry;[1]

(c) substitution of products acceptable to consumers, e.g. textured
     vegetable proteins instead of animal products, provided the taste is
     really comparable.

In practice, none of these possibilities offers great promise. If, for instance,
meat consumption in the rich countries declined, the chief result is likely to be a
fall in cereal output in those same countries, in response to contracting
demand.

(2) Non-agricultural food resources

It can be taken for granted that the world food problem is not going to be
solved by developing non-agricultural foods. Usable marine resources are
limited, and in some parts of the world overfishing is already making inroads
into fish stocks (e.g. North Sea herring). It seems that the best one can hope for
is to maintain output per head until the end of the century. The culture of yeast
on paraffin and other substrates encounters numerous difficulties, at the stage
of production and harvesting no less than of use. Even if these difficulties can
be overcome, yeasts can at best be expected to provide a useful protein
supplement; they will not solve the food problem.

There is more promise, perhaps, in the manufacture of certain amino-acids,
which would certainly do much to improve the nutritional value of grain. But
then one would first have to have the grain!

There is no doubt that in the foreseeable future agriculture will remain the
almost exclusive supplier of human food.

(3) Manpower

Extension work plays a crucial part in any programme for progress in
traditional agriculture. It is a *conditio sine qua non* of success. The problem is
how to train a sufficient number of competent and honest people with enough
tact and understanding to pass their knowledge on to others. This is of course
not a purely economic problem. There is no prospect of finding people of the
required quality unless agriculture occupies a high enough place in the scale of
values. Otherwise, it would need a saint to go and help farmers in their villages.
There are always saints everywhere, to be sure, but never enough of them.

---

[1]The transformation of vegetable products into animal products is very expensive, because it
yields only a small proportion of the calories and proteins of the original vegetable products.

(4) Energy

Modern agriculture consumes a lot of energy, which therefore stands high in the list of resources needed for the growth of food production.

There are calculations (based on the pell-mell summation of the calorie equivalents of petroleum, human labour, etc.) purporting to determine the quantity of energy that needs to be expended in order to produce, say, one calorie of cereals. These calculations are not without interest, provided no false conclusions are drawn from their results. It is hardly surprising to find that less and less calories of maize are obtained per calorie used up in maize production. But there is no point in trying to maximise that ratio. If this were the aim, it could best be achieved by a type of agriculture providing a living for at most a few hundred million people.

The more important thing to do is to work out the overall energy balance of agriculture, and to calculate what proportion of total energy consumption is attributable to agriculture. More precisely, what needs to be calculated is energy consumption throughout the whole of the farm-food complex ('agribusiness'), from the manufacture of agricultural inputs to the housewife's saucepan and refrigerator. In the United States, energy consumption in agriculture (including energy used in the manufacture of inputs) does not exceed one-fifth of total energy consumption in the farm-food complex. In France, the corresponding proportion is about one-quarter. If the American system were worldwide, it would take the equivalent of two thousand million tonnes of petroleum to feed today's world population. Since food production itself will inevitably require more and more energy in the future, it is downstream from farming that attempts will have to be made to reduce energy inputs. If energy resources are scarce, it may become necessary at some stage to choose between their use in the production of nitrogen fertilisers (a major consumer) and the production, storage and cooking of deep-frozen foods.

(5) Potentially arable land

The question of how much additional land can be taken into cultivation is perhaps the best example of widely divergent opinions and of hasty pronouncements made by people sitting at an office desk, far from what really happens.

The first point to note is that figures refer only to tilled land, because the unit yield of meadows and pastures is minute in most regions. Nevertheless it is regrettable that international statistics lump together the grasslands of semi-desert regions and the permanent meadows of the Netherlands.

Arable land, as the term is used in international statistics, covers some 15 million square kilometres. Estimates of potentially arable land range from 10 to 100 million square kilometres. The lower figure is the one used by those who argue that large areas of so-called marginal land should be withdrawn from cultivation.

These divergent estimates cannot be reviewed here. Let us take those recently published by the Food and Agriculture Organisation of the United Nations (FAO): 24 million square kilometres of potentially arable land, or 9 million more than is now under cultivation. But most of the additional land lies in the rain forest. Its development would raise formidable problems, such as the cost of clearing and of building infrastructures; mediocre yields; settlement (where are all those new farmers to come from?); the ecological risks involved in clearing millions of hectares of forest.

Quite definitely there are cheaper ways of increasing world agricultural production. The opening up of new land is to be contemplated only as a last resort. And then it will be a situation of rapidly rising costs for progressively smaller yields. Since, furthermore, the land withdrawn every year from farming for non-agricultural uses is often among the best, it seems vain to count on an increase in the cultivated area. In any event, if non-agricultural land uses are growing rapidly in developed countries today, they will no doubt do so even faster in the less developed countries, where the relevant *per caput* figures are very low at present.

(6) Water

Water is of immense importance in agricultural production. At an estimate, between 25 and 40 per cent of world agricultural output comes from irrigated land.

But we know even less, perhaps, about water resources than we do about land. The development of water resources often requires large-scale investment, which necessarily takes long to mature. Some calculations suggest that the great African rivers (the Niger, the Senegal, and others), which now simply discharge into the sea, could provide enough water to irrigate 100,000 square kilometres of land in the savannah zone. But at what price, and after how many decades? To be sure, it would be useful to carry out even a small fraction of such a programme, but its significance on the world scale would be small.[1]

Water resources can certainly be developed only at rapidly rising costs. Competition between agricultural and non-agricultural water uses is becoming so severe in some parts of the world that thoughts are turning more and more to desalination of sea water. But this involves costs of an altogether different order of magnitude than those now current (one-third of a dollar per cubic metre, which is a large multiple of the price now paid by farmers in countries of advanced agriculture). There is no technique in sight, at the moment, by which even in the distant future sea water might be desalinated at appreciably lower cost.

---

[1] In the short term, as opposed to the long term, there is much more to be said for giving priority to small irrigation schemes and to the improvement of existing distribution systems. This is the approach recommended by many experts.

However, it is not impossible to envisage a type of agriculture which would greatly reduce ecological risks. Modern agriculture, as it is today, with its enormous fields and its separation between crop farming and animal husbandry, has many drawbacks. A return to mixed farming would make animal excreta available again as manure for fields, instead of being a source of water pollution. This would also reduce fertiliser requirements. Similarly, pesticide requirements can be reduced by a combination of biological and chemical methods of pest control. The chemical industry itself must surely be capable of making products that are both more selective and less harmful. Such a system of agriculture would in no way be incompatible with the continuation of the present trend towards higher yields per unit of land, but it would be more costly (e.g. much more expensive pesticides,[1] wages for the spreading of manure, etc.).

(2) Rising costs

One can hardly go wrong in expecting the cost of certain agricultural inputs to go up very considerably. Energy will cost more, and so will phosphate and potash fertilisers as well as pesticides; desalinated sea water, if it comes to be used, will be much more expensive than water is now, etc. Farmers in developing countries should, of course, be able to employ less labour, but they will have to use growing quantities of costly industrial inputs. In the economically advanced countries, intensification of agriculture in some regions and the adoption of ecologically less hazardous methods may well raise labour requirements, so that the downward curve of the working farm population may at the very least flatten.

On the other hand, the need to exploit less and less conveniently situated resources will give new prominence to rent and hence will alter the distribution of income among countries, to the benefit of those endowed with resources easy of access. This may have dire consequences for the poorest countries.

(3) Limitations

Are there absolute limits to the growth of world food production? No doubt there are, even apart from those set by resources of land energy, fertilisers, and others. Plants will never be able to absorb more than a fraction of the solar energy that reaches the earth's surface. No-one, of course, can foresee the technologies of the year 2050, but it is possible to estimate the upper limit of yields obtainable with technologies now known. One such estimate, for temperate climates, sets a limit of the order of 25 tonnes of dry matter per hectare, which would correspond to about 12 tonnes of grains in cereal farming. These figures may cause concern to the handful of farmers who, in the

---

[1]Greatly increased research costs would be involved in the development of more selective and less harmful pesticides.

best-favoured regions, now already obtain yields not too far from the estimated maximum (8 tonnes of wheat per hectare, or 9 tonnes of maize); but on the world scale they leave a very considerable margin for improvement, especially in the rainy tropics, where two or more crops may be grown annually on the same land.

V. POTENTIAL WORLD FOOD PRODUCTION

In the following attempt to assess potential world production, I shall just set out my conclusions without detailed justification. I start from the assumption that the extent of cultivated area can be maintained, that fertiliser resources can be greatly increased and that water use can be much improved.

There is a considerable margin for expansion of output in all regions of traditional agriculture, even if top yields cannot be obtained everywhere. Furthermore, new technological progress can be expected in all departments of agronomy: new strains and breeds, more efficient crop-farming methods, more rational animal feeding methods, etc.

On this basis, and in the light of an analysis of the potential of the world's main regions, I have come to the conclusion that we may 'reasonably' consider as possible a fourfold or fivefold increase in world food production.[1] At that level, ten or twelve thousand million people could be fed very adequately, well beyond minimum requirements. This is not an estimate of the possible maximum, about which I refuse to speculate: the more valid approach is surely to stick to 'reasonable' prospects. I dismiss as totally irresponsible certain estimates which suggest that the earth could feed 150 thousand million people; apart from everything else, a population of this size would have to occupy the bulk of potentially arable land for non-agricultural uses alone.

Thanks to appropriate farming methods, the achievable high level of output could be maintained for a very long time without compromising the future of mankind by pollution and destruction of resources. If, however, world population were to grow much beyond twelve thousand million, the whole question would be wide open again.

VI. THE OUTLOOK

To know the resources available for increasing world food production is one thing; to put them to effective use is quite another. The solution of the world food problem depends on conditions which have little chance of coming about: a massive reduction of arms expenditure, a greatly increased flow of aid from the rich to the poor countries, a firm determination in poor countries to develop their agriculture, social transformations in these countries, efficient redistribution of the agricultural surplus of rich countries, definition of a scale

---

[1]This estimate falls far short of what could be obtained if yields reached their possible upper limit everywhere.

1

II. THE THREE METALS AND THEIR SOURCES OF SUPPLY

Mined ores and old scrap are the two basic sources of supply for metals. In terms of quantity, the former is by far the most important.[1] Since our interest is to clarify the price/cost effects of depletion of natural resources, our attention will centre on the primary supply. It is true that at each point in time, the stock of products in use guarantees a supply of old scrap metal for several decades to come. In this way, scrap has a crucial role as a shock absorber to temporary irregularities in primary supply. But since recovery can never be complete, old scrap supplies in a longer perspective are completely dependent on continued additions of primary metal. In the very long run, therefore, the course of events will be entirely determined by primary supply, and the role of scrap can be disregarded.

The selection of iron, aluminium and copper for the following exercises is easily justified. Both by weight and by value[2] they are incomparably more important than any other metals, and their leading positions are unlikely to be threatened in the foreseeable future. Table 7.1 shows that the three account for more than 80 per cent of total value and 98 per cent of total weight of the 13 major metals listed.[3] Cost and price changes for any other metal than the three would not have any major impact on total metal expenditure. Granted very small additions of other metal elements required for various steel alloys, the three metals together are sufficiently versatile to satisfy most of the functions for which metals are used.

The figures of Table 7.1 are also instructive in illustrating the impact on the world economy of possible changes in the price of the three major metals. The aggregate value, $88 billion, corresponds to 1.6 per cent of global GNP in 1974. A doubling of the price from the level which prevailed in that year, would imply a cost to the world economy equal to less than half a year's normal GNP growth. For comparison we may note that the oil price change in 1973, if assumed to have affected overall world crude production, corresponded to more than 3 per cent of the world's GNP in that year.

Pig iron, copper and aluminium are the results of an extended production process in which mining is only the first stage. If depletion of resources causes prices to increase, it can reasonably be taken to affect mining and concentrating only. A rough estimate of the value of iron ore, copper

---

[1]Data for the US suggest that roughly 25 per cent of final demand for steel and refined copper, and some 5 per cent of final demand for refined aluminium is satisfied by old scrap. See *Mineral Facts and Problems*, 1975 Edn (US Bureau of Mines, Washington DC, 1976).

[2]Value is defined here as price times quantity. An alternative measure of value could be the entire area underneath the demand schedule. The application of this measure might change our ranking by increasing the relative importance of indispensable metals with no close substitutes, and with very low price elasticities of demand. The problems of quantifying this alternative measure of value appear insurmountable.

[3]Only metals used mainly in their pure form have been listed. Thus, for instance, manganese, molybdenum and chromium, commonly used and traded in the form of concentrates, have not been included.

TABLE 7.1   WORLD MINE PRODUCTION OF MAJOR INDUSTRIAL METALS IN 1974

	Production, thousand tons	Price, dollars per ton	Value, million dollars	Cumulative value, million dollars	Cumulative value, %
Pig iron	513,000	116	59,160	59,160	56.4
Copper	7650	2054	15,713	74,874	71.4
Aluminium	13,810	940	12,981	87,854	83.8
Zinc	5910	1235	7300	95,154	90.7
Nickel	740	4410	3260	98,414	93.8
Lead	3570	590	2106	100,520	95.8
Tin	220	8180	1800	102,320	97.6
Silver	9	151,900	1367	103,687	98.9
Magnesium	270	1590	430	104,117	99.3
Antimony metal	40	4635	185	104,302	99.5
Mercury	10	18,180	182	104,484	99.6
Cobalt	25	7200	180	104,664	99.8
Cadmium	17	8490	144	104,880	100.0

NOTE Free market prices have been used where available.
SOURCE Metallgesellschaft.

equilibrium in the market studied, and available price data require a cautious interpretation. Even when the market is in equilibrium, an impending depletion of a resource may push up prices while leaving costs unaffected. In such cases, price will be the more relevant variable to study to disentangle the problem at hand.

Copper offers the best opportunity for such an investigation. The product is homogenous, international price series for the past 100 years are readily available, and the grades of ore mined have been reduced from 5–6 per cent at the turn of the century to less than 0.5 per cent in some mines in the 1970s. Research carried out elsewhere[1] suggests that technological progress has cheapened the cost of producing refined copper sufficiently to neutralise the upward cost push from the decreasing metal content in exploited ores. When studying Figure 7.1 which depicts real copper prices over this century, one should keep in mind that the extremely low levels between 1932 and 1946 are not representative of costs. Instead, they are the result, first of the world depression, and subsequently, of the severe war price controls. The high-price period of 1965–74 too, has little relation to the development of costs. More likely, it reflects a prolonged shortfall in supply, due to the politically induced output stagnation in the third world.[2] No long-run price trend at all can be discerned in the graph, when these disequilibrium periods are excluded.

The evidence from iron ore is more ambiguous. Meaningful price series over long periods of time are difficult to obtain. Until about 1960, the non-captive international market consisted, by and large, of the Swedish export supplies. Only from that time onward with the opening up of a number of large and rich mines in Australia, Africa and South America, did a truly international market develop. The metal content of exploited iron ores has not been falling over time. Any tendencies in that direction were completely reversed when these overseas mines came into production. The net economic advantage of the new supplies was of course reduced by the considerable lengthening of transport routes which ensued.

A further complication in long-term iron ore studies is that the product supplied by the mines has not been homogenous. To an increasing extent, beneficiation, pelletisation and other improvements take place before sales.

For whatever it is worth, we present in Figure 7.2 the development of real prices (fob) for iron ore exported from Sweden since the beginning of this century. The graph does not give any impression of a rising price trend, despite the fact that the product supplied has undergone considerable improvements over time. Early in the century, most of the ore was in lump, and the iron content varied between 25 and 45 per cent. In the 1970s, the ore is crushed, part of it is pelletised, and the iron content has increased to between 59 and 68

---

[1]O. C. Herfindahl, *Copper Costs and Prices 1870–1957* (Johns Hopkins, Baltimore, 1959) and M. Radetzki, 'Metal Mineral Resource Exhaustion and the Threat to Material Progress: The Case of Copper', *World Development* (Feb 1975).

[2]See M. Radetzki, *op. cit.*

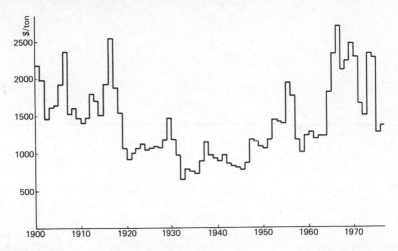

Fig. 7.1 The real price of copper (constant 1975 US $ per metric ton). Annual average copper prices in London, converted into US $ at current exchange rates, have been deflated by the US wholesale price index (1975 = 100).

NOTES The London copper price has been chosen because of its wide international significance.

The price has been expressed in $, first because this is the most important international currency, and second because of the great instability in the exchange rate of the £ since the late 1960s.

An international dollar price index would have been the most appropriate deflator for our purpose. In the absence of such an index for the entire period covered, we have instead deflated the prices with the help of the US wholesale price index.

SOURCES Copper price, £/metric ton, 1900–7 from H. G. Cordero and L. H. Tarring, editors, *Babylon to Birmingham* (Quin Press, London) C: a 1960, 1908–64 from Metallgesellschaft, 1965–76 from CIPEC Annual Reports.

$/£ exchange rate, 1900–8 from F. Pick and R. Sedillot, *All the Monies of the World* (Pick Publishing Corp, New York, 1971), 1909–28, Bank of Sweden statistics, 1929–51 UN Statistical Yearbooks, 1952–76 IMF.

US wholesale price index, 1900–20 *Historical Statistics of the United States*, US Bureau of the Census, Washington DC 1945, the BLS index, 1920–76, World Bank Report No. EC 166, the US General Wholesale Price Index.

per cent.[1] For a homogenous product, the price would indeed have been falling.

Sweden's price leadership ceased in the early 60s, and its iron ore prices have had to adjust in more recent times to those of the transcontinental mines.[2]

[1] Interview with Malmexport AB, Stockholm, March 1977.
[2] Other iron ore exporters experienced similar price falls in this period. See F. A. Tupper and F. I. Alvarellos, 'A Comparison of World Prices of Iron Ore and Steel 1950–1970', UNCTAD/CD/Misc 58 (21 Oct 1974).

TABLE 7.3   PROJECTED DEMAND OF THE THREE METALS UP TO 2000

	Demand 1974	Demand 2000	Annual growth per cent	Cumulative demand
Iron ore (million tons of fe content)				
Malenbaum	513	1086	2.9	20,590
USBM	513	1030	2.7	20,050
Historical	513	2450	6.2	33,710
Primary aluminium (million tons)				
Malenbaum	13.9^a	46.8	4.8	730
USBM^b	15.1	60.2	5.5	943
Historical^b	15.1	167.1	9.7	1734
Copper (million tons)				
Malenbaum^c	8.3^a	19.7	3.4	359
USBM^d	6.6	20.1	4.5	320
Historical^d	6.6^e	21.7	4.7	343

^{a}Metallgesellschaft.
^{b}Includes consumption of new scrap.
^{c}Consumption of refined copper, including that derived from old scrap.
^{d}Consumption of primary copper and new scrap.
^{e}Figure based on US Bureau of Mines.
SOURCES Metallgesellschaft, *Metal Statistics* (Frankfurt am Main, 1976).
US Bureau of Mines, *Mineral Trends and Forecasts* (Washington DC, October 1976) and *Mineral Facts and Problems*, 1975 Edn (Washington DC 1976).
W. Malenbaum, *Materials Requirements in the United States and Abroad in the Year 2000* (Wharton School of Finance and Commerce, University of Pennsylvania, March 1973).

shows that the 1974 reserve levels are considerably higher than any of the cumulative demand projections. Even if we take the extreme assumption that there will be no further additions to reserves, it is clear that the 1974 reserve stock is quite sufficient to satisfy demand up to the end of the century. And given the definition of reserves, the cost of supplies in the next quarter-century will be no higher than today.[1] The extremity of our assumption about

[1]In his valuable comment on this chapter at the Congress, Marcos Mamalakis rightly pointed out that while in the long run the conclusion reached here may be right, serious supply, and hence price, problems may arise in the less-than-long-run. Thus, supply may fail to grow at the rate required to satisfy demand at unchanged price, because governments expropriate too large a share of the return on investments in new mines or in technological progress, thereby restricting the amount of such investments. Supply may also become inadequate because of cartel action, made possible for instance by the uneven geographical spread of mineral resources. The OPEC actions provide a lively illustration.

unchanged reserves is illustrated by the factual developments between 1974 and 1976. In this two-year period, the creation of new reserves was several times higher than the simultaneous reserve exploitation. As a consequence, the 1976 reserves had risen by 2.8 per cent for iron ore, by 12.8 per cent for copper, and by 41 per cent for bauxite, above their 1974 level.[1]

IV. ADEQUACY BEYOND 2000

Judgements about mineral adequacy well into the next century and beyond require far more speculation than the exercises carried out so far. Conjectures are needed on such varied issues as future trends in population expansion, economic growth in the very long run, changes in the content of GNP, and the continued role of technological progress. Within the confines of a few pages, the treatment of the varied issues will by necessity be rhapsodic. We start out by an attempt to establish maximum annual global consumption figures for each of the three metals. We continue by considering how such consumption levels could be satisfied in the long run on the basis of current technology. The results obtained are then reassessed by assuming that technological progress will continue in the future.

The following computation of maximum global consumption is based on the presumption that the world's population will stabilise at the 10 billion level, and that irrespective of what will happen to long-run economic growth, per capita consumption of the three metals will eventually cease to expand. Our maximum global population figure is a pure conjecture. It has been chosen so as to provide ample time for the changes required to bring about zero population growth. It is also high enough to make it plausible that substantially higher levels of population would create a variety of constraints and discomforts, the effect of which would be to restrict further expansion. Since it is possible to take objection to the maximum global population figure assumed here, we should immediately make it clear that in the final analysis, our conclusions would not be drastically changed if, for instance, population continued to expand until it reached 20 billion rather than the 10 billion used in the computations which follow.

Our presumption about maximum global per capita consumption levels is more firmly founded. It is strongly supported by the data of Figure 7.3, which depicts per capita consumption of pig iron, primary aluminium and refined copper in the US in the past century.

For the two old metals, iron and copper, there is a continuous deceleration of per capita consumption growth till about 1950, and a complete stagnation

---

[1]*Commodity Data Summaries*, 1975 and 1977 edns (US Bureau of Mines, Washington DC). The main explanation to the exceptionally high rise for bauxite is probably the drastic royalty increase in Jamaica in 1974, and the consequent re-evaluation of reserves in countries whose tax levies rose less or not at all.

in the US since 1950, irrespective of what happens to the long-run growth of global GNP. Even if the metals may find new uses in the coming decades,[1] this assumption could hardly be an underestimate. By the time the majority of the world's population reaches per capita GNP levels comparable to those of the US in the post-war period, the further development of substitute materials and of materials savings techniques may well have reduced the level at which the per capita requirements of the two metals are saturated. For aluminium, the US consumption continues to grow, and the determination of maximum global consumption is therefore more tricky. By assuming the deceleration and stagnation path of aluminium consumption in the US to have a shape similar to those of copper and pig iron, we assess that the maximum per capita consumption of this metal in the US and elsewhere will not exceed 100 kg, e.g. about five times the present US level.

Table 7.4 summarises the figures of maximum consumption for the three metals, and compares them with current consumption levels. Maximum consumption will not occur until world population has reached the 10 billion mark and the poorest nations have attained per capita GNPs equal to those in the US around 1950. On the most bullish assumptions, this could happen by about 2060 at the earliest. Although world population could already reach 10 billion by around 2025 if its post-war annual growth of 1.9 per cent is maintained, it would take no less than 85 years for the poorest half of humanity (average per capita GNP in 1974 equal to $225) to reach the 1950 US per capita GNP level ($4000 of 1974 value), even on the exceedingly optimistic assumption of 3.5 per cent real per capita growth throughout this long period. The minimum lead time for mineral consumption to reach the levels indicated in Table 7.4, therefore, is considerable.

Rather than comparing the maximum consumption figures of Table 7.4 with current reserve and resource levels, it may be instructive to make use of the concept of 'back-stop technology', commonly employed in long-run analyses of depletable resources. This refers to the circumstances of production which would arise when all superior resources have been used up, and a very lean but effectively inexhaustible resource base is taken into use.[2] Such virtually inexhaustible resources have been defined for two of the three materials dealt with here.[3] Global availabilities of kaolin clays with some 20 per cent aluminium content appear to be sufficient to satisfy our maximum aluminium consumption figure for more than 1.5 million years. And the amount of iron contained in basalt and laterite (around 10 per cent metal content) would be enough for close to 0.5 million years' demand at the maximum level. In the case of copper, no corresponding resource with metal concentrations at a

[1] Important new fields for future copper consumption include desalination of water, solar energy generation and electric cars.
[2] R. Solow, 'The Economics of Resources and the Resources of Economics', *American Economic Review* (May 1974).
[3] See H. E. Goeller and A. M. Weinberg, 'The Age of Substitutability', *Science* (February 1976).

TABLE 7.4   WORLD ANNUAL CONSUMPTION OF THE THREE
MINERALS

	Actual consumption 1974		Maximum consumption in the future[a]		Maximum consumption as a multiple of actual consumption in 1974	
	per caput, kg	total million tons	per caput, kg	total million tons	per caput, kg	total million tons
Iron ore, Fe cont	132	513	380	3800	2.9	7.4
Aluminium[b]	3.9	15.1	100	1000	25.6	66.2
Copper[b]	1.7	6.6	8.3	83	4.9	12.6

[a]Assuming world population at 10 billion, per capita consumption of pig iron and copper equal to present levels in the US, and per capita consumption of aluminium equal to five times present level in the US.
[b]Including new scrap.

reasonably high multiple of overall crustal abundance and large enough to constitute a back-stop base, has yet been identified. Hence, we will assume a continuously declining trend in the metal content of copper ores used, with a consequent upward push on costs over time.

The background provided by the foregoing discussion enables us to proceed with our two-step approach towards the issue of supply adequacy for the three minerals in the very long run.

What would be the implications for adequacy, if the maximum demand computed above had to be satisfied on the basis of current technology? Aluminium offers the most straightforward result. The technology for extracting alumina from kaolin and other alumina clays is known. So far, bauxite has maintained a competitive advantage over the clays. Large-scale substitution in favour of clays can be expected if the cost of bauxite rises to levels where its competitive edge is lost. A recent study dealing with the prospects of a bauxite cartel[1] suggests that at bauxite prices just below $40 per ton (1976 prices), exploitation of clays becomes competitive. Delivered costs of bauxite in the US in the mid-70s vary between $25 and $28 per ton.[2] Given that bauxite accounts for between 10 and 15 per cent of the aluminium price, an increase in the cost for bauxite from $25 to $40 per ton, passed in its entirety on to the aluminium price, would add less than 10 per cent to the latter. This is all that is required to make the back-stop technology competitive in the case of aluminium.

[1]R. S. Pindyck, 'Cartel Pricing and the Structure of the World Bauxite Market', MIT Stencil, presented at the Ford Foundation World Commodities Conference, Airlie, Virginia, US, 18 March, 1977.
[2]R. Vedavalli, 'Market Structure of Bauxite/alumina/aluminum, and Prospects for Developing Countries', IBRD Commodity Paper No 24 (3/77).

copper costs and prices to double already within the next century. The technologically induced cost reduction needed to keep prices unchanged would now amount to 0.7 per cent per year. Even this higher rate appears to be extremely conservative by comparison with historical experience.

A third impact of technology on the adequacy of the three metals is through shifting their demand curves leftwards. In our discussion of consumption trends in the US, we pointed to the savings which resulted from improving qualities of these metals, and from emerging substitute materials. There is no sign of slow-down in these tendencies. Thus, there are considerable prospects of future savings in the use of iron, aluminium and copper from current developments of ingenious aluminium alloys, steel-based composites and so-called metal glasses.[1]

Despite its relative abundance in the earth's crust, and highly valued properties, e.g. lightness, corrosion resistance, ductility and strength, titanium has hitherto remained a minor metal. Absence of a suitable technology for titanium production on a mass scale is the primary explanation for the unimpressive performance of this metal. Sooner or later, a breakthrough is bound to come, just like it did in the case of aluminium in the latter half of the nineteenth century. From then onwards, titanium has prospects of becoming a major metal, substituting for many functions where iron, aluminium and copper are used today.

Technology also offers prospects of a forthcoming revolution in ceramics. These materials, obtained from an abundant and cheap resource base, have hitherto mainly been used in very high temperatures, at which most metals would melt. Recent developments in the production of ceramics suggest possibilities of shaping these materials to exacting specifications at swiftly falling costs.[1] The use of ceramics may experience a great expansion in coming decades, thereby bending the demand growth projections downwards for many metals.

A final example of a prospective substitute material is that of glass fibres. Some 20 per cent of total copper use is for communications wire and cable. Recent research results indicate that glass fibres, initially developed for uses in medicine, constitute a potentially far cheaper and abundantly more efficient substitute for copper in communications applications.[2] Wholesale replacement of copper in this field is expected in the late 80s, thus reducing any forthcoming pressures on copper resources.

In a way, the examples of prospective technological evolution brought out above are incongruous in a context of the very long run. The fact is that we know very little about the direction technology will have taken at the turn of the century and beyond. Past experience suggests that progress will continue,

[1] *Framsteg inom forskning och teknik 1975*, Swedish Academy of Engineering Sciences, Bulletin 194 (Stockholm 1975).
[2] *Copper Studies* (11 March 1977).

but it also suggests that attempts at predicting in precise terms its long-run direction will more often than not prove to be failures.

How certain can we be that technology will continue to advance in the very long run? It is of course conceivable, though very unlikely, that progress in technology might cease. Profound changes in our social systems and valuations would both precede and follow upon such an event. The ensuing consequences of such changes are completely outside the scope of the present paper. It suffices to note that both the level and growth rate of mineral demand would require a complete reassessment under the new circumstances which would emerge.

The tentative conclusion which can be derived from the varied speculations and conjectures contained in this section is that in all likelihood, the supplies of iron, aluminium and copper in the very long run will remain adequate, so that future demand can be satisfied at real price levels not much higher than those of the 1970s. Even if the resource base fails, and depletion causes prices to rise, we conjecture that technological efforts will result in the creation of substitute goods satisfying the functions of the depleting metal without any substantial cost increase to the users. Solow is probably right in presuming a high elasticity of substitution between natural resources on the one hand and labour-and-capital-goods on the other.[1] Indeed, the varied arguments pursued above point to a possibility of ever decreasing costs for the functions now performed by the three metals. Though it is conceivable that future costs will be lower than the current ones, we believe that there is a limit, beyond which further cost reduction is likely to cease. When the functions can be satisfied very cheaply, there is small incentive to devote further efforts to making them cheaper still, and technology will then be turned to other, more important assignments.

V. A SUMMARY OF CONCLUSIONS

The results of this paper are fairly optimistic. We set out to enquire whether demand for iron, aluminium and copper can be satisfied in the long run without substantial price increases. With some reservations, and accepting the necessary uncertainty surrounding the long-distant future, the answer seems to be affirmative.

After providing a broad survey of the three metals and the resources on which their supply is based (section II), we conclude (section III), that known high-quality reserves are fully adequate to satisfy any reasonable growth in demand up to the end of the century. Hence, there is no reason to expect any cost/price increase in the next 25 years, on account of a deteriorating resource base.

We then extend our time horizon beyond the year 2000. By necessity, much

---

[1] R. M. Solow, 'Intergenerational Equity and Exhaustible Resources', *The Review of Economic Studies*, Symposium Issue 1974.

8 Technology, Natural Resources and Economic Growth[1]

Nathan Rosenberg
STANFORD UNIVERSITY, CALIFORNIA

I. INTRODUCTORY

Not very many years ago a view seemed to be emerging in the
economics profession – it was never sufficiently widely held to be called a
consensus – that the Ricardian-Malthusian demons were finally being
exorcised, at least as far as the future of the industrialised West was concerned.
With respect to natural resources in particular, numerous studies suggested
that they had been playing a role of declining importance within the favoured
circle of industrialised countries. There was of course the compelling evidence
of the agricultural sector which, as Kuznets had authoritatively demonstrated,
had declined in relative importance in all economies which have experienced
long-term economic growth.[2] Within agriculture itself, the implicit assumption
that there were no good substitutes for land in food production had been belied
by a broad range of innovations which sharply raised the productivity of
agricultural resources and at the same time made possible the widespread
substitution of industrial inputs for the more traditional agricultural labour and
land – machinery, commercial fertiliser, new seed varieties, insecticides,
irrigation water, etc. As early as 1951 Ted Schultz called attention to the fact
that Harrod, in his notable book, *Toward a Dynamic Economics*, published in
1948, entirely omitted land as an input in the productive process.[3] Although it
is doubtful that many economists concerned with economic growth would
presently wish to go that far,[4] a growing sense of agreement did emerge with
respect to some weaker propositions. This became strikingly apparent in 1961
with the publication of a collection of conference papers in a volume titled

---

[1]The author wishes to thank Stanley Engerman and David Mowery for their valuable
comments on a range of issues pertinent to this paper.
[2]Simon Kuznets, *Modern Economic Growth* (Yale University Press, 1966) Chapter 3.
[3]Schultz's article bore the significant title 'The Declining Economic Importance of Land',
Economic Journal (December 1951). Schultz cites the following statement from page 20 of
Harrod's book: 'I propose to discard the law of diminishing returns from the land as a primary
determinant in a progressive economy ... I discard it only because in our particular context it
appears that its influence may be quantitatively unimportant'.
[4]Most of the growth literature of the 1950s in fact followed Harrod's practice in ignoring land
and resources. Indeed, even the early measures of factor productivity simply lumped land
together with capital.

the last several years really support the view that we have already entered the era of sharply-defined, inexorable constraints? What role can new technologies play in offsetting these resource constraints? What are the difficulties confronting the attempt to formulate an effective technology policy? It is with questions such as these that I will be primarily concerned.

Ever since the Arab oil embargo, of course, the energy problem has become a central preoccupation. There are good reasons, both of a short-term and of a long-term nature, why we should be especially concerned over this particular resource constraint. Aside from the obvious fundamental importance of energy in general to an industrial society, energy is also the key to the solution of many other materials problems. This is so because a large number of basic raw materials exist in abundance in nature in low concentration ores, and their extraction as well as subsequent refining is heavily dependent upon energy-intensive techniques.[1] Therefore in the latter part of the chapter I will focus primarily upon the energy problem and some of its ramifications.

I should also add that my discussion will centre upon the American experience, primarily because that experience is the one I happen to know best. I believe that my analysis, however, is applicable to that of all industrial societies which continue to have highly dynamic technologies at their disposal. Indeed, in many respects the Japanese economy would probably have been a much more appropriate one for my purposes, and I therefore regret that I cannot claim more than the most superficial acquaintance with its history. Because clearly the Japanese case is the case *par excellence* of a society very poor in natural resources, which has nevertheless managed to set a remarkable pace in the industrialisation process. Of course it is still possible to reply that Japan was in fact handicapped in that process by her poverty of resources. I confess I find that suggestion a bit mind-boggling. It is difficult to believe that an economy which grew for so many years at 11 per cent or so per year was suffering from *any* handicaps whatever. But perhaps that is just a failure of my culture-bound, occidental imagination.

II. THE NATURE OF TECHNOLOGICAL CHANGE

Technological change is a multidimensional phenomenon. There are many aspects of it which we might want to emphasise depending, of course, upon the problem at hand. What, after all, determines the startling differences in the apparent technological *capacities* of different societies, or the same society at different points in its own history? Even the most cursory survey of the economies of the world would reveal truly astonishing differences in the capacity to *generate* or to adopt technological innovations. The rate of innovative activity, as we know, varies greatly from one country to another.

---

[1]To some degree the energy-intensive nature of low-quality resource exploitation must reflect earlier price regimes which dictated the substitution of fuel for labour. The extent to which this is so, and therefore the extent to which it may be possible to substitute capital and labour for energy in the future is less clear.

The aspect of technological change which I wish to emphasise, however, is not simply its rate, but rather the manner in which technological change serves as a mechanism of *adaptation* to a world in flux. This aspect of technological change is peculiarly important in considering the relationship between the availability of natural resources and the prospects for future economic growth. The fact is that technological dynamic societies use their technological skills to adapt to changing patterns of resource availability over time. Although economics habitually makes a sharp distinction between shifts in the production function and movements from one *existing* technique to another in response to changing factor prices, I want for present purposes to discard that distinction. The justification for doing so is that I am interested in the dynamic process itself out of which new production possibilities are generated. If we are concerned with the historical circumstances out of which new technologies emerged, then the availability of these technologies obviously becomes part of the explicandum and cannot be taken as given. In this context the analytical distinction between technological change and mere factor substitution becomes distinctly fuzzy. For historically, establishing new possibilities for factor substitution has typically been the outcome of a search process involving substantial financial costs and the use of specialised knowledge and creative skills. The kinds of increments to knowledge underlying both substitution and innovation possibilities are, in other words, both the outcome of activities which may fairly be called research.[1] If, in response to changing resource supplies and prices, it is considered desirable to commit funds to establishing new optimal input mixes – to *extend* the isoquant into a new region – then the distinction between technological change and factor substitution loses its analytical value. Furthermore, of course, when a variety of substitution possibilities is already known, these possibilities are themselves the outcome of some past research activities. But the more general point is that the range of substitution possibilities which is possible within a *given* technology is often severely limited.

I have perhaps belaboured this point because the sharp distinction between opening up new production possibilities and 'mere' factor substitution is deeply embedded in our thinking about technological phenomena. As a result, it strongly shapes our thinking about alternative courses of action, about the options which are in some meaningful sense available to a society at any moment in time. And, as I will argue later on, it may be very misleading as a basis for thinking about questions of technology policy with which we need increasingly to be concerned. Specifically, it may induce us to underestimate drastically the cost – in both money and time – required to shift from one set of

[1] 'I shall define research as a specialized activity that requires special skills and facilities that are employed to discover and develop special forms of *new information*, a part of which acquires the properties of economic information. By this definition, such research is an *economic activity* because it requires scarce resources and because it produces something of value.' Theodore Schultz, *Investment in Human Capital* (New York, The Free Press, 1971), p. 203. The emphasis is Schultz's.

case, but was more a reflection of the nature of the technological diffusion process at work at the time.[1]

III. AMERICAN HISTORICAL EXPERIENCE OF TECHNOLOGICAL CHANGE

In considering the role of technological change in adapting to increasing natural resource scarcity, the American historical experience offers a very special set of circumstances. For, historically, American economic growth was strongly conditioned by a great diversity and abundance of natural resources. In the early stages of industrialisation there were two related features of American technology which are particularly worthy of notice. The first is that it represented a highly selective drawing upon the pool of existing European (primarily British) technology. Some technologies were borrowed very soon after their initial development abroad; others were borrowed but only with a lag of as long as several decades; and yet others were never utilised at all.[2] The second characteristic is that the available technology often underwent considerable modification in America. Both of these characteristics represented adaptive responses to a resource endowment and natural environment which was often strikingly different from and in some cases totally alien to the European experience. Although, for example, Europe had over the centuries developed an extensive wood-using technology, the availability of forest products during the period of industrialisation was never one which would have made it worth while to explore the highly resource-intensive end of the isoquant. In America the extravagant abundance of forest resources provided a strong inducement for the exploration of a wood-intensive technology.[3] The · point may be stated more generally: the adaptiveness of early American technology often consisted of searching out methods which were natural-resource-intensive – which substituted natural resources, wherever possible, for scarcer labour or capital. The characterisation of nineteenth-century American technology as labour-saving is common enough. It is less commonly noted that this same technology frequently had a resource-intensive bias. As economic growth and an expanding population eventually reduced the extent of this advantage, the technology also changed in a way which involved less intensive use of natural resources or shifted to a dependence upon more abundant resources.[4]

---

[1]This point may have some significance for LDCs and their efforts to acquire industrial techniques appropriate to their factor endowments. That acquisition process is often not assisted by the current institutional mechanisms for the diffusion of industrial technology, i.e. multinational firms and direct foreign investment.

[2]See 'Selection and Adaptation in the Transfer of Technology', Chapter 10 in Nathan Rosenberg, *Perspectives on Technology, op. cit.*

[3]Nathan Rosenberg, 'America's Rise to Woodworking Leadership', *ibid.*, Chapter 2.

[4]*Ibid.*, Chapter 14.

In agriculture as well, the distinctive feature of the American experience was resource abundance – a high ratio of land to labour. American farmers were often charged by European visitors with soil management practices of a wantonly profligate sort. They were accused of 'mining the soil' – cultivating lands with no effort to maintain soil fertility and then simply moving on to new lands when fertility declined, as it inevitably did.[1] More importantly, technological adaptation in the nineteenth and early twentieth centuries took the primary form of innovations which exploited the abudance of land by raising the acreage which could be cultivated by a single farmer. These innovations exploited the machine-making skills of the industrial sector in order to mechanise agricultural operations. The vast outpouring of innovations – cotton gin, steel plough, cultivator, reaper, binders, threshing machines and combine harvesters, and barbed wire fences – had the objective of reducing labour-intensive activities and of raising the feasible land/man ratio. Even the westward movement itself had a significant initial labour-saving effect, since it involved a movement from largely forested land to unforested land, and since the clearing of the latter naturally involved a much smaller labour cost per acre than the clearing of the former.

The twentieth century, in which land has become an increasingly scarce input and capital a more abundant one, presents a more complex picture. The process of mechanisation has continued, as in the case of the cotton picker, and especially in conjunction with the tractor and its growing family of attached implements, and associated changes in a whole range of new possibilities offered by electrification. Since 1940, however, American agriculture has been dominated by a wide range of innovations which have had the effect of raising output per acre as well as output per worker. The growing relative scarcity of land has been met by a series of improvements emanating from the life sciences and the chemical industries. As a result output per acre, which had not changed markedly since as far back as 1880, exhibited an upward movement for the major crops – wheat, corn and cotton – for which there is no earlier precedent.[2] The dominant factors at work here included the successful exploitation of the slowly-developing body of knowledge of the life-sciences, knowledge dealing with the fundamental biological processes of life and growth – especially genetics and biochemistry. A new capacity for breeding plants with specific characteristics raised productivity in many ways. Perhaps the most important was the development of new plant strains which were highly

---

[1]Even where land was abundant, however, farmers could not afford to be oblivious to the deterioration of soil fertility. The preparation of new land for cultivation may involve high costs, such as the initial cost of clearing.

[2]The US average output of corn per acre was 26.1 bushels in 1935–9, 68 in 1962–6 and 86.8 in 1971–5; wheat output rose from 13.2 bushels per acre in 1935–9 to 25.9 bushels per acre in 1962–6 to 31.3 in 1971–5; cotton output rose from 226 pounds per acre in 1935–9 to 501 pounds per acre in 1962–6 and was 472 in 1971–5. *Agricultural Statistics*, various issues. For the longer term trends see Yujiro Hayami and Vernon Ruttan, *Agricultural Development, op. cit.*, Figure 6–2, p. 117 and Appendix Table C–2.

responsive to fertiliser inputs. The employment of fertiliser inputs in agriculture had more than quadrupled between 1940 and the mid-1960s. This increase had in turn been induced primarily by a sharp fall in fertiliser prices relative to product prices and the prices of other inputs (Government acreage restrictions increased the incentive to employ these inputs). Underlying the relative decline in fertiliser prices, in turn, was a range of technological innovations not only in chemical engineering but in power production, since power is a major component in the cost of synthetic fertiliser. But the complementarity between these two sets of developments in the adaptive process needs to be emphasised: lower fertiliser costs would have yielded only modest benefits in the absence of the new fertiliser-responsive crop varieties.[1]

Thus there have been many technological changes in agriculture which have served to offset the increasing scarcity of land. But other forces have had even more pervasive, though perhaps less visible, effects in offsetting this growing scarcity. They have done this, most generally, by providing non-agricultural products which have served as effective substitutes for products from the agricultural (or primary) sector. The replacement of the horse by the automobile and tractor is an instance of massive importance, inasmuch as the feeding of horses (and mules) in 1920 is estimated to have required some 90 million acres, or roughly 25 per cent of all the cropland in the United States. Other instances have also been of great significance. The introduction of synthetic fibres as substitutes for cotton and wool, of chemical for natural fertilisers, of petroleum for wood as a fuel, or plastics for leather and wood, of synthetic for natural rubber – all of these innovations have meant a shift away from the products of the agricultural sector. Needless to say, these shifts have also been pregnant with other consequences, especially for their impact in increasing the demand for fossil fuels. But more of that later.

IV. THE METALLURGICAL INDUSTRIES

If the experience in agriculture demonstrates a highly successful set of responses to changing relative scarcities, technological change with respect to metallurgical resources emphasises another, and perhaps even more fundamental dimension of the process, a dimension of the greatest long-term significance. That is, the metallurgical industries have experienced a long sequence of innovations which have had the effect of progressively expanding the resource base of the industry. Indeed, the British industrial revolution was based on a series of innovations which had the effect of freeing the iron industry from its primeval dependence upon wood fuel and providing a new, vastly-enlarged mineral fuel base which made possible the spectacular

---

[1] In addition, of course, the energy-intensiveness of American agriculture increased dramatically after 1940 as a result of the growth of the direct consumption of energy associated with the increasing mechanisation of planting, harvesting and other operations, electrification of many non-field activities, the growing resort to irrigation, etc.

expansion of output in the nineteenth century. It is not too much to say that the industrial revolution was the direct product of the technological innovations which freed growing economies from the inevitably severe constraints imposed by the reliance upon forest sources of energy.

In the case of the iron industry, the shift to coal was merely the first, albeit critical, step in the use of technology to enlarge its limited resource base. From the 1850s on, a series of innovations occurred which continually altered the economic significance of natural resource deposits for the industry. Even the original (acid) Bessemer process had a narrow resource base. It could be used only to refine materials fulfilling certain precise chemical conditions – the process required iron free from phosphorus content (the later basic Bessemer process, by contrast, required ores of a *high* phosphorus content, but the United States did not possess large deposits of such ores, and the process never became a significant one in that country). The basic open hearth furnace of the 1880s, however, was capable of exploiting a very wide range of inputs in steelmaking (in addition to permitting a more precise degree of quality control than was possible with the Bessemer technique). In particular, it could utilise ore of almost any proportion of phosphorus content, and its availability made it possible to exploit a much wider band of the available spectrum of the gigantic Lake Superior iron ore deposits. Moreover, the process could utilise a high proportion of scrap as a material input, a consideration of great and increasing significance in locations with ready access to such supplies. The growing abundance and cheapening of scrap in the twentieth century induced research into methods of increasing the proportion of scrap used in oxygen converters. With the recent development of the electric furnace we now have a technique for producing steel entirely without iron ore, since such furnaces can operate with a 100 per cent scrap charge. Thus the potential supplies of inputs into the steelmaking process have been steadily widened, even to include the junkyards.[1]

The interaction between technological change and the natural resource base can be seen even more dramatically in Europe. The fact that Bessemer's methods could only refine materials which fell within certain narrow limits of chemical analysis had major economic consequences, imparting a strong comparative advantage to those regions possessing the non-phosphoric ores. Britain's (acid) Bessemer process grew rapidly upon the exploitation of her large deposits of non-phosphoric haematite ores. On the other hand, Germany and France had only very limited deposits appropriate for the Bessemer technique and Belgium had none. The Bessemer technique was useless for the exploitation of Europe's massive deposits of high-phosphorus ore in Lorraine and Sweden.

---

[1] In this respect the steel industry has already taken giant strides in the direction of recycling. It is worth noting that some of America's earliest rail mills did some recycling, in effect reducing reliance upon iron ore and permitting somewhat greater locational flexibility.

This British advantage, however, proved to be short-lived. The Thomas–Gilchrist technique, introduced in 1879 after a long search for methods which permitted the exploitation of phosphoric ores, drastically altered comparative advantage in favour of Continental steel producers. Their introduction of a 'basic' lining for an 'acid' one vastly expanded the range of ores which could be utilised in modern steel-making technologies – making possible the intensive exploitation of Europe's great phosphoric ore deposits. The Thomas–Gilchrist technique thus made possible a vast expansion of steel production in Germany, France and Belgium after 1880 – an expansion involving both the basic Bessemer and basic open hearth methods. Thus, what appears as a rather insignificant and humdrum technological event – the 'mere' substitution of a new material for an old one in the lining of the furnace – was, in fact, an event of immense economic and geopolitical significance. Germany's swift and spectacular emergence as an industrial power was based directly upon the rapid growth of her steel industry in the 1880s and 1890s – a growth which had, in turn, been made possible by the introduction of the basic lining and the drastic redefinition of the natural resource base which flowed from it.[1]

The gradual exhaustion of the richest iron ore supplies in the US and elsewhere in the twentieth century shifted the economic payoff away from the earlier concern over phosphorus content and toward the development of methods which would make possible the exploitation of low-grade iron ore. The result has been the growth of a highly sophisticated technology focusing upon the use of poor-quality inputs. Ores with a low iron content are now subjected to a process of beneficiation – an upgrading of their iron content before they are introduced into the blast furnace. Waste materials such as clay, gravel and sand are removed and the ores are crushed and washed, so that the material entering the blast furnace is cleaner and more uniform in quality. The implications of such techniques have been very great because they have made possible the utilisation of huge resource supplies which would formerly have been ignored. New methods have made possible the exploitation of taconite, a hard rock containing only around 22 per cent iron in fine particle form, and which exists in great abundance in the area around Lake Superior. The eventual exploitation of such ores, in pelletised form, was closely connected with the gradual exhaustion of richer ore deposits in the twentieth century. And yet the development of the appropriate techniques for processing the ore and determining the optimal characteristics of the pellets for their function within the blast furnace turned out to be an extremely tedious, time-consuming process stretching back from their first successful commercial use in 1960 to the 1920s and even to the years before the First World War. Separate machines had to be devised for crushing, grinding, magnetic separation,

---

[1] See J. C. Carr and W. Taplin, *A History of the British Steel Industry* (Harvard University Press, 1962), Chapter XIX, appropriately titled 'Lost Pre-eminence'.

filtering, concentrating, and, finally, pelletising in a furnace.[1] Although foreign ores were less costly to extract and were of a high degree of chemical purity, pellets won their way to commercial acceptance in the 1960s because they offered certain distinct offsetting advantages. They were tailormade to offer the blast furnace operator not only the chemical analysis required for his operation, but also the precise size and shape of ore particles which is most exactly suited to his specifications. Thus the perfecting of taconite technology has vastly enlarged our resource base to include some billions of tons of previously worthless ores in northern Minnesota. Although a greater sense of urgency (i.e. more rapid depletion of higher grade ores) would doubtless have compressed the development time from the several decades over which it actually stretched, the design of a sequence of complex machines for the processing of highly refractory materials and the dovetailing of their separate operations, as well as the experimentation with the final product in the blast furnace, was unavoidably a time-consuming activity. In no useful sense could such a technology have been regarded as 'on the shelf' in 1920, 1930 or 1940.

The developments in iron and steel are by no means unique. Although discussions of the impact of new technologies usually concentrate upon resulting improvements in productivity, it is essential to note that the main technological innovations in this industry over the past century also had the immensely important effect of greatly widening the range of usable natural resource inputs. Indeed, our identifiable iron reserves are much larger today than they were twenty-five years ago. New techniques elsewhere have, in effect, similarly augmented our 'dwindling' supply of other minerals in parallel ways. The flotation process, originally developed in copper mining, made it possible to exploit ores of as low as 0.4 per cent, whereas the lower limit in 1900 had been around 3.0 per cent. The technique has been applied to a wider range of ores, both of lower mineral content and more complex forms. Techniques of selective flotation have played a major role in offsetting the decline in the quality of available resources, not only for copper, but for such important materials as lead, zinc and molybdenum as well. Indeed, even the use of such modifiers as 'high grade' or 'high quality' are often misleading since they refer to chemical composition and describe properties which may or may not have

---

[1]The story is told in detail in E. W. Davis, *Pioneering with Taconite* (Minnesota Historical Society, St. Paul, 1964), especially Chapter 4. The author was appointed as superintendent of the Mines Experiment Station of the University of Minnesota back in 1918 and was subsequently involved in the development work for many years. Some of the difficulties which were encountered are suggested in the following passage: 'As it worked out, our second round of research on Babbitt taconite was divided into two general projects. The first involved fine grinding and magnetic concentration to produce at least a 64 per cent iron product. The second had to do with the agglomeration of these fine particles of concentrate into the rounded well-oxidized lumps that the blast furnace operators had specified. The processing of taconite is simple in theory but complex in execution. The extremely hard rock must be crushed and ground to a fineness resembling flour. This fine grinding liberates the small particles of high-grade magnetite. These are caught and removed (or concentrated) by magnetic separation. The particles must then be put back together (agglomerated or pelletized) to make pieces large and hard enough for shipping and smelting . . .' *Ibid.*, p. 69.

economic significance, or whose economic significance may change over time as a result of changing technology. Thus, anthracite coal has usually been regarded as higher quality than bituminous coal because it has little gas and other impurities, such as sulphur. But from the point of view of its use as a blast furnace fuel, the low gas content was, for many years, a serious disadvantage because it rendered ignition very difficult. As a result, the rich anthracite deposits in eastern Pennsylvania were unusable in the blast furnace until the introduction of Neilson's hot blast in the 1830s.[1] Even so, this 'high-quality' coal was soon displaced by large 'low-quality' bituminous deposits when the westward movement of population made these deposits (such as those in western Pennsylvania) more readily accessible.

V. PROSPECTS FOR GROWTH

Given the time constraints, let me allow these brief references to agricultural and metallurgical history to serve as proxies for the ways in which technological change has interacted with changing natural resource scarcities in the past.[2] How then are we to account for the pervasive pessimism which has come to dominate the discussion of economic growth prospects in the past several years? Are we just going through yet another of those recurrent cycles of pessimism which seem to have afflicted us at intervals in the past, or is there something genuinely new and different about our present state?[3]

There are many possible levels at which an answer to this question might be

---

[1]Neilson's preheated blast also made possible the more efficient smelting of poorer quality ores than possible with a cold blast. It also, of course, sharply reduced fuel requirements per ton of iron output.

[2]For a more general treatment see 'Innovative Responses to Materials Shortages', Chapter 14 in Rosenberg, *Perspectives on Technology, op. cit.*

[3]The ease and speed with which perceptions may shift is worth noting. In the post-Second World War period up to the early 1960s, it was almost universally believed that the United States enjoyed some sort of decisive and unassailable technological superiority over the other highly industrialised nations of the world. Although the notion of a 'technological gap' was never precisely defined, it was widely accepted that the United States possessed an unquestioned technological advantage and that this advantage was fraught with the most dangerous economic and political consequences for other countries, particularly those of western Europe. At the very least, the view was widely held in western Europe that only a drastic overhauling of political machinery would make it possible to face up to 'The American Challenge', as J.J. Servan-Schreiber characterised it in his widely-discussed book bearing that title which was published in 1968. Failing some decisive action, western Europe was destined to slip into the status of an American colony, totally dependent upon the United States for both economic and technological leadership.

The speed with which these dominating views were displaced by something approaching their polar opposite was breathtaking. Within a couple of years the view of American technological hegemony gave way to the view that the United States was being overtaken throughout a wide range of high technology exports by the burgeoning economies of western Europe and Japan. By 1974 a distinguished American economist published an article bearing the somewhat ominous title 'An American Economic Climacteric?' (*Challenge*, January–February 1974) and proceeded to suggest an affirmative answer to his question.

attempted. A mere economic historian cannot offer an explanation for the persistent tendency, in our society, to predict dismal futures quite different from a more illustrious past. He can, however, point to certain distinct ways of modelling reality, certain intellectual artifacts with which we attempt to probe the future. But I do not propose even to attempt to account for the popularity of such models or artifacts in the face of the abundant historical evidence which should cast them into instant disrepute (it must be readily admitted that the last decade has not been the most spectacularly successful in our history. But neither, I hasten to add for the benefit of those under forty years of age, is it the first bad decade we have ever had).

I would like to emphasise one dimension which seems to loom very large in the differing assessments of the prospects for future economic growth. That dimension is in fact implicit in my discussion up to this point. Optimistic assessments of future growth prospects are usually founded upon the conception of the economy as a social system with at least a substantial capacity for adaptation to changing conditions; whereas pessimistic assessments are based upon models in which the capacity for such adaptation is either understated or ignored. Alternatively, the issue may be expressed in terms of substitution possibilities. The pessimists see no significant substitution possibilities for natural resources, whereas for the optimists the elasticity of substitution of capital and labour for natural resources is very high. The Club of Rome model is simply one extreme end of this spectrum. It is, indeed, a model whose essential feature is precisely the *lack* of a capacity to adjust. Not only is there no technical change in the model; neither is there a process generating the discovery of new resources or new substitution possibilities, nor even the most rudimentary elements of a price mechanism to induce the substitution of abundant for scarce resources. That such a system soon encounters inexorable limits to growth should be neither surprising nor alarming.

Although the Club of Rome model simply excludes new technologies and other mechanisms which can generate adjustments, others recognise the existence of those forces but deny that they can serve as effective adjustment mechanisms. Many of those who view the future with deep alarm seem to treat both science and technology as totally autonomous forces, unlinked and unresponsive to social or economic considerations. Thus, Mishan has stated:

Notwithstanding occasional declarations about the unlimited potentialities for social betterment science is not guided by any social purpose. As with technology, the effects on humanity are simply the by-products of its own self-seeking. As a collective enterprise science has no more social conscience than the problem-solving computers it employs . . . [1]

In some important respects Mishan's view is not unrepresentative of the one

[1]Ezra Mishan, *Technology and Growth* (Praeger, New York, 1969), p. 129.

which dominated almost the entire economics profession until very recently. With a few distinguished exceptions such as Marx and Schumpeter, economists neglected technological change shamelessly for generations. The subject has received extensive consideration only since Abramovitz and Solow awakened us from our dogmatic slumber twenty years ago by calling attention to the great apparent quantitative importance of that phenomenon in the American growth process. But it was Jack Schmookler's[1] work which powerfully and persuasively argued that inventive activity had major economic causes as well as consequences, that the allocation of inventive effort among different commodity classes could be explained in terms of economic forces to which inventors were responsive. Specifically, Schmookler argued that demand considerations, through the influence which they exercise upon the size of market for particular classes of inventions, are the principal determinant of the allocation of inventive effort.[2]

Schmookler's analysis constituted a major step forward, but it still needs to be extended by further work which will integrate his study of the forces controlling the allocation of inventive resources with a more systematic examination of the economic consequences *flowing* from that allocation. The point at issue is that Schmookler's work illuminates the demand side but not the supply side. For his purposes he was content to operate with the simplifying assumption that the supply schedule of inventive activity is perfectly elastic, at the same price, in all industries.[3] But, clearly, if we are centrally concerned with the adjustment mechanism through which the economy responds to changing conditions of resource scarcity, then the position and shape of the invention supply curve in each relevant commodity class needs to be examined. For it is precisely the differential capacity to generate inventive responses which has to be explained. And, for policy purposes, we need to inquire into the possibilities for *altering* certain response capabilities. For our purposes, if not

[1] Jacob Schmookler, *Invention and Economic Growth* (Cambridge, Harvard University Press, 1966).

[2] Schmookler also asserted that science, as well as technology, was shaped by the demand for final products. 'Thus, independently of the motives of scientists themselves and with due recognition of the fact that anticipated practical uses of scientific discoveries still unmade are often vague, it seems reasonable to suggest – without taking joy in the suggestion – that the demand for science (and, of course, engineering) is and for a long time has been derived largely from the demand for conventional economic goods. Without the expectation, increasingly confirmed by experience, of "useful" applications, those branches of science and engineering that have grown the most in modern times and have contributed most dramatically to technological change – electricity, chemistry and nucleonics – would have grown far less than they have. If this view is approximately correct, then even if we choose to regard the demand for new knowledge for its own sake as a non-economic phenomenon, the growth of modern science and engineering is still primarily a part of the economic process.' *Ibid.*, p. 177. See also Jacob Schmookler, 'Catastrophe and Utilitarianism in the Development of Basic Science', in Richard Tybout (ed.), *The Economics of Research and Development*, (Columbus, Ohio State University Press, 1965).

[3] This, as well as other aspects of Schmookler's analysis, is dealt with in *Perspectives on Technology*, *op. cit.*, Chapter 15, 'Science, Invention and Economic Growth'.

Schmookler's, the behaviour of the supply schedule is the essence of the problem.

In this context, it is now possible to point to certain ways in which the world has changed in the past ten or fifteen years which are significant for our purposes – and this even before the most fundamental change of all associated with the emergence of OPEC after October 1973 as what may prove to be the most successful cartel in history. Perhaps the most inclusive way of expressing it is that we have been experiencing a broadening of goals and concerns as a result of which the 'alternative ends' which we seek have an ever-expanding non-material component. I am inclined to see this as a product of our growing affluence. A sufficiently large proportion of American society has been attaining to income levels at which they are revealing a high-income elasticity of demand for 'products' which were not previously on their shopping lists – e.g. a non-polluted environment.[1] However intrinsically desirable these other things may be, I merely want to insist that their attainment is costly in a variety of ways and that, as a result, the adaptation process has been subjected to additional and often very expensive constraints.

Consider the growth of the vast constituency which is now intensely concerned with problems of pollution and the improvement of environmental quality – a concern which is now institutionalised not only in the Sierra Club but in the federal Environmental Protection Agency. Perhaps what is most astonishing about this movement is that it took so unconscionably long in coming, and I cannot repress the speculation that the abusive manner in which Americans have treated their natural environment has been yet another inheritance of our historical experience in an environment of abundant resources. Everyone has his own favourite litany of the ways in which industrial man has managed to foul his own nest, and I will not inflict my own upon you. The present point is simply that a major concern over environmental impact seriously affects the speed and the cost with which we can respond to a sudden rise in fuel prices by strip-mining western coal, drilling for off-shore oil, or constructing a nuclear power plant. The requirement that utilities introduce stack gas scrubbers as a means of protecting the environment from sulphur dioxide emissions involves not only considerable cost but an array of additional complexities.[2] Further, government regulations, however well-intentioned and

---

[1] In 1900, Americans said that the large cities were dirty, noisy, crowded, and unpleasant to live in, but that was the way they had always been. In the 1960s Americans said that the large cities were dirty, noisy, crowded, and unpleasant to live in, and the situation was intolerable and something should be done about it.' Gerald Gunderson, *A New Economic History of America,* (New York, McGraw-Hill Book Company, 1976), p. 451.

[2] It is no secret that the power industry has, to varying degrees, been reluctant to adopt scrubbers. The equipment is expensive – $75 to $125 per kilowatt, a substantial fraction of the cost of the power station itself . . . Scrubbers also consume as much as 5 per cent of the power output of a generating plant and introduce a whole new order of complexity, that of chemical processing, into the operation.' Allen L. Hammond, 'Coal Research (IV): Direct Research Lags Its Potential', *Science* (8 October 1976), p. 172. It is also pointed out: 'Despite the unresolved problems, stack gas scrubbing has much to recommend it – not least that it now appears to be a far cheaper way of cleaning up coal for power generation than conversion of the coal to a synthetic fuel.' *Ibid.,* p. 173.

even when they are effective in some important respects, are likely to have the effect of increasing still further the uncertainties concerning the future which can act as a serious deterrent to decisive action. The uncertainties over future regulatory directions are likely themselves to become an independent force discouraging innovation. Thus, a great deal of the uncertainties in the development of non-petroleum energy sources derive from a present lack of coherence in environmental protection regulations. Just how strict are safety regulations going to be for nuclear power generating plants? How restrictive will government regulations with respect to air pollution in urban areas be for the utilisation of coal in electric power generation? When federal legislation is eventually enacted, how will it affect the costs of strip-mining operations? Will automobile emission standards be strengthened or relaxed in the future?

Thus, I am suggesting that the attainment of relative affluence in the industrial economies has led to a greater public demand (through the addition of new arguments to individual utility functions, or the greater subjective weights assigned to such arguments) for goods of a sort not previously demanded with much fervour, such as clean air and water, relative quiet, etc. As it happens, many of these new 'goods' are inherently not amenable to provision through the market mechanism. Their public good nature entails governmental intervention and regulation. Now, the *fact* of this growing governmental regulation of certain private activities has, itself, generated substantial uncertainties for private business. The uncertainty is really a central aspect of what is in fact an adaptation process which is being mediated through the political rather than the market mechanism. Such a process of the political achievement of certain goals through the detailed regulation of private market activity inevitably introduces its own peculiar lags and frictions into the adaptation process – a condition which is further aggravated by the fact that the technologies for the achievement of these goals are not well-specified.

Although environmental concerns have become very conspicuous since the 1960s, other concerns have also served to weaken our earlier, more single-minded pursuit of (a very narrowly defined) economic efficiency. Some of these overlap substantially with purely environmental considerations but nonetheless warrant separate recognition. I include here the emergence, strongly associated with Ralph Nader, of a consumerist movement committed to the improvement of product safety. I include also the increasing assumption, especially on the part of government regulatory agencies, of responsibility for matters concerning public health. I would also include the multitude of ways in which questions of worker morale and job satisfaction are leading to a reorganisation of the productive process in ways which may have important implications for economic efficiency. However laudable these goals are individually and collectively, their presence necessarily means that we have lost some degrees of freedom in adapting to changing economic circumstances.

In attributing these recent developments to a kind of inexorable working out of Engel's Law, I do not mean to suggest that that is the whole story, but merely a most important part of it. I would not want to deny, for example, that the scale, power and intensity of many new technologies have often resulted in objectively-measurable, more disruptive ecological effects. On the other hand, it is also true that some highly pollution-intensive technologies have been displaced or have vastly declined in importance – for example, horses and coal fires – and we unfortunately have no single, unambiguous index with which we can trace the overall rise or decline of pollution.[1] There is, however, a related and more subtle point. Improvements in scientific knowledge expand our awareness of inter-relationships and therefore enhance our ability to perceive and to anticipate *possible* costs which *may* be associated with specific new technologies. Often these relationships cannot be firmly established because many of the putative consequences appear to be slow-acting but cumulative in nature. Thus an improved but still highly imperfect understanding tends to be consistently biased in terms of raising our assessment of some of the possible costs involved in the exploitation of new technologies. Perhaps it is right to err on the side of caution, but it needs to be remembered that caution, too, may have substantial costs in terms of opportunities foregone and flexibility sacrificed.

Our recent difficulties have, of course, been exacerbated by government policies which, by placing restrictions upon the upward movement of prices, have artificially encouraged the development of and increasing reliance upon energy-intensive technologies. Government policies have also served to increase the reliance upon higher quality fuels – especially cheap, clean natural gas – while simultaneously weakening the incentives to exploration. At the same time government priorities resulted in pouring vast resources into R & D for just one new energy technology – nuclear power – while neglecting other potential energy technologies for which we possess an immense natural resource base – particularly shale oil and coal gasification. As nuclear power turned out to be wracked with unexpected difficulties – including but not only those of an environmental and safety nature – our dependence upon highly vulnerable petroleum and natural gas supplies increased sharply. The eventual consequence of this dependence for all the industrial countries in the past four years is too familiar to require any recounting. But it does seem fair to state that what is loosely called an 'energy crisis' is really an oil and natural gas crisis – a very different thing.

VI. A MAN-MADE CRISIS

The burden of the foregoing discussion is that we are currently suffering from an unfortunate conjuncture of circumstances. The emergence of a 'taste' for higher environmental quality and injudicious government energy policies (which also weakened the incentives to adopt energy-saving techniques) have

---

[1] There have been some highly successful instances of dealing with urban pollution – e.g. in Pittsburgh and London – but for some reason improvements do not seem to be regarded as newsworthy.

combined to dampen our capacity to respond to shifting patterns of resource scarcities at the same time as our growing dependence upon imported petroleum has increased our vulnerability to those in a position to manipulate supply. We are still making our adjustments to this new regime of high oil prices, and we will continue to do so for some time. The point which I want to insist upon, however, is that the post-1973 energy 'crisis' is fundamentally political in its origins. It is man-made. It does not represent some sudden discontinuity which has been inflicted upon us by nature. Those who have long argued that we were in imminent danger of running out of oil have no business taking the new OPEC-imposed price of oil as confirmation of their views. Of course we *will* run out of oil one day. And of course the market *would*, eventually, have begun to reflect future growing oil scarcity in the absence of OPEC (and domestic natural gas prices would surely already have reflected it in the absence of price ceilings). But the quadrupling of oil prices after the embargo was obviously *not* due to rising costs of oil extraction. The long-run average cost curve for OPEC oil has not shifted upward. In some parts of the Middle East the cost of extraction is still below twenty-five cents a barrel. Far from the new oil price regime constituting evidence of a drastic shift in resource scarcity, it is simply a measure of abnormal profits extracted by those in control of supply, with costs essentially unchanged.[1]

I conclude from this that the events of the last ten or fifteen years do not warrant a major revision in the earlier optimism about the adequacy of natural resources to support economic growth in the long run. But the qualification 'in the long run' is all-important. There are no adjustment mechanisms in our economic system which can insulate us against sudden random shocks or perturbations, especially of a kind which are politically inspired and the *timing* and *severity* of which could not have been anticipated either by an examination of economic data or long-term natural resource trends. The basic point is a simple one. One doesn't search for substitutes for commodities which are expected to remain cheap for a long time, just as one does not search for new reserves of a mineral when known reserves are already very abundant relative to expected demand. We did not search widely for substitute fuel technologies when oil was selling at pre-embargo prices and dramatic changes were not

---

[1] Of course if the goal is solely the conservation of oil supplies, the monopoly price is to be preferred to the competitive one. Indeed, the Shah of Iran could even suggest to an interviewer (presumably with a straight face) that, by raising further the price of oil, he deserved to be accorded all the accolades due to a saviour of western civilisation. '. . . he was still insistent that the price of oil was too low, and he would keep it up, he blandly explained, for the West's own sake: "It would really be weak and short-sighted, and it would not help the world at large: because you will start to go again into a false euphoria of cheap oil, and forget about extracting your coal and searching for new sources of energy. It would be the biggest mistake which would be made to our (sic!) civilization. I won't be part of that mistake." ' Anthony Sampson, *The Seven Sisters* (London, Hodder and Stoughton, 1975), p. 292.

anticipated.[1] At some point, such search expenditures would surely have become warranted as a function of revised expectations concerning future prices and (appropriately discounted) revenue flows. But sudden and drastic *alterations* in expectations can create serious problems, particularly when very long lead times are required in switching to alternative technologies.[2]

As a result, we need to recognise the likelihood of natural resource problems of some degree of intractability in the short run. Moreover, if I am right, we are going to have to accept the likelihood that the short run, in the present context, may represent a calendar time of twenty or thirty years. Adapting to changing patterns of resource scarcity is a highly time-consuming activity, and I have already suggested some forces at work in recent years which are having the effect of further slowing down that process. In addition, the time-consuming nature of the adjustment process brings with it many problems and complexities which will bedevil the attempt to formulate effective policies for the future. We will therefore need to pay particular attention to some of the implications of the Marshallian dictum that 'the element of Time . . . is the centre of the chief difficulty of almost every economic problem . . .'. But I invoke this bit of Marshallian wisdom to emphasise my own point that the difficulties which we currently confront are imposed primarily by the considerable length of time involved in making the adjustments which need to be made. For I am suggesting a view which is precisely the opposite of that offered by the Club of Rome and the 'Limits to Growth' school. I suggest, in other words, that for the advanced industrial economies of the world, the difficulties are of a short-run and not a long-run nature.

I characterise our present historical juncture as one where we have been caught 'off-track' or, more accurately, one where we have been *bumped* 'off-track', and where devising and undertaking the utilisation of an appropriate new track will be a slow and perhaps painful adjustment. Alternative energy technologies exist and we possess the natural resource endowment for utilising them. But the alternative technologies are by no means 'on the shelf' and there are many uncertainties – including their eventual costs – associated with each of them. Once again it is essential to realise that the replacement of one natural resource for another is more than 'mere' factor substitution. The achievement

---

[1] Additionally, we have abandoned the search for synthetic fuel technologies in the past when new information concerning the abundance of natural sources became available. 'Unsuccessful attempts to launch a synthetic fuels industry in the United States have been made twice before, in the 1920s and again following World War II. The first was abandoned after discovery of the large East Texas oil fields undermined any hope of commercial success. The second, which included about $100 million in federal R & D work and construction of several successful pilot plants at Louisiana, Missouri, between 1948 and 1953, was scuttled by the realization of the magnitude of the vast Middle East oil reservoirs.' Allen L. Hammond, 'Coal Research (I): Is the Program Moving Ahead?' *Science* (20 August 1976), p. 667.

[2] For a discussion of some of the implications of various kinds of expectations concerning changes not in price but in technology see Nathan Rosenberg, 'On Technological Expectations', *Economic Journal* (September 1976).

of the conditions necessary for that substitution may involve many elements for which we regularly employ the term 'technological change'. While these are being developed, it will be necessary to take recourse in the short run to a variety of adjustments including, most obviously, eliminating price controls so that higher prices may restrict consumption, stimulate exploration and the exploitation of higher-cost supplies, shifting the output mix and product design in the direction of less energy-intensive goods, etc. Some of these adjustments are, in any case, intrinsically desirable.[1]

Again, the central problem is the element of time. It takes as much as a decade to place a nuclear power plant on line and perhaps half that time to instal a coal-fired plant. And these are cases where we are dealing with known technologies. For some of the most feasible alternative resource bases, the appropriate technologies are simply not yet established. Although, if environmental regulations permitted it, we could substitute coal for oil or natural gas at an electric power station with minimum difficulty, the substitution of coal for gas via gasification or liquefaction or the exploitation of our oil shale supplies is another matter entirely. None of these technologies is sufficiently advanced to be of significant service in the immediate future. They each require very extensive – although varying degrees of – development. Their development costs are certain to be very high and the length of time involved in bringing them to the stage of commercial availability, where they can make a significant contribution to our energy requirements, is more likely to be a matter of decades than years.

Thus, the point which has to be emphasised is that our options are presently more constrained by time than by the emptiness of nature's larder. Nevertheless, the problems with which the time element confronts us are real enough and their severity should not be underestimated. We are dealing with large investment projects whose financial requirements are immense.[2] Lead times in planning and construction are very great even for the more conventional technologies, and therefore investors are required to make commitments into a very distant future (the length of these lead times has of course been increased by regulation). Not only is the gestation process a long one, but the capital asset itself – whether a power plant or coal mine – has a

---

[1] There has been a good deal of questioning of the effectiveness of higher prices as a means of restricting consumption, in view of evidence suggesting that the demand curve for energy is highly inelastic, at least in the short run. Less attention has been devoted to the critical question of the elasticity of the energy supply curve. Although higher prices will undoubtedly elicit greater production, it is not at all clear how responsive energy supplies are likely to be to higher prices. The ordinary practice of the US Geological Survey is to estimate proven reserves at prevailing prices and existing technology. However, there is a great deal of evidence that there may be large supplies of less accessible oil, and perhaps much larger supplies of natural gas, which it would be commercially feasible to exploit at substantially higher prices.

[2] A full-size commercial facility to produce 250,000,000 cubic feet of synthetic natural gas per day is now estimated to cost $1 billion.' Allen L. Hammond, 'Coal Research (II): Gasification Faces An Uncertain Future', *Science* (27 August 1976), p. 750.

very long life and slow payout period. In the case of the new and as-yet-untried technologies, there are many great uncertainties over the functioning of the technologies themselves, there are alternative possible solutions to numerous problems which require separate exploration, and there are innumerable uncertainties over the performance characteristics of individual components. All of these difficulties require a willingness to make decisions with respect to a very long time horizon, and a willingness to coax out solutions to technical problems with large and steady libations of R & D expenditures over an indeterminate number of years. Given what we know about the time horizons of decision-makers in private industry – a notoriously myopic world – the R & D funds for the critical technology development activities are unlikely to be forthcoming.[1] There is a serious gap here, a discrepancy between what appears to be socially profitable on the one hand, and what appears to be privately profitable in the business world with its own peculiar incentive systems, heavy discount of the future, etc., on the other. In a world of myopic businessmen, long lead times and numerous and costly technological uncertainties requiring resolution, the effectiveness of private signalling is considerably weakened.

It is difficult at this time not to invoke the government as the far-sighted *deus ex machina* which can make and enforce the socially necessary decisions which private industry cannot. Unfortunately, (because no superior alternative is ready to hand) there are compelling reasons for myopia in government, particularly in a democracy, when the kinds of decisions which would presumably be made by those taking the necessary long view for society are likely to be intensely unpopular in the short run.

But there is one more element to all this, and it is perhaps the most formidable difficulty of all. Potential entrants into the energy industry, or present members who are contemplating expansion, require above all some degree of assurance that oil prices will remain high for a period of time sufficiently long to permit them to recover their investments. But when dealing with an industry dominated by a cartel as resourceful as OPEC, the risks involved are much greater than can be conveyed by referring to the normal uncertainties concerning future prices. Potential energy suppliers must deal with the fact that the cartel is devising a strategy which will maximise its *own* long-run income stream. It is therefore clearly in the interest of the cartel to discourage new entrants into the energy field. Thus there is the continual threat of temporary price cutting to discourage new entrants. Moreover, the cartel may reasonably be assumed to be monitoring carefully the progress which is being made in the development of substitute technologies. It may therefore also

[1]Ed Mansfield points out that, in the chemical and petroleum industries for example, R & D expenditures tend to be limited to activities which will affect profits in less than five years. Ed Mansfield *et al., Research and Innovation in the Modern Corporation* (W. W. Norton & Co., New York, 1971), pp. 19–33. See also 'R & D and Economic Growth: Renewed Interest in Federal Role', *Science* (17 September 1976), 1101–1103.

be expected to move with greater circumspection as it approaches the price levels at which certain high-cost technologies begin to become commercially feasible.

Ironically, one of OPEC's greatest strengths in discouraging potential competitors, aside from the difficulties confronting new entrants which have already been mentioned, may be the expectation that it will collapse in the not-too-distant future! That expectation probably was a significant force in the immediate post-embargo period. Collapse of OPEC would surely drive down prices. On the other hand, the continued survival of a strong OPEC offers the alternative hazard of temporary price cutting to drive out prospective new entrants. From a social point of view, the ideal situation would be for prospective energy producers to *believe* in the continued survival of a strong cartel, maintaining reassuringly high prices, but for the cartel actually to collapse under eventual pressure from these competitors, if it did not do so sooner. Clearly this is an unlikely scenario.

The uncertainties over future prices are such a serious deterrent that some system of price guarantees would seem to be unavoidable. No economist will recommend such guarantees lightly, but it seems to be the one direct and obvious way of strengthening the willingness of private enterprise in the face of genuine, deep-rooted uncertainties and in a situation where there is a broad consensus that the social payoff is likely to be very high. The prospects are that the perceived risks associated with uncertainty over future oil prices will probably persist. And, so long as they do persist, they may be expected to exercise a paralysing effect over long-term investment decisions. Some form of minimum assurance over price therefore seems unavoidable.

VII. SOME CONCLUDING OBSERVATIONS

This is not the place to engage in a detailed discussion of what precise shape government policies ought to take in dealing with resource problems in general and energy in particular.[1] However, a few general observations, and especially some cautionary ones, may be appropriate. The short-term time horizons within which business operates identify an important range of activities where there is a vital social interest which is not adequately accommodated through the incentives of the market place. Some more extensive system of government subsidy will need to be developed to articulate society's legitimate longer-term R & D needs and to strengthen the incentives of business in technology development involving more distant payoffs. New energy systems, as we have seen, are especially likely to fall beyond the planning and investment horizons of private firms. Public agencies, however, are almost certainly not the appropriate institutions for attempting to carry these technological

---

[1]For a discussion of the broad issues involved in government technology policy, see Nathan Rosenberg, *Thinking About Technology Policy for the Coming Decade*, prepared for the Joint Economic Committee, USGPO, 1976.

developments to the stage of commercial applicability. Such agencies are likely on the one hand to make specific commitments too early, and on the other hand to have insufficient incentive to terminate projects as evidence accumulates of their excessive costliness. Where the evidence seems favourable that a developing technology may be commercially viable, and as the time horizons shorten, arrangements should be made to shift the technology over to private enterprise for commercial exploitation.

In general, the great uncertainties which still persist as to which energy source will be most satisfactory in the long-run supports the position that the government should not confine itself to any single alternative or even to a very small number of alternatives. Indeed, it is most unlikely in any case that a single source will, in the near future, emerge as decisively superior to all alternatives for all purposes. In any case, it should be an explicit goal of government policy to keep a variety of options open, and it can best do this by a broad-based programme which explores possibilities wherever informed judgement indicates that there may be promising prospects. An eventual narrowing of the alternatives can come most effectively out of the information eventually generated by further research.

As a related but separate point, the government-supported research programme ought to attach a particularly high priority to research which holds out the promise of widening the range of substitutability. The dangers of heavy dependence upon a single resource, for which no close substitutes are readily available, have been forcefully underlined by OPEC. Although it is doubtful that the success of that cartel can be emulated with respect to any other resource category (partly because there *are* no comparable other resource categories) there is wisdom in cultivating a capacity for flexibility, especially in relation to productive activities characterised by long lead times. Such flexibility in turn would require some minimum, ongoing research activity at the engineering and technological levels, and possibly even some support of pilot or demonstration plant projects in specific cases, in order to facilitate the capacity to shift from one resource base to another more rapidly than often appears to be possible at present. And, of course, the more abundant the materials whose substitution possibilities are being expanded, the better.[1]

In considering the possibilities for dealing with specific raw materials scarcities through substitution, it is essential that this substitution process be conceived in a broad way. One may simply substitute one material for another – as, for example, aluminium for copper in electric transmission systems, or concrete blocks for timber in housing construction. But, more broadly, one can often perform a specific function or activity in quite a variety of different ways.

---

[1]The energy problem intrudes itself here as well because many of the more abundant minerals in the earth's crust have highly energy-intensive processes associated with their extraction and subsequent refining. High energy costs are currently a serious obstacle to the expanded use of aluminium and magnesium and they have also become a major deterrent to the utilisation of lower-grade ores.

Microfilm represents a highly materials-saving (as well as space-saving) technique for the storage of information. Adhesives can replace the use of nuts and bolts for certain joining purposes. The telephone substitutes for the postal service as a means of transmitting information. Laser beams may soon transmit telephone conversations through tiny glass fibres rather than copper wires. Improved techniques of telecommunications may soon serve as a substitute for transportation in meetings, conferences and even to some extent for social intercourse where face-to-face communication is highly desired. Aside from the many remarkable developments which have been based upon it over the past quarter century, including the computer, the development of the transistor and solid-state components has represented a materials- and energy-saving substitution over the vacuum tube. The integrated circuit, happily, is based upon the second most abundant of all elements, silicon.[1] Miniaturisation, as it has been developing in recent years, holds out a wide range of prospects for economising upon both materials and energy. Computerised electronic control of the automobile engine offers an excellent prospect both for greater gas economy and for improved emission control. Biological research may well create new grain varieties which, among other things, can fix their own nitrogen, as the legumes already do – a development which would dramatically reduce the energy requirements of modern agriculture. Somewhere farther down the road, electronics may offer practical techniques for the photoelectric conversion of solar energy.

If some of the possibilities held out by electronics and genetic engineering occasionally seem to verge on science fiction, it is well to recall Simon Kuznets' admonition that science fiction writers have had a better track record over the years in sensing what might become technically feasible in the future than the professional specialist whose vision has often been clouded rather than enlarged by his technical expertise. Finally, it needs to be recalled that, in America, with our long history of resource abundance, relatively little attention was given to the development of resource-saving technologies. Indeed, as I suggested earlier, in the nineteenth century we were much concerned to develop resource-*intensive* technologies. The friendly neighbourhood public utility, which now publishes daily 'Helpful Hints' in local newspapers on how to economise on electricity bills, had spent the previous seventy years assiduously plying the American public with wave after wave of gadgetry which just happened to require plugging in to an electric socket (often as well the gadgetry was very badly designed with respect to efficient electricity use). The point is that many of the resource problems which currently concern us, as we consider the prospects for continued growth, are problems to which we have only just begun to address our scientific and technological capacities in a serious way. It is therefore probably still much too early to perceive with any clarity what the

---

[1] More generally, one of the more promising aspects of the electronics revolution is its relatively modest energy or materials demands.

eventual possibilities may be.[1] Nevertheless, our ability to adjust to different kinds of resource problems in the past would seem to justify reasonable confidence that our present resource problems can also be made to yield to systematic research and organised ingenuity.[2] How rapidly they will yield will depend partly upon how singlemindedly we pursue that single goal to the exclusion of other desirable goals, such as improvement of environmental quality. However, getting back upon an appropriate technological track will under no circumstances be easy or quick. It will not be achieved in one or two or even ten years. And, if the past is any guide at all (which of course it may not be) technological solutions, when achieved, will produce a whole new generation of other problems. But that sequence of events, I am afraid, is in the nature of technologically dynamic societies, if not in the nature of the human condition itself.

[1]Although there has been a good deal of research within the university community in developing materials with specific properties or performance characteristics, such as were required in the space programme – heat resistance, electrical conductivity, etc. – relatively little has been done to deal with problems of materials shortages. Not much has been done to explore the possibilities of resource saving by redesign, by recycling, or by specifically designing products for longer life. In some cases, as in the attempt to lengthen product life, there are serious conflicts with capitalist values, which in the past have been so heavily geared to planned obsolescence and annual model changes. Academic work in Materials Science has been concerned, quite naturally, with working out its own paradigms relating to the physical properties of materials. It would require considerable reorientation in order to undertake work of immediate relevance to the problems posed by prospective materials shortages. See Robert Huggins, 'Basic Research in Materials', *Science* (20 February 1976).

[2]In the academic world this will probably involve some changes in the incentive system to create a greater problem focus as opposed to the present powerful focus upon individual disciplines. Along with a greater problem orientation is an increasing emphasis upon interdisciplinary research. In some respects this runs deeply counter to trends which have been highly successful in the twentieth century – particularly the increasing specialisation of knowledge within narrow, well-defined disciplinary boundaries. Nevertheless, it appears to be a fact that an increasing number of crucial technical problems are now emerging the solutions to which do not lie completely within single academic disciplines. It is also apparent that such problem-oriented, interdisciplinary research has been organised and managed with spectacular success in a few instances, as in the development of the high-yield rice varieties at the International Rice Research Institute in the Philippines.

9 The Role of Technological Change in United States Economic Growth[1]

Edwin Mansfield
UNIVERSITY OF PENNSYLVANIA

I. INTRODUCTION

During the past twenty years, there has been a continuing interest among economists in the relationship between technological change and economic growth. After many decades of relative neglect, there began in the mid-1950s a series of investigations of various aspects of this relationship, the purpose being both to extend the range and power of economic analysis and to help guide public policy. In the present chapter, my purpose is to summarise briefly some of the major findings of this research and to relate these findings to some of the key questions concerning science and technology policy that have been prominent in the United States in the past ten or fifteen years.

II. TECHNOLOGY AND AMERICAN ECONOMIC GROWTH

In August 1957 – just twenty years ago – Robert Solow published a seminal article [29] calling attention to the importance of technological change in American economic growth. Assuming that there were constant returns to scale, that capital and labour were paid their marginal products, and that technological change was neutral, Solow attempted to estimate the rate of technological change for the non-farm US economy during 1909–49. His findings indicated that, for the period as a whole, the average rate of technological change was about 1.5 per cent per year. Based on these findings, he concluded that about 90 per cent of the increase in output per capita during this period was attributable to technological change, whereas only a minor percentage of the increase was due to increases in the amount of capital employed per worker.

Solow's measure of the effects of technological change also included the effects of whatever factors were omitted, such as economies of scale, improved allocation of resources, changes in product mix, increases in education, or improved health and nutrition of workers. To obtain a purer measure, Edward Denison [3] attempted to include many inputs – for example, changes in labour quality associated with increases in schooling – that had been omitted, largely

[1]The research on which this paper is based was supported by grants from the National Science Foundation. Much of the material concerning public policy toward civilian technology is taken largely from work done for the Joint Economic Committee of Congress. For a more complete discussion, see [14].

or completely, by Solow and others (such as Abramowitz and Fabricant). Since it was relatively comprehensive, Denison's study resulted in a relatively low residual increase in output unexplained by the inputs he included. Specifically, he concluded that the 'advance of knowledge' – his term for the residual – was responsible for about 40 per cent of the total increase in national income per person employed during 1929–57 in the United States.

In 1973, Zvi Griliches published a paper [11] that attempted to estimate the contribution of public and private research expenditures to the growth in the residual as conventionally measured. Assuming a Cobb–Douglas production function with labour, capital, and the stock of R & D capital as inputs, he showed that

$$f = \lambda + \rho I_\eta / Q, \tag{1}$$

where f is the rate of growth of total factor productivity, λ is the rate of disembodied 'external' technological change, ρ is the rate of return to research expenditures (i.e. the marginal product of the stock of R & D capital), and I_η / Q is the net investment in R & D divided by total output. Based on very rough estimates of ρ and I_η / Q, he concluded that about 2/10 of one percentage point of the rate of growth of US output was due to R & D expenditures.

In 1976, Denison published a paper [4] in which he presented his estimates of the contribution of advances in knowledge to the rate of growth of output per unit of input in the United States during various periods. These estimates, which were the residual in his model, amounted to 1.34 per cent per year in 1948–53, 1.13 per cent per year in 1953–64, and 1.15 per cent per year in 1964–69. In his forecasts for 1969–80, he assumes that the advance of knowledge will result in a 1.16 per cent annual increase in output per unit of input in the United States.[1]

III. SOCIAL RATES OF RETURN FROM INVESTMENTS IN NEW AGRICULTURAL TECHNOLOGY

From the point of view of public policy, economists have been interested in the social rates of return from past and prospective investments in new technology. In response to the need for such information, a variety of microeconomic studies of the returns from R & D (and related investments in new technology) have been carried out in the past 20 years. To estimate the social benefits from an innovation, economists generally have used a model of the following sort. If the innovation results in a shift downward in the supply curve for a product (such as from S_1 to S_2 in Figure 9.1), they have used the area under the product's demand curve (DD[1]) between the two supply curves – that is, ABCE

---

[1]Needless to say, all of the studies cited in this section (as well as a substantial number of additional papers on this topic that we lacked the space to include) are subject to a variety of limitations and difficulties. In the available space, it is impossible to summarise these limitations. For a discussion of some of them, see [15].

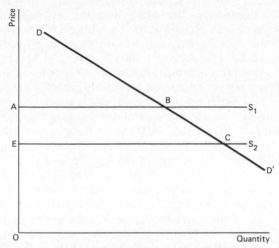

Fig. 9.1 Measurement of social benefits from technological innovation

in Figure 9.1 – as a measure of the social benefit during the relevant time period from the innovation. If all other prices remain constant, this area equals the social value of the additional quantity of the product plus the social value of the resources saved as a consequence of the innovation. Thus, if one compares the stream of R & D inputs relating to the innovation with the stream of social benefits measured in this way, it is possible to estimate the social rate of return from the R & D investment.

An early investigation that used this approach was Griliches' study of hybrid corn [9]. Based on data concerning the increase in yields resulting from hybrid corn, the value of corn output each year, and the price elasticity of demand for corn, he could estimate the area corresponding to ABCE in Figure 9.1 each year. Then using data concerning the amount spent each year on hybrid corn research, he could estimate the rate of return from the investment in hybrid corn research, which turned out to be 37 per cent. Clearly, a 37 per cent rate of return is high. However, in evaluating this result, it is important to bear in mind that this is the rate of return from an investment which was known in advance to have been very successful. Thus, it is not surprising that it is high.

A later study, based on much the same principles, was carried out by Peterson [26] to estimate the rate of return from poultry research. This study, unlike the previous one, looked at the rate of return from all research in this particular area, successful or not. In other words, it included the failures with the successes. The resulting rate of return was 18 per cent, which again is a rather high figure. However, as would be expected, this figure is lower than that for hybrid corn. A further study [27], by Schmitz and Seckler, used basically the same kind of techniques to estimate the social rate of return from the investment in R & D pertaining to the tomato harvester. The result depends on how long workers displaced by the tomato harvester remained unemployed, but the authors report that, even if the tomato workers received compensation of $2–$4 million per year for lost jobs, the net social rate of return from the harvester would still have far exceeded 100 per cent.

Note that all of the rates of return cited so far are average rates of return. For many purposes, a more interesting measure is the marginal rate of return, which is the rate of return from an additional dollar spent. Using econometric techniques, a number of studies have estimated the marginal rate of return from agricultural R & D. One study [10], by Griliches, investigated the relationship in various years between output per farm in a state and the amount of land, labour, fertiliser, and machinery per farm, as well as average education and expenditures on research and extension in a State. The results indicate that, holding other inputs constant, output was related in a statistically significant way to the amount spent on research and extension. Assuming a 6-year-lag between research input and its returns, these results indicate a marginal rate of return from agricultural R & D of 53 per cent. Another study [6], by Evenson, uses time-series data to estimate the marginal rate of return from agricultural R & D, the result being 57 per cent. Also, Peterson's study [26] of poultry R & D indicates that the marginal rate of return for this type of agricultural R & D is about 50 per cent. Schultz's study [28] indicates a marginal rate of return of 42 per cent.

To sum up, every study carried out to date seems to indicate that the average social rate of return from agricultural R & D tends to be very high. The marginal social rate of return from agricultural R & D also seems to be high, generally in the neighbourhood of 40 to 50 per cent. Of course, as stressed above, these studies are based on a number of simplifications, and it would be very risky to attach too much significance to them, since they are rough at best. All that can be said is that the available evidence, for what it may be worth, suggests that the rate of return from agricultural R & D has been high.

IV. SOCIAL RATES OF RETURN FROM INVESTMENTS IN NEW INDUSTRIAL TECHNOLOGY

Let us turn now to the available results concerning the social rate of return from R & D in industry. Recently, a study was made by Mansfield, Rapoport, Romeo, Wagner and Beardsley [17] of the returns from 17 specific industrial innovations. These innovations occurred in a variety of industries, including primary metals, machine tools, industrial controls, construction, drilling, paper, thread, heating equipment, electronics, chemicals and household cleaners. They occurred in firms of quite different sizes. Most of them are of average or routine importance, not major breakthroughs. Although the sample cannot be regarded as randomly chosen, there is no obvious indication that it is biased toward very profitable innovations (socially or privately) or relatively unprofitable ones.

To estimate social rates of return from the investments in each of these innovations, my colleagues and I used a model somewhat like that described in Figure 9.1, except that we extended the analysis to include the pricing behaviour of the innovator, the effects on displaced products, and the costs of uncommercialised R & D and of R & D done outside the innovating organisation. The results indicate that the median social rate of return from the investment in these innovations was 56 per cent, a very high figure. On the other hand, the median private rate of return was 25 per cent. (In interpreting the latter figure, it is important to note that these are before-tax returns and that innovation is a risky activity.)[1]

TABLE 9.1   SOCIAL AND PRIVATE RATES OF RETURN FROM INVESTMENT IN 17 INNOVATIONS.[a]

| | Rate of return (per cent) | |
Innovation	Social	Private
Primary metal innovation	17	18
Machine tool innovation	83	35
Component for control system	29	7
Construction material	96	9
Drilling material	54	16
Drafting innovation	92	47
Paper innovation	82	42
Thread innovation	307	27
Door control innovation	27	37
New electronic device	Negative	Negative
Chemical product innovation	71	9
Chemical process innovation	32	25
Chemical process innovation	13	4
Major chemical process innovation	56	31
Household cleaning device	209	214
Stain remover	116	4
Dishwashing liquid	45	46
Median	56	25

[a]For a more detailed description of the model and data on which these results are based, see [17] and [19].

Also, my colleagues and I obtained very rich and detailed data concerning the returns from the innovative activities (from 1960 to 1972) of one of the nation's largest firms. For each year, this firm has made a careful inventory of the technological innovations arising from its R & D and related activities, and it has made detailed estimates of the effect of each of these innovations on its profit stream. We computed the average rate of return from this firm's total investment in innovative activities during 1960–72, the result being 19 per cent,

[1]For a detailed description of seven of these case studies, see Chapter 9 of [19].

138   *Economic Growth and Resources*

which is not too different from the median private rate of return given in the previous paragraph. Also, we computed lower bounds for the social rate of return from the firm's investment, and found that they were about double its private rate of return, which also agrees with the results in the previous paragraph.[1]

These results pertain to the average rate of return. In earlier investigations based on econometric estimation of production functions, Mansfield [18] and Minasian [21] estimated the marginal rate of return from R & D in the chemical and petroleum industries. Mansfield's results indicated that the marginal rate of return was about 40 per cent or more in the petroleum industry, and about 30 per cent in the chemical industry if technical change was capital embodied (but much less if it was disembodied). Minasian's results indicated about a 50 per cent marginal rate of return on investment in R & D in the chemical industry.

More recently, Terleckyj [30] has used econometric techniques to analyse the effects of R & D expenditures on productivity change in 33 manufacturing and non-manufacturing industries during 1948–66. In manufacturing, the results seem to indicate about a 30 per cent rate of return from an industry's R & D based only on the effects of an industry's R & D on its own productivity. In addition, his findings show a very substantial effect of an industry's R & D on productivity growth in other industries, resulting in a social rate of return greatly exceeding that of 30 per cent. No evidence was found, however, demonstrating that government contract R & D has any effect on the productivity increase of the industries performing it.

In another recent study, Griliches [12] has carried out an econometric study, based on data for almost 900 firms, to estimate the rate of return from R & D in manufacturing. His results pertain only to the private, not the social, rate of return. He finds that the private rate of return is about 17 per cent. It is much higher than this in chemicals and petroleum, and much lower than this in aircraft and electrical equipment. He finds that the returns from R & D seem to be lower in industries where much R & D is federally financed.

From his calculations for the economy as a whole, Denison [3] concluded that the rate of return from R & D was about the same as the rate of return from investment in capital goods. His estimate of the returns from R & D was lower than the estimates of other investigators, perhaps due to his assumptions regarding lags. In his presidential address to the American Economic Association, Fellner [7] estimated the average social rate of return from technological-progress activities, his conclusion being that it is 'substantially in excess' of 13 or 18 per cent, depending on the cost base, and that this is much higher than the marginal rate of return from physical investment at a more or less given level of knowledge.

In sum, practically all of the studies carried out to date indicate that the

[1]Much of this work is contained in George Beardsley's unpublished Ph.D. thesis at the University of Pennsylvania. Also, see [19].

average social rate of return from industrial R & D tends to be very high. Moreover, the marginal social rate of return also seems high, generally in the neighbourhood of 30–50 per cent. As in the case of agriculture, there are a variety of very important problems and limitations inherent in each of these studies. Certainly, they are very frail reeds on which to base policy conclusions. But recognising this fact, it nonetheless is remarkable that so many independent studies based on so many types of data result in so consistent a set of conclusions.

V. GOVERNMENT SUPPORT OF CIVILIAN TECHNOLOGY

During the past twenty years, a question has continually arisen in the United States concerning the adequacy of existing Federal programmes in support of civilian technology. A number of economists have pointed out that, because it is often difficult for firms to appropriate the benefits that society receives from new technology, there may be a tendency for too few resources to be devoted to the development of new technology [1, 20, 23]. It is also generally agreed that the extent to which these benefits are appropriable is probably related to the extent of competition faced by the potential innovator and to the kind of research or development activity in question. In particular, the more competition there is and the more basic the information, the less appropriable it is likely to be. (However, this argument is blunted somewhat by the obvious fact that some inventive activity is carried on with little or no economic motive. Clearly, inventors and technologists are not motivated solely by dollars and cents.) Economists also seem to agree that, because R & D is a relatively risky activity, there may be a tendency for firms to invest too little in it, given that many firms seem to be averse to risk and that there are only limited and imperfect ways to shift risk.

Another reason why there may be an underinvestment in particular kinds of R & D is that they may be characterised by significant indivisibilities. In other words, they may be characterised by economies of scale that prevent small organisations from undertaking them efficiently. This argument seems much more applicable to development than to research. It is important to recognise that, while firms may have to be a certain minimum scale to do many kinds of R & D effectively, this scale may be a relatively small share of the market. Furthermore, it is important to recognise that small firms have been responsible for many important innovations, while many big firms have concentrated on more minor improvement innovations. Nonetheless, bearing these qualifications in mind, it is often argued that some industries are so fragmented, they cannot do the proper amount of R & D.[1]

Although the preceding arguments have a considerable amount of force, they by no means prove that there is currently an underinvestment in civilian

[1]For a discussion of the factors in this and the previous paragraph, see [1], [2], [8], [14], [20], [22], [23], [24], [25], and [8a].

technology. For one thing, these arguments generally are based on the supposition that markets are perfectly competitive, whereas in fact many important markets are oligopolistic. In oligopolistic markets, many economists believe that firms often stress product improvement as a form of rivalry, rather than direct price competition. Because of tacit agreement among the firms, this may be the principal form of rivalry, with the result that more may be spent on research and development than is socially optimal. This is not, however, a proposition that is easy to prove or disprove.

Another reason why there may be no underinvestment in various forms of civilian technology is that the government is already intervening in a large number of ways to support civilian technology. For example, in particular industries such as aircraft, there are a host of government influences promoting R & D and technological change. The government has paid for R & D related to aircraft, and it has increased the demand for new airplanes by providing subsidies to the airlines and by regulating the airlines in such a way as to discourage price competition. Of course, the aircraft industry is hardly typical in this regard, but, as detailed in [14], there is considerable government support for R & D of various kinds in the private sector, and it is not obvious, on *a priori* grounds, that the Government has not already offset whatever latent underinvestment in R & D was present in particular parts of the economy [5].

Going a step further, some economists [13] have argued that, even in the absence of oligopoly or government invervention, a private enterprise economy might not underinvest in R & D. For example, it has been pointed out that the inventor might be in a position to predict and thus speculate on price changes resulting from the release of his new technology. In principle at least, this might offset the fact that he could not appropriate all of the benefits directly. But it is important to recognise how difficult it is to foretell what price changes will be, particularly since there are many factors other than the technology to be considered.

In sum, there are several important factors, related to the inappropriability, uncertainty and indivisibility of R & D that seem likely to push toward an underinvestment in R & D by the private sector. But these factors may be offset, partially or fully, by oligopolistic emphasis on non-price competition, by existing government intervention, or by other considerations. Thus, on *a priori* grounds, it is impossible to say with any reasonable degree of certainty whether there is an underinvestment in R & D in particular parts of the private sector.

VI. SOME POLICY ALTERNATIVES

As pointed out in previous sections, existing evidence is too weak to indicate with any degree of certainty whether there is an underinvestment in civilian R & D of various sorts. All that can be said is that practically all of the studies carried out to date conclude that the average and marginal social rates of return from R & D have tended to be very high. Nonetheless, most economists who have studied the question seem to feel, on the basis of the existing evidence, that it is likely that some underinvestment of this sort exists [23, 2]. And there have been suggestions that tax credits for R & D be adopted, that more Federal contracts and grants be used in support of civilian technology, that the government initiate and expand work of the relevant kinds in its own laboratories, that the government insure a portion of private credit to firms for R & D and other innovation costs, that the government use its own purchasing procedures to encourage technological change in the private sector, and that the government use its regulatory policies to try to encourage R & D in the private sector.

In evaluating these and other policy alternatives, a number of considerations should probably be kept in mind. To begin with, it seems fair to say that most economists who have studied this problem have come away with the impression that a general tax credit for R & D would be a relatively inefficient way of increasing Federal support for R & D in the private sector. This is because it would reward many firms for doing what they would have done anyway, and it would be likely to encourage the same sorts of R & D that are already being done. Further, it would be an invitation to firms to redefine various activities as research and development. A tax credit for increases in R & D spending would be less objectionable on these grounds, but it too is frequently regarded as inefficient because it is not sufficiently selective, and it too runs into the problem that firms could redefine R & D. To get the most impact from a certain level of Federal support, it seems to be generally agreed that a more selective technique would be desirable.

However, to utilise more selective techniques, some way must be found to determine where the social payoff from additional Federal support is greatest (or at least relatively high). The way that most economists would approach this problem is to use some form of benefit-cost analysis to evaluate the payoff from additional Federal support of various kinds of R & D. Unfortunately, although such methods are of some use, they are not able to provide very dependable guidance as to how additional Federal support for civilian technology should be allocated, due in large part to the fact that the benefits and costs from various kinds of R & D are very hard to forecast. As the Department of Defense knows so well, it is difficult indeed to forecast R & D costs. And even major corporations have difficulty in using various forms of benefit-cost analysis for R & D project selection, even though they have a much easier benefit concept to estimate than do most government agencies [16].

Thus, the choice between the general and more selective forms of support is not as simple as it may seem at first. And when one recognises that the estimates constructed to guide the selective forms of support may be biased for parochial, selfish or political reasons, the choice becomes even more difficult. As Eads [5] has pointed out, the organisations and individuals that benefit from, or have a positive interest in, a certain R & D programme may inflate the benefits estimate by claiming various 'secondary' or 'external' benefits that in fact are spurious or at least exaggerated. Given that it is so hard to estimate with reasonable accuracy the true social benefits of various R & D programmes, the result could be a distortion of social priorities, if the estimates are taken seriously. And if they are not taken seriously, it would be difficult to prove them wrong.

Another consideration also bears on this choice. Some studies [30] have concluded that an industry's R & D expenditures have a significant effect on its rate of productivity increase, but that the amount of federally financed R & D performed by an industry seems to have little or no such effect. In part, this may be due to the possibility that output measures in industries like aircraft are not reliable measures of social value. But it may also be due to a difference in the effectiveness of federally financed and privately financed R & D. At present, there is no way to tell how much of the observed difference is due to the latter effect; but if it turns out to be substantial, this would seem to favour tax credits rather than increased Federal contracts and grants.

Given the difficulties in more selective forms of supports, it would probably be sensible to supplement them with more general forms of support, if a programme of this sort were adopted. But unfortunately so little is known about the quantitative effects of general R & D tax credits (either for R & D or for increases in R & D) that it is difficult to tell whether they would be worthwhile. And, as noted above, there are problems in selective forms of Federal support. Thus, to a considerable extent, economists, both inside and outside the government, have been rather cautious in their recommendations. As practically everyone recognises, we have only limited and tentative findings concerning the extent to which more Federal support is needed, and even less information concerning the net effects of various kinds of programmes on the rate of innovation [22].

VII. SOME BROAD AREAS OF AGREEMENT

Despite the limited knowledge in this area, there seem to be at least five important points on which there is considerable agreement among US economists in this area. First, based on Congressional testimony and reports, it seems to be generally agreed that, to the extent that such a programme were selective, it should be neither large-scale nor organised on a crash basis. Instead, it should be characterised by flexibility, small-scale probes and parallel approaches. In view of the relatively small amount of information that is available and the great uncertainties involved, it should be organised, at least in part, to provide information concerning the returns from a larger programme. On the basis of the information that results, a more informed judgement can be made concerning the desirability of increased or, for that matter, perhaps decreased amounts of support.

Second, any temptation to focus the programme on economically beleaguered industries should be rejected. The fact that an industry is in trouble, or that it is declining, or that it has difficulty competing with foreign firms is, by itself, no justification for additional R & D. More R & D may not have much payoff there, or even if it does, the additional resources may have a bigger payoff somewhere else in the economy. It is important to recall the circumstances under which the government is justified in augmenting private R & D. Practically all economists would agree that such augmentation is justifiable if the private costs and benefits derived from R & D do not adequately reflect the social costs and benefits. But in many industries there is little or no evidence of a serious discrepancy of this sort between private and social costs and benefits. Indeed, some industries may spend too much, from society's point of view, on R & D.

Third, most American economists who specialise in this area seem to believe that, except in the most unusual circumstances, the government should avoid getting involved in the latter stages of development work. In general, this seems to be an area where firms are more adept than government agencies. As Pavitt [25] has put it, government programmes in support of civilian technology 'should be managed on an incremental, step-by-step basis, with the purpose of reducing key scientific and technical uncertainties to a degree that private firms can use the resulting knowledge to decide when (with their own money) they should move into full-scale commercial development'. Although there may be cases where development costs are so high that private industry cannot obtain the necessary resources, or where it is so important to our national security or wellbeing that a particular technology be developed that the government must step in, these cases do not arise very often. Instead, the available evidence seems to indicate that, when governments become involved in what is essentially commercial development, they are not very successful at it [8a].

Fourth, in any selective government programme to increase support for civilian technology, it is vitally important that a proper coupling occur between technology and the market. Recent studies of industrial innovations point repeatedly to the key importance of this coupling. In choosing areas and projects for support, the government should be sensitive to market demand. To the extent that it is feasible, potential users of new technology should play a role in project selection. Information transfer and communications between the generators of new technology and the potential users of new technology are essential if new technology is to be successfully applied. As evidence of their importance, studies show that a sound coupling of technology and marketing is one of the characteristics that is most significant in distinguishing firms that are relatively successful innovators from those that are relatively unsuccessful innovators [8a].

Fifth, most US economists seem to be impressed by the advantages in this area of pluralism and decentralised decision-making. Technological change, particularly of a major or radical sort, is marked by great uncertainty. It is difficult to predict which of a number of alternative projects will turn out best. Very important concepts and ideas come from unexpected sources. Consequently, there seems to be a widespread feeling that it would be a mistake for a programme of this sort to rely too heavily on centralised direction.

REFERENCES

[1] Arrow, K., 'Economic Welfare and the Allocation of Resources for Invention', *The Rate and Direction of Inventive Activity* (Princeton, 1962).

[2] Capron, W., 'Discussion', *American Economic Review* (May 1966).

[3] Denison, E., *The Sources of Economic Growth in the United States* (Committee for Economic Development, 1962).

[4] ——, 'Sources of Growth Accounting as the Basis for Long-term Projection in the United States,' in T. Khachaturov, *Methods of Long-Term Planning and Forecasting* (Macmillan, 1976).

[5] Eads, G., 'U.S. Government Support for Civilian Technology: Economic Theory vs. Political Practice', *Research Policy* (1974).

[6] Evenson, R., 'The Contribution of Agricultural Research and Extension to Agricultural Production', Ph.D. thesis, University of Chicago, 1968.

[7] Fellner, W., 'Trends in the Activities Generating Technological Progress', *American Economic Review* (March 1970).

[8] Freeman, C., *The Economics of Industrial Innovation* (Penguin, 1974).

[8a] Gilpin, R., *Technology, Economic Growth, and International Competition* (Joint Economic Committee of Congress, 1975).

[9] Griliches, Z., 'Research Costs and Social Returns: Hybrid Corn and Related Innovations', *Journal of Political Economy* (October 1958).

[10] ——, 'Research Expenditures, Education, and the Aggregate Production Function', *American Economic Review* (December 1964).

[11] ——, 'Research Expenditures and Growth Accounting', in B. Williams (ed.), *Science and Technology in Economic Growth* (Macmillan, 1973).

[12] ——, 'Returns to Research and Development Expenditures in the Private Sector', Conference on Research in Income and Wealth, 1975.

[13] Hirschleifer, J., 'The Private and Social Value of Information and the Reward to Inventive Activity', *American Economic Review* (1971).

[14] Mansfield, E., 'Federal Support of R and D Activities in the Private Sector', in *Priorities and Efficiency in Federal Research and Development* (Joint Economic Committee of Congress, 1976).

[15] ——, 'Contribution of R and D to Economic Growth in the United States', *Science* (4 February 1972).

[16] ——, 'Technological Forecasting', in T. Khachaturov, *Methods of Long-Term Planning and Forecasting* (Macmillan, 1976).

[17] ——, J. Rapoport, A. Romeo, S. Wagner and G. Beardsley, 'Social and Private Rates of Return from Industrial Innovations', *Quarterly Journal of Economics* (May 1977).

[18] ——, *Industrial Research and Technological Innovation* (W. W. Norton for the Cowles Foundation for Research in Economics at Yale University, 1968).

[19] ——, J. Rapoport, A. Romeo, E. Villani, S. Wagner and F. Husic, *The Production and Applications of New Industrial Technology* (W. W. Norton, 1977).

[20] Matthews, R., 'The Contribution of Science and Technology to Economic Development', in B. Williams (ed.), *Science and Technology in Economic Growth* (Macmillan, 1973).

[21] Minasian, J., 'Research and Development, Production Functions, and Rates of Return', *American Economic Review* (May 1969).

[22] National Science Foundation, *Technological Innovation and Federal Government Policy* (Washington, DC, January 1976).

|23| Nelson, R., M. Peck and E. Kalachek, *Technology, Economic Growth, and Public Policy* (Brookings, 1967).
|24| Noll, R., 'Government Policy and Technological Innovation', unpublished, 1975.
|25| Pavitt, K., 'A Survey of the Literature on Government Policy Towards Innovation', unpublished, 1975.
|26| Peterson, W., 'Returns to Poultry Research in the United States', *Journal of Farm Economics* (1967).
|27| Schmitz, A. and D. Seckler, 'Mechanized Agriculture and Social Welfare: The Case of the Tomato Harvester', *American Journal of Agricultural Economics* (1970).
|28| Schultz, T., *The Economic Organization of Agriculture* (McGraw-Hill, 1953).
|29| Solow, R., 'Technical Change and the Aggregate Production Function', *Review of Economics and Statistics* (August 1957).
|30| Terleckyj, N., *Effects of R. and D. on the Productivity Growth of Industries: An Exploratory Study* (National Planning Association, 1974).

10 R & D, Knowledge, and Externalities: An Approach to the Puzzle of Disparate Productivity Growth Rates Among Manufacturing Industries[1]

Richard R. Nelson
INSTITUTION FOR SOCIAL AND POLICY STUDIES, YALE UNIVERSITY

I. INTRODUCTION

In several other papers I have commented upon the considerable dispersion in rates of productivity growth across manufacturing industries. Without question these differences are due largely to differences in the pace of technological progress, which in turn reflect disparities in R & D spending and in the effectiveness of R & D. The question addressed in this paper is this: What explains these variations in R & D inputs and effectiveness?[2]

In attempting to explain the allocation of R & D inputs and R & D effectiveness economists have considered a number of variables. In order to set the stage for the model I will develop here, it is useful to review briefly some of that analysis, and some of the analytic difficulties.

Principally as a result of Jacob Schmookler's work, it is now well documented that the size of the market for a product is an important determinant of R & D input.[3] Schmookler explained the relationship in terms of derived demand for invention; market size chains back to influence the perceived returns to R & D aimed at improving the product or the processes used to produce it. However, there are other things going on as well. For example, market size almost certainly is correlated with the number of people who are familiar with the technology and its strengths and weaknesses; hence growth of a market may shift the supply curve for inventions as well as the demand curve. In any case, at least within manufacturing industries (the focus

[1]This paper is part of a larger endeavour to develop an evolutionary theory of firm behaviour undertaken jointly with Sidney Winter. I am indebted to him, to the members of Yale's Micro Economic Workshop, and especially to Richard Levin, for helpful comments on an earlier draft.

[2]These papers have been written jointly with Sidney Winter. See in particular our 'In Search of Useful Theory of Innovation', *Research Policy* (Winter 1977).

[3]See Jacob Schmookler, *Invention and Economic Growth* (Harvard University Press, 1966). For a more general discussion, see R. Nelson, M. J. Peck and E. D. Kalachek, *Technology, Economic Growth and Public Policy* (Brookings, 1969), Chapter 2.

of this paper) R & D expenditures, direct and indirect, are correlated with the sales of an industry. And shifts in the pattern of sales tend to pull the allocation of R & D inputs in the same direction.

Economists also have considered factors influencing the ease of inventing in different industries. One factor, differences in knowledge, has been stressed by several scholars. Among economists, both Nathan Rosenberg and I have argued that knowledge relating to certain technologies is better than for others, and this facilitates technical invention.[1] However, it has proved difficult to formalize this sensible proposition in a persuasive way. It has been proposed that knowledge can be associated with formal science and that advances in science 'trigger' significant advances in technology in the sense both of making them possible and inducing efforts on them. However, when this hypothesis has been explored in studies 'tracing' the scientific antecedents of a number of inventions, it has been found that in most of the cases it was demand side-factors that triggered the effort, and that the science involved in the solutions tended to be rather 'old'.[2] As a rule (there are important exceptions) science might be better viewed as there behind the scenes influencing the ability of inventors to see good alternatives or solve certain problems. But even this broad metaphor is not fully satisfactory. In the first place, the association of knowledge with formal science is shaky. Much of the knowledge used by engineers and applied scientists in guiding what they try to do and how they do it seems more like semi-codified past experience than formal science. In the second place, the proposition begs the question of just how knowledge influences the technological possibilities inventors try to attack, and their success in these attacks. The role or roles that knowledge plays in invention has not been very well articulated.

Economists have recognised that research and development activity differs from physical investment in that externalities are more persuasive. While many economists have discussed R & D externalities theoretically, recent research, particularly by Mansfield, has begun to assess their quantitative importance empirically.[3] The empirical studies suggest a large average gap between private and social returns, but also a lot of variation in the gap. Externalities certainly influence R & D allocation and effectiveness.

There are significant differences in R & D spending across industries with roughly the same value of sales. These may be explained in part by differences in the extent to which inventors can appropriate the benefits created by their inventions. Whether a large demand for a product generates a high private

[1]His sharpest statement is contained in his 'Science, Invention, and Economic Growth', *Economic Journal* (1974). My earlier thoughts on the matter were presented in Nelson, Peck and Kalachek, Chapter 2.

[2]E. Mansfield, J. Rapoport, A. Romeo, S. Wagner and G. Beardsley, 'Social and Private Returns from Industrial Innovations', *Quarterly Journal of Economics* (1977).

[3]R. Evanson and Y. Kislev have worked with a model that is similar in some respects. See their *Agricultural Research and Productivity* (Yale University Press, 1975). However, their treatment of knowledge is very different from mine.

return for an invention that significantly reduces costs or improves quality depends on the extent to which an inventor can appropriate the returns. Firms can capture the benefits created by their R & D projects if they can establish property rights on their inventions, or can keep their technologies secret for a while, or if they do not have any competitors. The extent to which R & D returns are internalised thus depends on such variables as the effectiveness of patent protection and the organisation of the industry. These variables differ from industry to industry and surely influence the volume of R & D spending pulled forth by a given level of product demand.

Patent protection and the organisation of the industry do much more than merely affect the level of R & D spending. They influence the kinds of R & D that firms find it profitable to do, and the number of different independent sources of R & D initiative. That is, they affect the nature of the R & D portfolio, and hence the effectiveness of the R & D effort as well as its magnitude.

The externalities from R & D clearly are related to the nature of the knowledge inputs and outputs. The failure of economists to pin down the role of knowledge in R & D is thus associated with a certain sloppiness and eclecticism among economists in their theoretical discussions of externalities. In some analyses invention itself is characterised as 'new knowledge' in the form of a template. In others, externalities have been associated with knowledge created by an invention and goes beyond providing a template. For example, it often has been argued that one can invent around a patent, implying that scrutiny of a particular invention provides a basis for thinking about variants. It also has been posited that one invention lays the basis, in some sense, for subsequent ones. One might conjecture that these different kinds of 'externalities' would affect R & D allocation in different ways, for a given structure of patent protections and market organisation.

It seems clear that the role of knowledge in influencing the ease of invention, the knowledge that flows from R & D, the nature of the externalities created in a given regime of markets cum patents, and the level and effectiveness of R & D that will be generated by such a regime, are closely connected topics. If the connections were understood better, some headway might be made towards understanding the differences in R & D expenditure and effectiveness across industries. However, by and large, economists have treated these as disjoint subjects, ignoring the connections. This paper aims to sketch them out. The approach will be theoretical, although the theorising will be strongly influenced by my understanding of the empirical literature. In section II I will examine the nature of knowledge as an input to R & D, and as an output. In section III externalities, patents and market structure will be considered.

II. A FAMILY OF R & D MODELS

In this section I shall discuss a family of R & D models designed to illuminate the character and the role of knowledge in the R & D process. Thus, consider a class of product (defining an industry) which can be produced with any member of a given set of technological possibilities. God (and the theorist) knows them all. Each possibility is associated with certain product attributes (in what follows I shall usually consider product attributes as constant over the set) and inputs of various factors of production per unit of output (I shall assume that all technologies have constant returns to scale). God knows these, and the economic profits associated with each possibility for any set of attribute and input prices. He can readily identify the best (most profitable) technology for any market condition (a best one exists).

But man (or woman) is not blessed with such knowledge. He is working with a given technology, the best that he knows. He knows also that it is far from the best possible, and he can do R & D to try to find a better one. The question under consideration is: What are the factors that will influence the R & D undertaken and its effectiveness?

The assumed institutional context is a firm that aims to maximise profits. But the difference between man and God means that while God knows how to do this, man does not. While man knows that there are better technologies than the one he is employing, he does not know which of the untried technological alternatives is best; he does not even know which ones are better than the prevailing technology. He knows some of the technological characteristics of various alternatives, where technological characteristics are differentiated from economic attributes in involving dimensions such as molecular structure or thermodynamic cycle employed or mode of construction, rather than attributes directly associated with cost of production, such as input per unit of output, or product attributes directly related to what consumers would be willing to pay, such as durability. He knows something of how these technological dimensions map into economic dimensions, but his knowledge of this is very imperfect.

The subsequent analysis will resemble the traditional economic theory of behaviour in that the decision-maker will be assumed to be trying to do as well as he can. Further, it will be assumed that his understanding of the situation is at least roughly responsive to the variables that will be varied theoretically. He may even try to 'model' the situation facing him and pick a strategy that looks optimal, or at least good, within that model. However, the analysis will depart from traditional theory in that it is not assumed that the decisions made are actually optimal in any non-sophistical sense. The inventor–decision-maker must be seen as grappling with a problem he does not fully comprehend.

Different inventors would model (see) the problem in different ways, and make different choices. This essential complication can be ignored, however, until the following section. For the present consider a world of a single R & D decision-maker who sees his problem as described below and tries to do as well as he can.

A simple two-stage model

A surprising amount of intellectual mileage can be made by modelling the R & D process in a way similar to the models often used to explore the process of searching for a good job or a good buy. While the analysis is somewhat forced, it is sharp, and the subsequent elaboration of the model to better suit R & D proceeds rather smoothly. The focus is on the effect of demand-side variables and 'knowledge' on the quantity, allocation, and effectiveness of R & D.[1]

In order to isolate the effect of knowledge, assume initially that while the R & D decision-maker knows some of the technological attributes of all members of the set, he knows absolutely *nothing* of the relationship between these technological characteristics and economic characteristics (unit costs). Under this extreme assumption he only knows (somehow) the probability distribution of economic attributes over the set and his knowledge of technological attributes of particular members provides no help in discriminating likely high-payoff members from low-payoff ones. However, there exists a way of finding out about the economic attributes of any alternative, and of accurately assessing its net profitability. The netting here may be interpreted as encompassing costs that must be incurred to develop a particular technology to the point where it can be used, after a decision has been made to do this. (A more sophisticated concept of development will be presented later.) The way of finding out about an alternative may be thought of as doing a test or study, and will be called 'doing research'.

Assume that the cost of a test which provides complete and reliable information is the same for all technologies and independent of the number of technologies tested. For the present assume a single period, and that at most only one technology will be developed. At least two different kinds of strategies have been studied for decision problems of this kind. One strategy involves prior commitment to a certain number of tests. The decision-maker draws a sample of given size from the population, tests each member to find its profitability if developed, and picks the best member of that sample as the R & D project to run. The second strategy involves a precommitment to a certain target level of net profit. The decision-maker samples and tests sequentially until a project is found whose profitability meets or exceeds the target level. That project is selected for development. Under the first strategy one can calculate the optimal number to sample, under the second the expected number sampled at an optimal cut off. And under either strategy one can calculate the expected advance achieved from employing an optimal strategy. Given the standard behavioural assumptions, these are the predictions of research input and technical advance achieved (say in the sense of unit cost reduction, or productivity growth).

Consider the effect of the 'size of the market' upon the R & D it will be profitable to undertake. The greater the quantity produced the greater the amount of output to which a technology is applied. The advantages, plus or minus, of any new technology over the prevailing one are magnified when the

---

[1]For a description of pharmaceutical research see David Schwartzman, *Innovation in the Pharmaceutical Industry* (Johns Hopkins, 1976). A roughly similar discussion of certain kinds of agricultural research is contained in Evanson and Kislev.

market is large, or has grown, compared with the situation in a small market, or before growth. It is well known that in models of this kind, both the optimal number to sample and the expected advance achieved from an optimal strategy then are larger. (A simple proof is contained in the appendix to this paper.) Thus the model leads to a prediction that an increase in demand (a large demand) will lead both to greater research spending and to a faster rate of unit cost reduction (productivity growth) than before (a small demand). This is quite in keeping with the empirical findings of Schmookler and others.

If the technologies involved vary with respect to product attributes, an increase in the sales of versions with one attribute relative to versions with another may or may not increase the number of elements sampled (the amount of research that is done). However, if more than one element is sampled, the effect will be to increase the likelihood that the project chosen for development will score well on the attribute whose demand has increased. A similar conclusion applies to changes in relative factor prices. Thus an increase in the price of labour may or may not induce more sampling. However, such a shift increases the probability that the technology developed will be relatively labour-saving.

Notice that in the analysis above market forces have no influence on the direction (in some sense) of search. This is because in the simple model the decision-maker cannot discriminate between different kinds of projects to sample and test. It is exactly here that one can introduce a meaningful concept of knowledge into the model.

Preserve the simplistic sequential structure above, but augment the model as follows. Assume that the decision-maker knows more than merely the probability distribution of economic payoffs over the set. Assume that he knows also the distribution conditional on the values taken by certain technological attributes. These attributes may be continuous or discrete. Thus expected economic payoff may vary with volume, with a well-defined size such that expected payoff is maximised. Blue projects may be better than yellow projects. These correlates in general will not be foolproof guides, but they can enable the researcher to do better than he could merely by random sampling. Assume for the present that these attributes are obvious ex-ante, or can be observed without cost.

In contrast to the case where such correlations are not known, the effect of such knowledge on inventive activity is to focus attention on certain parts of the set of alternatives, before engagement in the costly part of the endeavour – the actual expensive testing or studying. This characterisation seems to capture what is going on when engineers think of designing an engine to operate at a particular temperature and pressure, when chemists look for their compound in a particular class of chemical rather than another class, etc. The portion of the set actually sampled will on average have better projects than the portion of the set ignored. Stronger knowledge (in this sense) leads to lower expected cost (smaller number sampled) of achieving an advance of given magnitude.

It is well known that the better the choice set (in the sense of stochastic dominance) the better the expected outcome (the greater the expected technical advance) from an optimum strategy. However, there is not necessarily any more sampling (R & D input) in the optimum strategy. See the appendix for a more formal analysis. The conclusions here are compatible both with those of researchers like Schmookler who have argued that 'stronger science' does not necessarily lead to more inventive input, and with the arguments of researchers like Rosenberg who argue that stronger knowledge means more progress.

Notice also that, within this model, the sensitivity of inventive effort to changes in demand variables depends on the state of knowledge (in the sense described above). Consider, say, R & D projects whose economic payoffs can be described in terms of reduction of various input coefficients from the status quo. If there is no ability to prefocus or do cheap screening tests, the sensitivity of R & D outcomes to changes in factor prices will depend on the number of alternatives sampled prior to commitment. But if knowledge permits prefocus on certain correlates of factor input reduction, then research (full-scale testing) can be shifted to regions judged particularly likely to generate input reductions of certain kinds. The same argument obviously obtains for changes in the demand for various product attributes.

In the discussion above, it has been assumed that certain technological attributes are costlessly observed, and that 'knowledge' is of the relationship between these variables and economic payoff variables. It may not be that all technological variables can be observed without cost. Then the usefulness of knowledge of a correlational sort depends not only on the strength of the correlation, but also on how easy or cheap it is to observe the technological variables of the correlation. Under the obvious extension of the model, we can interpret the proposition often made that strong knowledge 'facilitates problem solving'. Knowledge enables a set of cheaper first stage tests to guide what is done at the more costly second stage.

Some scholars have put forward the proposition that enhanced knowledge enriches the set of technological alternatives (possible R & D projects). Is the foregoing interpretation of knowledge compatible with that language? The basic model loses its structure unless the set of alternatives is, in some sense, taken as given. However, quite in the spirit of the model, R & D decision-makers may see certain regions as possibly possessing some attractive projects, but as possessing mostly unattractive ones. If there are no known cheaply observable correlates of high economic payoff to guide looking into the region, and if the cost of observing known reliable correlates is high, then the whole region might well be ignored, not thought about, not really perceived. If new knowledge permits better discrimination or cheaper pretesting within that region, and this is known, then it pays to pay attention to the region. And in this sense, the set of real alternatives, alternatives perceived as thinkable to explore, has been enriched. Notice that attention is focused on regions where good alternatives can be identified relatively cheaply. This may be the result of the fact that a large fraction of blue projects are very good. But it could be that most blue projects are not good bets, but blue projects with stripes are, and it is cheap to test for stripes.

More complex sequential structure

The discussion above has implicitly extended the original simple model to involve more complex sequential structure: an original prefocus, a round of inexpensive tests to further screen alternatives, and then a final commitment. While the simple search model is a somewhat forced representation of R & D, with a more complex sequential structure the model can be tailored and interpreted to characterise a wide range of R & D, at least metaphorically. The basic idea that knowledge can be described in terms of cheaply observable known correlates of economic performance, and that stronger knowledge means more effective research and development, while taking on a more complicated form than in the simpler models, holds up. It is worthwhile to work through a couple of examples.

In many industries R & D is describable in terms of a search that is homing in on something, say a pharmaceutical product with certain properties. The decision maker knows that certain technological attributes are associated with what is desired economically, but he cannot 'see' them without testing. He knows he wants something that is heavy, blue and striped, where in pharmaceutical research the first two attributes might refer to chemical characteristics and the last the safe performance when tested on mice. R & D proceeds by first finding a number of heavy compounds, then screening these for colour, then testing for stripes.[1]

Another quite common form of R & D has the following characteristics. The R & D decision-maker does not know ex-ante the population statistics about the correlates of good economic performance, but only knows his past experience from sampling. As an example, consider the set of technological possibilities defined by various mixes of ingredients. On the basis of past experience the decision-maker believes that a significant increase in the amount of one of these relative to others will yield an economically superior product. But he is not sure, and does not know how much more to add. A sensible R & D strategy might involve first testing the economic attributes of a mix somewhat richer than the prevailing one, then if the results are favourable trying out an even richer mix, etc., in effect hunting for the top of the hill.[2] In general a good strategy will stop the R & D project somewhere short of the top of the hill because the economic attributes achieved are good enough, and the

---

[1] For a discussion in this spirit see Y. Hayami and V. Ruttan, *Agricultural Development* (Johns Hopkins, 1971), pp. 82–5. The formal statistical discussion of the theory of this kind of hill climbing has been provided by several people, but notably G. Box, see his *Evolutionary Operation*. Barry Galef is currently writing a thesis on R & D on this sort of approach employing a modified Box model.

[2] For a description of development, and a discussion of development strategy in this spirit, see T. Marschak, T. Glennan and R. Summers, *Strategy for R & D* (Springer Verlag, 1967).

gains from varying the mix in one way or another are not expected to be worth the cost of performing another test. However, notice that in this case knowledge has been changed in the course of undertaking the R & D project. And this will have implications, which I will discuss shortly, for the next round of R & D projects.

In many industries which produce hardware, as in the aircraft industry, R & D may be represented as a gradual commitment to the details of an overall rough design idea with the course of design being guided by a series of studies and tests.[1] In the later stages these involve prototype versions of the actual new hardware. In endeavours of this sort the metaphor of 'alternatives out there' is somewhat forced. Man is building a technological variant that was not in existence before (except in the eyes of God) and finding out about how it works. Information is being acquired not only in activities that are incidental to accomplishing, but also in the course of creating and learning about something new. In general, the new design will involve a large number of sub-design elements or components. Regarding each of these there may be certain 'design problems' to solve, in the sense that certain technological parameters need to be achieved. Knowledge can facilitate the problem-solving, in the way mentioned earlier, by guiding the effort towards promising design alternatives. And knowledge can facilitate overall design by indicating what problems may be hard, or easy, and guiding strategy towards configurations that do not require that the former kind be solved. As was the case with the search for a better chemical mix discussed above, a successful development project creates more than a discrete practical invention. Today's new hardware represents a set of solutions to design problems and provides a new starting point for the next round of research and development efforts.

I could easily extend the list of variants on the basic theme, but there is no point in doing that here. What I want to stress is that the simple basic model of R & D is capable of being tailored to fit a wide variety of descriptions of R & D. While R & D in pharmaceuticals differs in important respects from R & D in aviation, in both cases a sequential search and learning model seems to characterise the essential elements of what is going on. And discussion of the last two examples leads in a natural way to the concept of cumulative technologies.

Cumulative technologies

It is possible to explain continuing technological progress with a simple search model of the sort with which we started under the assumption that today's round of R & D projects is independent of what happened during the last round, except for the fact that what was achieved in the last round forces the

[1]'In Search of Useful Theory of Innovation'. Rosenberg earlier put forth a similar idea in his 'The Direction of Technological Change: Inducing Mechanisms and Focussing Devices', *Economic Development and Cultural Change* (October 1969).

sights to be set higher in this round. If the set of possible technologies is bounded in the space of economic dimensions, and if product demand and factor supply curves remain constant over time, this model will display diminishing expected returns to R & D, and after a point R & D will cease to be profitable. Growth of demand can extend this period, perhaps indefinitely, although the achieved advances will become progressively smaller per unit of R & D input.

This characterisation may capture what is going on in certain technologies, but it fails to explain the cumulative nature of technological advance in many sectors. In many technological histories the new is not just better than the old; in some sense the new evolves from the old.

The models discussed in the preceding sub-section provide an interpretation of this phenomenon. In these models the achieved technology represents the outcome of sequential narrowing down of search, or a particular fine structure of a package of design elements. There is a neighbourhood concept of a quite natural variety. Technological successes of yesterday provide natural starting places for searching close-by in certain directions.

If last period's search of blue striped compounds yielded an important new pharmaceutical product, one's confidence that there are good things to be found in the blue striped subset is enhanced. But perhaps it is more than that. Last period's R & D demonstrated that potency continued to increase with the density of stripes, at least in the region sampled. It seems a good strategy this period to consider even more densely striped substances. In hardware technologies, one can think of varying a few elements in the design of last period's aircraft, trying to solve problems that still exist in the design or which were evaded in a compromising way, etc. In these latter examples technological advance builds on itself in a quite literal way, through accumulation of knowledge, and through progressive modification of design.

In another paper I suggested that in many technologies there appear to be 'natural trajectories' that represent the unfolding of a technology in a particular direction.[1] Examples are the progressive exploitation of latent scale economies in certain technologies, or the progressive increase of operating pressures and temperatures in others. These trajectories undoubtedly reflect the mechanisms described above. Engineers exploit what was learned in the last round (for example, the returns to increasing operating temperature still seem to be considerable), build from the last round of technical advances (let us see if we cannot design a higher temperature burner for our new boiler) and they work on the problems that have emerged (for example, corrosion problems are severe at high temperatures). These trajectories represent paths taken through the set of possibilities towards some local optimum (which may never be achieved). Since today's successful R & D projects not only set the hurdles

---

[1]For a discussion of some of the issues, see R. Nelson and S. Winter, 'Dynamic Competition and Technical Progress' in B. Balassa and R. Nelson (ed.), *Economic Progress, Private Values, and Public Policy* (North-Holland, 1977).

higher for tomorrow's, but also provide some inputs and some knowledge useful to tomorrow's R & D, there is a partial offset to the mining out of alternatives that characterised the simple search models. However, under the assumptions above, ultimately the technological returns to further R & D along each trajectory must fall.

This trajectory idea also provides an interpretation of certain phenomena observed in many technological histories: occasional sharp shifts in the nature of R & D done and technological advance achieved, associated with a jump in the rate of return on R & D, and (often) the rise of new firms to technological leadership and the decline of old firms. Consider a set of technological possibilities that consists of a number of quite different classes of technology, say engines employing different thermodynamic cycles, different technologies for the generation of electric power, etc. Within any of these classes of technology, technological advance may follow a particular trajectory. At any given time all the R & D may be focused on one class of technologies (the blue ones) with no attention being paid to the yellow technologies because the structure of knowledge (the ability effectively to explore within the subset) is weak there. Along the prevailing trajectory there will be a tendency for returns to fall. Assume, however, that knowledge is occasionally created (perhaps from activities other than the applied R & D going on) that significantly improves the structure of knowledge regarding the portions of the set where knowledge previously had been weak and hence which applied research tended to ignore (striped yellow technologies tend to be very effective, dotted yellow ones ineffective). Then one would observe the phenomena in question. There will be a significant shift in the nature of the R & D that goes on, and old experience and knowledge would become obsolete. The R & D game would become very different, perhaps requiring people of different kinds of backgrounds, different kinds of firms, and so on.

III. EXTERNALITIES, PATENTS, INDUSTRY STRUCTURE AND THE ALLOCATION OF R & D RESOURCES

Preserve the perspective of no sources of R & D outside of the industry, but now abandon the assumption that only one firm does the R & D. The view of the role of knowledge in guiding R & D, and of the knowledge output of R & D, developed in the preceding section leads to some conclusions about the effect of patents and market structure upon the effectiveness of R & D that are quite striking, and somewhat at variance with traditional economic thinking.

As suggested earlier, there is a problem in pinning down what traditional thinking really is. Economists are of several different minds regarding the problems latent in relying on a regime of markets cum patents to motivate industrial R & D. In some articles analysis of R & D allocation proceeds as if R & D did not differ from any other kind of investment; externalities and publicness are ignored. In another body of literature externalities from R & D are recognised, but often rather mechanically, and associated with knowledge in a sense of templates. In this literature market structure is almost always assumed to be competitive. Patents may or may not be considered. Still another body of writing stems from Schumpeter and is concerned with the question whether a degree of market power might not be a requirement for, or a consequence of, technological innovation.[1] I do not intend to summarise or criticise past writings. Rather my purpose is to explore the implications of the view of R & D sketched in the last section regarding the nature of the externalities and the kinds of misallocations that market incentives are likely to generate.

Consider an industry consisting of a large number of competing firms, each doing its own R & D. Then there are several different kinds of 'market failure' that need to be recognised. First, if firms have less than perfect ability to exclude other firms from using their technology, there is the well known 'template externality' that stems from the chances of imitation by other firms of the technology that is being found (created) by one. If patents prevent direct mimicking, but there is a 'neighbourhood' illuminated by the invention that is not foreclosed to other firms by patents, the externality problem is there in modified form. Second, and less well recognised in the literature, there is a problem akin to that of multiple independent tappers of an 'oil field'; individual companies can make money from projects which would not be worthwhile had they access to the best technologies developed by others, projects which yield little social value. There are incentives for a firm to duplicate the prevailing best technology patented by another firm, in a way that does not infringe on patents. More generally, there are incentives for a firm to develop a technology even if it is worse than the current best one, if it is better than the one it has and the best is blocked by patents. The first problem tends to repress total R & D spending to a level below a social optimum. The second may spur R & D spending, but towards an allocation of effort that is socially inefficient. If patent rights are stronger the second problem rises in importance, and the first diminishes.

Still another allocational problem emerges if technologies are cumulative. In the competitive situation there would appear to be a problem regarding R & D similar to that described by Hotelling in the case of location decisions. Where the returns to a firm from a technical advance must be assessed against the technology it is currently using, rather than against the best technology in the industry, and where the rough location of the best available technology is known and the neighbourhood looks both promising and unprotected by patents, there are incentives placed in the system for everybody to cluster around the same broad opportunity. If one considers how technology will evolve over a long time horizon, too much attention is focused on particular parts of the landscape and not enough real diversification of effort is achieved.

[1]An important implicit assumption is that there is friction in the system so that a firm employing an inferior technology can survive, at least for a time. For a discussion of the larger modelling context, see the Nelson–Winter papers listed in other footnotes.

Using the externality language, the knowledge externality created by one firm pulls other firms to doing roughly the same thing. If a firm explores new terrain it is less likely to come up with something. And if it does, it knows that other firms will soon cluster around.

Monopolise the industry. Assume away any economics of scale in doing the R & D and consider only differences in the incentive structure. Now both the template externality and the incentive for doing R & D which would not be profitable if one had access to the best technology go away. And the knowledge externalities that come from successful exploration of uncharted regions of the set are now internalised. While in the model of the preceding section the stress was on knowledge won as a by-product of an R & D effort aimed at a particular advance, for a firm that plans to be around for a while it might make sense to go after that knowledge directly – to engage in research to discover new correlations, pin down relationships more tightly, identify new promising regions for search – independently of any applied quest. But this kind of an effort also only makes sense if one has considerable market power.

Thus far the discussion has focused on the 'internalisation' advantages of a concentrated industrial structure. There may be cost-side advantages as well. For many kinds of R & D there are certainly economies of scale, at least up to a point, from several different sources. Certain kinds of R & D inputs, and outputs, are lumpy; a significant quantity of R & D effort must be directed to a project if there is to be any hope of success. A small-scale R & D effort may not be able to achieve success at all, and if it does, will achieve it significantly later than an effort where funding is at a higher rate. There are also portfolio advantages of a large-scale research and development effort. Multiple attacks on particular objectives can be mounted. A large and diversified range of projects can help guard a company from the economic disadvantages of a long dry spell between R & D successes. And, to the extent that the rate of growth of capital or sales of a firm is limited, there is an 'economy of scale' associated with the fact that a big firm can quickly apply a new technological development to a larger quantity of output and capital than can a small firm.

What are the debits of concentrated structure to be charged against these credits? Traditional theory would argue that the size of output in the industry would be lower. This causes the traditional triangle loss. It also feeds back to R & D incentives by reducing the size of the output to which R & D applies. It is hard to say whether there would be more or less R & D undertaken in the monopolised case than in the competitive case. The greater degree of internalisation and the smaller scale of output pull in different directions. Also, it should be considered that there will be less incentive in the monopolised case to do R & D that is profitable in the competitive case only because someone else has a patent. While this is another factor that acts to pull down the R & D level in the monopolised case relative to the competitive case, it suggests that the most important difference in the two regimes is the efficiency of R & D allocation. If the monopolist can be assumed to be a profit maximiser and if the consequences of choosing any R & D projects are more or less obvious, there are strong arguments that monopoly would generate a better portfolio of R & D projects than a regime of competition.

However, introduce the facts that different people see alternatives in different ways, and that organisations as individuals have tendencies to adopt simplified decision-making styles. Then a centralised regime looks less attractive in terms of the portfolio of projects it would be likely to carry, and a competitive regime more attractive. However, the argument against monopoly and for competition here is not the standard one of textbook economic theory. It does not derive from the logic of maximising choices or from arguments that have a family relationship to the proposition that it is socially desirable to set the level of output where marginal cost equals price. Rather the argument is that differences in perception as to what are the best bets will have a greater chance to surface and be made effective in terms of diversity of R & D projects in a competitive regime than in a monopolised one. Any regime of competitive R & D is bound to involve some waste and duplication. The costs and dangers of monopoly are principally those of reliance on a single mind for the exploration of technological alternatives.

One is tempted to look to a regime of oligopoly – involving neither the R & D incentive problems of a multitude of small producers, nor the pricing and single source reliance problem of a true monopoly – as a happy compromise. Many prominent economists, from Schumpeter to Galbraith, are associated with this position. And oligopolistic structure has the potential of combining the best aspects of competition and pluralism, and of R & D benefit internalisation. But such a structure also has the potential for combining the worst features of monopoly and competition. In many oligopolistic industries, a considerable amount of R & D done by firms seems to be 'defensive' and aims to assure that a firm has available a product similar to that developed by a competitor, rather than aiming to come up with something significantly different. Small numbers may yield considerable duplicative R & D without any real R & D diversity.

IV. CONCLUSIONS

The analysis in the last two sections has only scratched the surface of the puzzle: how to explain the apparent great differences across industries in R & D inputs and effectiveness. The focus has been single-mindedly on only a single variable – knowledge – and its interaction with institutional structure. The conceptual framework employed in this exploration has been highly stylised. Only market institutions have been considered. But I hope I have nudged analysis of the puzzle forward a little bit.

APPENDIX: Quick Proofs of Some Features of Order Statistics

Some of the assertions made in the text to the effect that certain features of search models are 'well known' are amenable to quick simple proofs. These are sketched below.

To begin with, recognise that the customary expression for the mean of a bounded variable $X_* \leqslant X \leqslant X^*$ can be rewritten as follows:

$$E(X) = \int_{X_*}^{X^*} Xf(X)\, dX = \int_{X_*}^{X^*} Xd(F(X)), \tag{1}$$

where $f(X)$ is the density function of X, and $F(X)$ is the cumulative frequency distribution. Integrating by parts:

$$E(X) = X^* - \int_{X_*}^{X^*} F(X)\, dX \tag{2}$$

Let $Y(n)$ be the maximum of a sample of size n with each member drawn from $F(X)$. Then

$$E[Y(n)] = X^* - \int_{X_*}^{X^*} F(X)^n\, dX \tag{3}$$

It is obvious that the two terms in equation (3) are the counterparts of those in equation (2), when the variable under consideration is Y as defined above. For $n \geqslant 2$ the first difference is as follows:

$$\Delta E[Y(n)] = \int_{X_*}^{X^*} [F(X)^{n-1} - F(X)^n]\, dX \tag{4}$$

Since $F(X) < 1$ except at X^*, Δ is clearly positive. And the second difference must be negative.

Consider two distributions of X, $F(.)$, the second of which is more spread out in the sense that $G(\lambda X) = F(X)$, $\lambda > 1$. Let X^{**} and X_{**} refer to the largest and smallest values of X with non-zero probability under $G(.)$. Then

$$E[Y(n) : G(\cdot)] = X^{**} - \int_{X_{**}}^{X^{**}} G(X)^n dX$$

$$= \lambda X^* - \int_{\lambda X_*}^{\lambda X^*} F\left(\frac{X}{\lambda}\right)^n \lambda d\left(\frac{X}{\lambda}\right)$$

$$= \lambda E[Y(n) : F(\cdot)] \tag{5}$$

And obviously for $n \geqslant 2$, ΔE is also multiplied by λ in the case of $G(.)$ compared with $F(.)$.

Now consider two distributions of X, $F(.)$ and $G(.)$ the second of which is 'shifted to the right' such that $G(X + u) = F(X)$, $u > 0$. Then, considering $E[Y(n)]$ under the two distributions it is clear that

$$E[Y(n) : G(\cdot)] = X^{**} - \int_{X_{**}}^{X^{**}} G(X)^n dX$$

$$= X^* + u - \int_{X_* + u}^{X^* + u} F(X - u)dX$$

$$= X^* + u - \int_{X_*}^{X^*} F(X)dX \tag{6}$$

It follows that for $n \geqslant 2$

$$\Delta E[Y(n) : G(.)] = \Delta E[Y(n) : F(.)]. \tag{7}$$

Define an optimal strategy as an n^* such that

$$\Delta E[Y(n^*)] < C < \Delta E[Y(n^* - 1)].$$

Then the results above show:

(a) If the underlying distribution is 'spread out' in the sense of the above paragraph, n^* is increased (if the spread is great enough) and $E[Y(n^*)]$ is also increased.
(b) If the underlying distribution is 'shifted' in the sense above, while $E[Y(n^*)]$ is increased but n^* is not (unless n^* originally was zero).

The first of these propositions is relevant to analysis of the effect of a larger market on incentives for R & D aimed at reducing cost, where R & D is viewed as sampling from a distribution of new technologies which differ from the existing technologies in terms of unit costs. Both expected payoff from an optimal strategy, and optimal n, are greater under $G(.)$. The second proposition is relevant to analysis of the effect of knowledge which enables one to sample from a 'better' sub-population. Whichever expected payoff for an optimal strategy is greater under $G(.)$, optimal n is the same.

11 Induced Innovation in Agriculture

Vernon W. Ruttan, Hans P. Binswanger and Yujiro Hayami[1]

I. INTRODUCTION

The 1970s have been a period of renewed uncertainty with respect to the long-run prospects for economic growth and human welfare. We were confronted in the early 1970s with a convergence of scientific opinion and ideological perspective which insisted that the world was fast approaching both the physical and cultural limits to growths. There is a continuing concern that advances in man's capacity for scientific and technical innovation have not been matched by the institutional innovations needed to enable him to manage and direct this capacity for his own welfare.

The tools of the economist are relatively blunt instruments with which to confront the grand theme of epochal growth and decline. Until a few decades ago comparative statics was the most powerful tool available to the economist as a guide to empirical knowledge. Even modern neo-classical growth theory has been based primarily on an application of the tools of comparative statics to the analysis of alternative growth paths. In the simple Harrod–Domar–Mahalanobis models which dominated growth theory in the 1950s, increases in the capital/labour ratio represented the only source of increase in per capita income. Even in the more sophisticated models that have been available in more recent years the growth of output is narrowly determined by growth of the labour force and of physical capital and by technical change and improvements in the quality of human capital. Technical change continues with few exceptions to be treated as exogenous to the economic system.

On the other hand, outside of growth theory proper, substantial progress has been made in the effort to interpret the process of technical change as endogenous rather than exogenous to the economic system. In this view technical change represents a dynamic response to changes in resource endowments and in the social and economic environment. The induced innovation perspective implies a much more optimistic view of the relationship between resource endowments and the possibilities for economic growth than the view that progress in science and technology is essentially autonomous and hence unresponsive to social and economic forces (Mishan, 1970). The induced innovation perspective suggests that 'the fundamental significance of technical

[1]Vernon W. Ruttan is President of the Agricultural Development Council (New York and Singapore); Hans P. Binswanger is an Associate of the Agricultural Development Council, International Crops Research Institute for the Semi-Arid Tropics (ICRISAT) (Hyderabad, India); and Yujiro Hayami is Professor, Tokyo Metropolitan University (Tokyo). The authors are indebted to Dr Wen-Lee Ting of the University of Singapore for comments on an earlier draft of this paper.

change is that it permits the substitution of knowledge for resources, or of less expensive and more abundant resources for more expensive resources, or it releases the constraints on growth implied by inelastic resource supplies' (Ruttan, 1971, p. 708).

In this paper we review the evolution of thought on induced technical change. We then summarise the series of attempts to test the theory of induced technical change against the history of agricultural development in the United States, in Western Europe, and in Japan. Finally, an attempt is made to draw on the history of agricultural development to suggest some of the elements of a theory of induced institutional innovation. Both the literature review and the empirical tests are reported in greater detail in Hayami and Ruttan (1970 and 1971), Yamada and Ruttan (1975), in Binswanger (1974a and 1974b) and in Binswanger and Ruttan (1978).

II. THE THEORY OF INDUCED TECHNICAL CHANGE

The theory of induced technical change represents an attempt to clarify the impact of relative resource endowments, as mediated through factor and product markets, on the rate and direction of technical change. The term 'induced innovation' was first used with reference to bias in the direction of technical change by Sir John Hicks in his *Theory of Wages* (1932). Hicks argued that changes in factor prices induce biases in the direction of technical change which save the progressively more expensive factors. He did not attempt to specify the mechanism of induced innovation.

Interest by economists in the issue opened up by Hicks lagged until the 1960s. In 1960 W. E. G. Salter objected to the Hicks formulation on the grounds that there is no incentive for competitive firms to develop new knowledge designed to save a particular factor.[1] While Salter's criticism diverted attention from work on the theory of induced innovation it did encourage the emergence of a body of work on the choice of technology (Sen, 1959, 1962).

Greater interest in the process of induced innovation emerged in the early 1960s as a result of efforts to explain the apparent stability of the shares of capital and labour, in spite of a rising capital/labour ratio, in the United States

---

[1]'If . . . the theory implies that dearer labor stimulated the search for new knowledge aimed specifically at saving labor, then it is open to serious objections. The entrepreneur is interested in reducing costs in total, not particular costs such as labor costs or capital costs. When labor's costs rise, any advance that reduces total costs is welcome, and whether this is achieved by saving labor or capital is irrelevant. There is no reason to assume that attention should be concentrated on labor-saving techniques, unless, because of some inherent characteristic of technology, labor-saving knowledge is easier to acquire than capital-saving knowledge.' (Salter, p. 43).

Salter then stated that engineers, given existing knowledge, design machines so that they use optimal amounts of factors, given the existing factor prices. But he argued that this is not induced innovation. This amounted to eliminating induced innovation by definition.

(Fellner, 1961). A second source of interest in the theory of induced innovation grew out of a concern with technology policy in the field of economic development. During the late 1960s and early 1970s it was gradually perceived that technology policies based on a choice of technology perspective represented an inadequate response to a situation where the available agricultural and industrial technologies had been developed under conditions of factor endowments and factor prices that were sharply different from those in many underdeveloped economies.

We now turn to a brief review of the several schools or traditions that have emerged in the literature on induced technical change since the mid-1960s.

Growth theory approaches

The most fully developed attempt to construct a theory of induced innovation involved an attempt by Kennedy (1964), Samuelson (1965), and Drandakis and Phelps (1966) to incorporate the process of technical change into modern growth theory.[1] It was primarily the implications of factor share stability which interested Kennedy and the other growth theorists. They were apparently not interested in the issue of research resource allocation.

The staggering burden of assumptions which the Kennedy growth model approach to induced innovation carries has been examined by Nordhaus (1967, 1973), Wan (1971), and in Binswanger and Ruttan (1978). First, there is the assumption of an exogenously given budget for research and development of new techniques that is unresponsive to the productivity of research investment and hence to changes in the size of the firm which occur as a result of successful technical innovation. Second, there is the assumption of a given 'fundamental' trade-off or transformation function (which Kennedy termed the innovation possibility frontier (IPF)) between the rate of labour augmentation (or reduction in labour requirements) and the rate of capital augmentation (or reduction in capital requirements) which is stable over time and is therefore independent of achieved levels of labour or capital augmentation.

Although the Kennedy growth theory approach to induced innovation was developed to permit technical change to occur endogenously – as a result of the working of economic factors rather than by postulation – it attempted to achieve this result by postulating an IPF in which technical change turns out to be just as exogenous as in a growth model without an IPF. It is hard to escape

---

[1]The growth theory approach to induced technical change is relatively simple. Assume that it is equally expensive to develop a new technology which would either reduce labour requirements or capital requirements by 10 per cent. If the capital share is equal to the labour share entrepreneurs will be indifferent as between the two courses of action and technical change will be neutral. If, however, the labour share is 60 per cent entrepreneurs will choose the labour-saving alternative. If the elasticity of substitution between capital and labour is less than one this process will continue until labour and capital shares are equal – provided that technical change does not alter the elasticity of substitution between labour and capital. An implication of the model is that factor shares can be stable even if the capital/labour ratio changes over time.

the conclusion that there is no real world research and development process which is consistent with a Kennedy type IPF. This inadequate microeconomic foundation accounts for the lack of any significant empirical research on induced innovation along the lines suggested by Kennedy, Samuelson, and Drandakis and Phelps.

Microeconomic approaches

A microeconomic approach to induced innovation can be built directly on Sir John Hicks' original observation that changes on factor prices induce biases in the direction of technical change which save the progressively more expensive factors. The first attempt to develop a microeconomic approach to induced innovation was by Ahmad in a seminal article in 1966.

Ahmad employed the concept of a historical innovation possibility curve (IPC) which is the envelope of all unit isoquants of the subset of potential processes which an entrepreneur might develop given the existing state of knowledge in science and technology and a given research and development budget. Each process in the set is characterised by an isoquant with a relative low elasticity of substitution between capital and labour.[1]

[1]Ahmad developed a graphic exposition of his approach along the following lines (Figure 11.1). Assume that at time t a firm is employing a technology described by I_t. The IPC corresponding to I_t is IPC_t. Given the relative factor prices of the line P_tP_t, I_t is the cost-minimising process. Once I_t is developed, the remainder of its IPC becomes irrelevant because, for period $t + 1$, the IPC has shifted inward to IPC_{t+1} and because it would take the

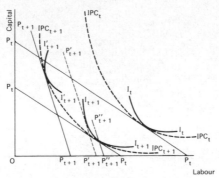

Fig. 11.1 Ahmad's induced innovation model

SOURCE   Syed Ahmad, 'On the Theory of Induced Invention', *Economic Journal*, 76 (1966), Figure 1, amended.

same amount of expenditure to go from I_t to any other technique on IPC_t as to go from I_t to any technique on IPC_{t+1}. If factor prices remain the same, entrepreneurs will develop the process I_{t+1} for the next period. If the IPC shifts neutrally, the technical change will be neutral. (But Ahmad recognises that the IPC may shift inward non-neutrally, which would result in biases even at constant factor prices.) If, however, factor prices change to $P_{t+1}P_{t+1}$, then it is no longer optimal to develop I_{t+1} and instead the process corresponding to I'_{t+1} becomes optimal. In the graph, $P_{t+1}P_{t+1}$ corresponds to a rise in the relative prices of labour. If the IPC has shifted neutrally, I'_{t+1} will be relatively labour-saving in comparison to I_t.

The Ahmad model shares one fundamental limitation with the Kennedy model. Neither model treats research and development as a resource-using activity. It is clear, however, that research and development are resource-using investments that lead to benefits which accrue over time. The rate of technical change is a function of investment in research and development and the direction of bias is a function of the mix of labour-saving or capital-saving research projects in the R & D portfolio of a firm (or an industry or a nation). From an investment perspective factor prices (including the rate of interest), product prices and the size of the market should be included among the factors which determine the optimum R & D investment portfolio and hence the rate and direction of technical change.

An attempt to extend the Ahmad model to incorporate the allocation of research resources to achieve technical change was introduced by Hayami and Ruttan (1970, 1971). Their attention was directed to the process of induced

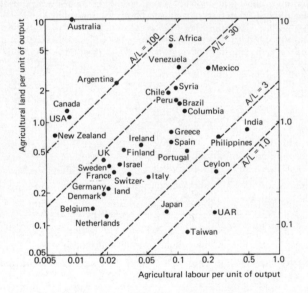

Figure 11.2 Input–output and land–labour ratios in agriculture

NOTES   Output is measured in wheat units. A/L = land–labour ratio.
SOURCE   Yujiro Hayami and Vernon W. Ruttan, *Agricultural Development: An International Perspective* (Baltimore: Johns Hopkins University Press, 1971), Table 4-2, p. 73.

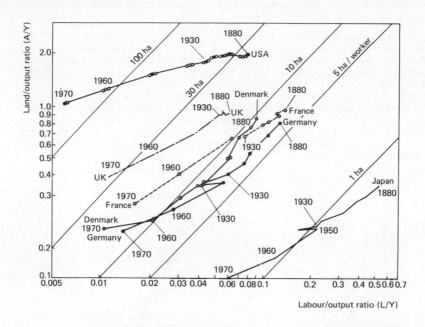

Fig. 11.3 Input–output ratios for six countries, 1880–1970 (In Logs). Diagonals are land/labour ratios.

innovation as a result of a study of historical differences in the rate of productivity growth over time and of differences in productivity levels among countries in the agricultural sector (Figures 11.2 and 11.3). It appeared completely unreasonable to expect that the enormous differences in land/labour ratios could be explained by ordinary factor substitution.[1] Rather it appeared reasonable to conclude that the enormous differences in factor ratios over time and among countries represented a process of dynamic factor

[1]For example, in the early 1960s, the US had a land/labour ratio of 141 hectares per worker while Japan's ratio was 1.74 hectares per worker. The US ratio exceeded the Japanese ratio by a factor of 81. However, Japan's land/labour price ratio exceeded the US ratio by a factor of less than 30 during the same period. To explain the difference in factor ratios by factor-price effects, the elasticity of substitution between the two factors would have to be 3 or more. Evidence from micro-level production functions suggested that an elasticity of substitution of this level is highly unrealistic.

substitution along innovation possibility curves in response to changing relative
factor prices.[1]

[1]In the Hayami–Ruttan model the process of advance in *mechanical technology* is
illustrated in the left-hand portion of Figure 11.4. I_0^* represents the land/labour isoquant of
the metaproduction function (MPF) at time zero; it is the envelope of less elastic isoquants
such as I_0 that correspond, for example, to different types of harvesting machinery. I_1^* is the
innovation possibility curve (IPC) of time period 1. A certain technology – a reaper, for
example – represented by I_0, is invented when the price ratio BB prevails for some time.
When this price ratio changes from BB to CC, another technology – such as the combine –
represented by I_1, is invented. The new technology represented by I_1 which permits an
expansion in land area per worker, is generally associated with higher animal or mechanical
power inputs per worker. This implies a complementary relationship between land and
power, which may be illustrated by the line [A, M]. It is hypothesised that mechanical
innovation is responsive to a change in the wage rate relative to the price of land and
machinery and involves the substitution of land and power for labour.

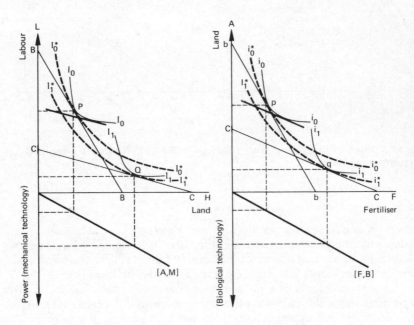

Figure 11.4 Factor prices and induced technical change

SOURCE   Adapted from Yujiro Hayami and Vernon W. Ruttan, *Agricultural
Development: An International Perspective* (Baltimore: Johns Hopkins University Press,
1971), p. 126.

The process of advance in *biological technology* is illustrated in the right-hand portion of
Figure 11.4. Here i_0^* represents the land/fertiliser isoquant of the metaproduction function.
The metaproduction function is the envelope of less elastic isoquants, (for example, i_0) that
represent advances such as crop varieties characterised by different levels of fertiliser
responsiveness. A decline in the price of fertiliser is seen as inducing plant breeders to develop
more fertiliser-responsive crop varieties – which might be described by the isoquant i_1 along
the IPC i_1^* – and as inducing farmers to adopt the new varieties as they become available.

An investment approach

If the theory of induced innovation is to become productive of empirical research and useful as a guide to research resource allocation it would seem desirable that it be reformulated in an explicitly investment form. Hayami and Ruttan stressed the significance of research as an investment activity but did not formally develop the investment component of their model. In 1973 de Janvry extended the Ahmad and Hayami–Ruttan graphical model to show how the effect of introducing research costs modifies the effects of relative factor prices on research resource allocation and the direction of bias in technical change. More recently Binswanger has reformulated the microeconomic approach explicitly to introduce both research costs and expected payoff functions (1974a; Binswanger and Ruttan, 1978). In this reformulation it is shown that the Ahmad, Hayami and Ruttan, and de Janvry approaches, as well as the static Kennedy approach, are special cases of the more general investment model.

The investment approach builds on the work of Evenson and Kislev (1975). In their analysis of crop-breeding research they treat research as a sampling process. A probability distribution of potential yield increases is assumed in which the potential yield increases are determined by nature, the state of basic science, and plant-breeding techniques. Research is viewed as drawing successive trials from this distribution. The Evenson–Kislev view of the research process is related to the induced innovation process by identifying the research objective as shifts in the factor demand curves (per unit of output) corresponding to a given production process.[1] Research resource allocation decisions are not cast in terms of deciding to pursue different lines of research which result in the reduction of factor demands. Each research activity reduces labour and capital demands to a different extent so that the research activities can be ordered according to the extent to which they move the production process in alternative factor-saving directions.[2] An investment model is then built in which the entrepreneur chooses a portfolio of research activities.

In the investment model biases and rates of technical change are determined jointly by the following factors: (a) the relative productivity of alternative research lines; (b) changes in the cost of capital-saving (labour-saving) research; (c) changes in the scale of output; and (d) changes in the *present value of factor costs*. A rise in the wage rate, or the initial labour–output ratio,

---

[1] This builds on recent advances in the theory of duality between production functions and cost functions and the one-to-one correspondence between factor demand curves and cost functions (see, for example, Jorgenson and Lau, 1973).

[2] For example, only by coincidence would the factor into which the new quality is embodied be the only factor whose productivity is augmented. A new rice variety will not only augment the productivity of the seed in which the new productive capacity is embodied but it will also augment the productivity of the land and the labour used to produce rice. The Binswanger model is designed to cope with this problem by permitting each research activity to affect each factor augmentation coefficient.

tends to increase labour-saving lines of research, relative to other lines. In general this will lead to a more pronounced labour-saving bias.

Demand and the rate of technical change

The theory of induced innovation has been directed primarily to efforts to understand the role of resource endowments and factor prices on the direction of technical change. At the microeconomic level empirical work on demand-induced innovation began with the work of Griliches (1957) on hybrid corn and with the work of Schmookler on the railroad, petroleum, paper and agricultural equipment industries (1966, 1972). Griliches demonstrated the importance of demand in determining the location and diffusion of the invention of hybrid corn varieties. Schmookler concluded, from an exhaustive study of patent statistics, that the rate of return to inventive activity was of far greater importance than advances in the state of knowledge in explaining technical change in the four industries that he studied.

At the macroeconomic level the responsiveness of technical change to final demand was first empirically tested and confirmed in a study by Lucas (1967). Ben Zion and Ruttan (in Binswanger and Ruttan, 1978) show that the rate of input saving technical change is higher in periods of growing demand than in periods of stable or declining demand in the US economy.

An evolutionary approach

All of the approaches to the theory of induced innovation discussed in this section, both those in which technical change is induced from the supply side and those in which it is induced from the demand side, represent attempts to extend the neo-classical theory of the firm to incorporate the process of technical change. The evolutionary simulation models developed by Richard Nelson and Sidney Winter (1973, 1974) and with Schuette (1972) represent an interesting attempt to reach beyond the neo-classical theory to describe the process of technical change.

The Nelson–Winter simulation models do not contain a production function in the usual sense and do not make a distinction between moving along a given production function and shifts in the production function. Firms produce with fixed-proportion techniques in any given period of time. In the early versions of the model (1973, 1974), firms start to search for new techniques of production if profits fall below a certain margin. The models assume that in this search the firms draw samples from a distribution of input–output coefficients in somewhat the same manner as described by Evenson and Kislev. Except for the profitability check, research outcomes are random in their early versions. The inducement mechanism comes about through competition, selection and growth of the successful firms, not through an elaborate maximisation scheme.[1]

What is remarkable about these models is that the induced innovation results obtain even under these minimal assumptions about the behaviour of firms. Thus the basic inducement mechanism must be very robust.

In the more recent versions of the model (1975, 1977), Nelson and Winter move beyond the satisficing assumptions and explicitly introduce directed search, while continuing to emphasise the importance of uncertainty surrounding the research process.[2] This brings their models much closer to the Ahmad–Hayami–Ruttan–Binswanger microeconomic investment model. We continue to view investment models with directed search as having the greatest potential for generating fruitful empirical research.

III. TESTING THE INDUCED TECHNICAL CHANGE HYPOTHESIS

We will now turn to a review of the efforts to establish the plausibility of the induced technical change hypothesis by testing it against historical experience of agricultural development in the United States, Western Europe and Japan. Primary interest will focus on the issue of whether changes or differences in relative factor prices are associated with bias in the direction of technical change. With the exception of one test reported by Fellner (1971) all of the empirical tests available to us are drawn from the agricultural sector.[3]

[1] Paul A. David (1975, pp. 50–91) has developed a model of induced innovation which has some features that are similar to Nelson and Winter's model. His model is primarily concerned with the interaction of learning by doing and ordinary price-induced switches in production techniques.

[2] One criticism of the early Nelson–Winter models was that firms start to do research only when profits fall below a certain level. It thus predicted that an increase in demand for the product of an industry, while leading to greater profitability of every firm in that industry, will also lead to a reduction in research effort. This is inconsistent with much of the empirical evidence and indicates that at least those firms who do respond to profit incentives cannot behave according to any satisficing model.

[3] Fellner attempted to test the induced technical change hypothesis against historical trends in the capital/labour ratio, output per unit of total input, and output per unit of labour input and relative factor shares in the United States for the period 1920–1966. Fellner argued that the evidence which he examined suggests that during most of the 1920 to 1966 period the labour-saving bias of technical change was sufficient to keep the factor share to labour approximately unchanged except during the period in the 1950s when the capital/labour ratio was rising at an exceptionally rapid rate. He interpreted his results as consistent with induced innovation. The labour-saving bias, resulting from rising wage rates, was sufficient to keep factor share stable even though the capital/labour ratio was rising. The Fellner test can not, however, be regarded as definitive since it is not able to reject the hypothesis of exogenous labour-saving bias sufficient to offset the effect of the rise in the K/L ratio.

The Hayami–Ruttan type tests

Hayami and Ruttan first tested the induced innovation hypothesis against the historical experience of agricultural productivity growth in Japan and the United States for the period 1880–1960 (1970, 1971). The analysis was later extended by Wade (1973) to include the United Kingdom, France and Denmark and by Weber (1973) to include Germany. The time period has been also extended to permit the test to cover the period 1880–1970.[1]

The tests involve an analysis of the relationships between factor prices and the pattern of factor use associated with growth in both output per hectare and output per worker in the six countries (Tables 11.1 and 11.2).

TABLE 11.1   AGRICULTURAL OUTPUT, FACTOR PRODUCTIVITY, FACTOR ENDOWMENTS AND FACTOR PRICE RATIOS IN SIX COUNTRIES, 1880–1970

	Year	Japan	Germany	Denmark	France	United Kingdom	United States
Agricultural output	1880	100	100	100	100	100	100
index (Y)	1930	223	192	279	146	111	204
	1960	334	316	422	235	185	340
	1970	428	412	459	334	236	403
Agricultural output per male	1880	1.89	7.9	10.6	7.4	16.2	13.0
worker in wheat units (Y/L)	1930	4.60	16.0	24.1	13.2	20.1	22.5
	1960	8.41	35.4	47.5	33.4	45.3	88.8
	1970	15.77	65.4	94.4	59.9	87.6	157.4
Agricultural output per	1880	2.86	1.25	1.19	1.06	1.10	0.513
hectare of agricultural land	1930	5.06	2.47	2.95	1.50	1.18	0.555
in wheat units (Y/A)	1960	7.44	4.01	4.65	2.48	1.94	0.811
	1970	10.03	5.40	5.27	3.70	2.61	0.981
Agricultural land per male	1880	0.659	6.34	8.91	6.96	14.7	25.4
worker in hectares (A/L)	1930	0.908	6.46	8.18	8.80	17.0	40.5
	1960	1.131	8.83	10.21	13.44	23.3	109.5
	1970	1.573	12.20	17.92	16.19	33.5	160.5
Days of labour to buy one	1880	1.874	967	382	780	995	181
hectare of arable land	1930	2.920	589	228	262	189	115
(P_A/P_L)	1960	2.954	378	166	166	211	108
	1970	1.315	244	177	212	203	108

NOTES One wheat unit is equivalent to one ton of wheat. The method of constructing output measures in terms of wheat units is described in Yujiro Hayami and Vernon W. Ruttan, *Agricultural Development: An International Perspective* (Baltimore: Johns Hopkins Press, 1971), pp. 308–25.
Definitions of agricultural land are not strictly comparable among countries and over time, but generally include all land in farms, including crop land used for crops, pasture and fallow plus permanent pasture.
In Denmark the land price includes the value of agricultural land and buildings.

SOURCE Hans P. Binswanger and Vernon W. Ruttan, *Induced Innovation: Technology, Institutions and Development* (Baltimore: Johns Hopkins University Press, in press) Appendix 3.2.

The model of *biological technology* outlined earlier in this paper (Figure 11.4) suggests that a decline in the price of fertiliser relative to the price of land can be expected to induce advances in crop technology, such as the development of more fertiliser-responsive crop varieties, which can be characterised by new short-run production functions (such as i_1 below and to the right of i_0). A decline in the price of fertiliser relative to the price of labour can also be expected to induce technical changes leading (a) to the substitution

[1]The results of the several studies are presented in a consolidated form in Binswanger and Ruttan (1978, Chapter 3) and in Yamada and Ruttan (1975).

TABLE 11.2   ANNUAL RATES OF CHANGE IN AGRICULTURAL OUTPUT, FACTOR PRODUCTIVITY, AND FACTOR ENDOWMENTS IN SIX COUNTRIES, 1880–1970

	Japan	Germany	Denmark	France	United Kingdom	United States
1880–1970						
Agricultural output (Y)	1.63	1.59	1.71	1.35	0.96	1.56
Output per worker (Y/L)	2.39	2.48	2.46	2.35	1.89	2.81
Output per hectare (Y/A)	1.40	1.64	1.67	1.40	0.96	0.72
Land per worker (A/L)	0.97	0.73	0.78	0.94	0.92	2.07
1880–1930						
Agricultural output (Y)	1.62	1.31	2.07	0.76	0.21	1.44
Output per worker (Y/L)	1.79	1.42	1.66	1.16	0.43	1.10
Output per hectare (Y/A)	1.15	1.37	1.83	0.70	0.14	0.16
Land per worker (A/L)	0.64	0.04	−0.17	0.47	0.29	0.94
1930–1970						
Agricultural output (Y)	1.64	1.93	1.25	2.09	1.91	1.72
Output per worker (Y/L)	3.13	3.81	3.47	3.85	3.74	4.98
Output per hectare (Y/A)	1.73	1.97	1.44	2.28	2.00	1.43
Land per worker (A/L)	1.38	1.60	1.98	1.54	1.71	3.50
1930–1960						
Agricultural output (Y)	1.36	1.67	1.39	1.60	1.72	1.72
Output per worker (Y/L)	2.03	2.68	2.29	3.14	2.75	4.68
Output per hectare (Y/A)	1.29	1.63	1.53	1.69	1.67	1.27
Land per worker (A/L)	0.73	1.05	0.74	1.42	1.06	3.37
1960–1970						
Agricultural output (Y)	2.51	2.69	0.84	3.58	2.45	1.71
Output per worker (Y/L)	6.49	6.35	7.11	6.02	6.82	5.89
Output per hectare (Y/A)	3.03	3.02	1.26	4.08	3.01	1.92
Land per worker (A/L)	3.35	3.29	5.79	1.88	3.69	3.90

NOTES One wheat unit is equivalent to one ton of wheat. The method of constructing output measures in terms of wheat units is described in Yujiro Hayami and Vernon W. Ruttan, *Agricultural Development: An International Perspective* (Baltimore: Johns Hopkins Press, 1971), pp. 308–25.
Definitions of agricultural land are not strictly comparable among countries and over time, but generally include all land in farms, including crop land used for crops, pasture and fallow plus permanent pasture.
In Denmark the land price includes the value of agricultural land and buildings.

SOURCE Hans P. Binswanger and Vernon W. Ruttan, *Induced Innovation: Technology, Institutions and Development* (Baltimore: Johns Hopkins University Press, in press) Appendix 3.2.

of fertilisers, or other chemical inputs such as herbicides and insecticides, for more labour-intensive husbandry practices and (b) to the substitution of chemical fertilisers for farm-produced fertilisers such as animal manures and green manures.

A strong negative relationship was observed between the fertiliser/land price ratio and fertiliser use per hectare in all six countries (Table 11.3). A positive relationship between the price of labour relative to land and fertiliser use per hectare was also observed, although the relationship appears to have emerged later in France and Germany than in the other four countries. Given the enormous differences in the cultural and physical environments in which crops are produced among the six countries the similarity in the fertiliser/land price (P_F/P_A) response coefficients is quite remarkable. The implication is not only that farmers have responded in a roughly comparable manner to similar factor/factor price ratios but that farmers have been able to respond in a similar manner as a result of comparable shifts in the short-run production function. This implies a similar institutional response in the allocation of research resources to make more fertiliser crop varieties available to farmers. A second test of the model of induced innovation in biological technology was

TABLE 11.3   RELATIONSHIPS BETWEEN FERTILISER USE PER HECTARE AND RELATIVE FACTOR
PRICES IN SIX COUNTRIES

Country and period	Coefficient of prices of		Coefficient of determination	Standard error of estimate	Degrees of freedom
	Fertiliser Relative to land	Labour Relative to land			
	(P_F/P_A)	(P_L/P_A)	(R^2)	(S)	
Japan (1880–1960)[a]	−1.274*	0.729*	0.974	0.0810	14
	(0.057)	(0.220)			
Germany (1880–1913)[b]	−1.806*	0.083	0.943	0.289	13
	(0.009)	(0.515)			
(1950–1968)	−0.377*	0.799*	0.954	0.100	15
	(0.098)	(0.093)			
Denmark (1910–1965)[c]	−1.20*	0.958*	0.87	0.310	9
	(0.348)	(0.430)			
France (1870–1965)[d]	−0.950*	−1.375*I	0.56	0.776	17
	(0.332)	(0.362)			
(1920–1965)	−0.664*	0.485	0.386	0.538	7
	(0.259)	(0.733)			
United Kingdom (1870–1965)[e]	−1.130*	1.010*	0.92	0.218	17
	(0.025)	(0.080)			
United States (1880–1960)[f]	−1.357*	1.019*	0.970	0.083	14
	(0.102)	(0.168)			

NOTE Equations are linear in logarithms. The numbers inside the parentheses are the standard errors of the estimated coefficients.
*Significant at 0.5 level; I: inconsistent with simple induced innovation hypothesis.
    (one-tail test)

SOURCES

[a]Yujiro Hayami and Vernon W. Ruttan, *Agricultural Development: An International Perspective* (Baltimore: Johns Hopkins Press, 1971).
[b]Adolph Weber, 'Productivity in German Agriculture: 1850 to 1970', (St. Paul: University of Minnesota Department of Agricultural and Applied Economics, Staff Paper 73–1, August 1973), p. 23.
[c]William W. Wade, *Institutional Determinants of Technical Change and Agricultural Productivity Growth: Denmark, France and Great Britain, 1870–1965* (Minneapolis: University of Minnesota Graduate School, Ph.D. Thesis, August 1973), p. 128.
[d]William W. Wade, *Institutional Determinants*, pp. 134, 136.
[e]William W. Wade, *Institutional Determinants*, p. 149.
[f]Hayami and Ruttan, *Agricultural Development*. p. 132, Regression (W 15).

made on the relationship between feed concentrates and factor prices. In animal agriculture feed concentrates play a role analogous to fertiliser in crop agriculture. The results are shown in Table 11.4.

The model of *mechanical technology* outlined earlier suggests that a decline in the price of land relative to labour can be expected to induce advances in mechanical technology leading to an expansion in the area cultivated per worker. Technical change leading to a decline in the price of machinery relative to labour would also contribute to an expansion in the area cultivated per worker.

The results of the empirical tests of induced innovation hypothesis were not as clear cut in the case of mechanical as in the case of biological technology (Tables 11.5 and 11.6). The hypothesis that land area per worker is negatively related *both* to the price of land relative to labour and to the price of machinery relative to labour was confirmed in the historical experience of the United States and in the United Kingdom and in Germany after 1850. In all six countries, except Germany during 1880–1913, land area is, as hypothesised, negatively related to the price of machinery relative to labour. The hypothesis that power per worker is negatively related *both* to the price of land relative to

TABLE 11.4   RELATIONSHIP BETWEEN USE OF FEED CONCENTRATES PER HECTARE AND FACTOR PRICES

Country and period	Coefficient of prices of		Coefficient of determination	Standard error of estimate	Degrees of freedom
	Concentrates Relative to land	Labour Relative to land			
	(P_O/PA)	(P_C/PA)	(R^2)	(S)	
Germany (1880–1913)[a] (Net oil cake imports)	−3.333* (0.569)	3.974* (1.221)	0.712	0.337	31
(1950–1968)	−1.567* (0.254)	2.381* (0.255)	0.973	0.337	15
Denmark (1880–1925)[b] (All imported concentrates per hectare)	−0.680* (0.300)	0.494* (0.124)	0.590	0.030	7
United Kingdom (1870–1965)[c] (All concentrates per hectare)	−3.642* (0.331)	3.634* (0.331)	0.970	0.137	17

NOTE Equations are linear in logarithms. The numbers inside the parentheses are the standard errors of the estimated coefficients.
*Significant at P = 0.05 (one-tail test).

SOURCES
[a]Adolph Weber, 'Productivity Growth in German Agriculture: 1850 to 1970', (St. Paul: University of Minnesota Department of Agricultural and Applied Economics, Staff Paper) 73–1, (August 1973), p. 23.
[b]William W. Wade, *Institutional Determinants of Technical Change and Agricultural Productivity Growth: Denmark, France and Great Britain, 1870–1965* (Minneapolis: University of Minnesota Graduate School, Ph.D. Thesis, August 1973), p. 128.
[c]William W. Wade, *Institutional Determinants*, p. 149.

TABLE 11.5   RELATIONSHIPS BETWEEN LAND[a] PER WORKER AND RELATIVE FACTOR PRICES IN SIX COUNTRIES

Country and period	Coefficients of prices of		Coefficient of determination	Standard error of estimate	Degrees of freedom
	Land relative to labour	Machinery relative to labour			
	(P_A/P_L)	(P_M/P_L)	(R^2)	(S)	
Japan (1880–1960)[b]	0.159† (0.110)	−0.219 (0.041)	0.751	0.016	14
Germany (1880–1913)[c]	−0.264* (0.066)	0.066*I (0.018)	0.393	0.012	31
(1950–1968)	−0.177 (0.139)	−0.476* (0.087)	0.975	0.083	15
Denmark (1910–1965)[d]	0.148† (0.084)	−0.357* (0.072)	0.910	0.030	9
France (1870–1965)[e]	0.398*† (0.202)	−0.088 (0.141)	0.323	0.189	17
(1920–1965)	0.050† (0.226)	−0.498* (0.166)	0.460	0.164	7
United Kingdom (1870–1925)[f]	−0.129* (0.033)	−0.139* (0.070)	0.610	0.041	17
(1925–1965)	0.279† (0.159)	−0.065 (0.256)	0.440	0.110	6
United States (1880–1960)[g]	−0.451* (0.215)	−0.486* (0.120)	0.826	0.084	14

*Significant at P = 0.05 (one-tail test)
†Inconsistent with simple induced innovation hypothesis

NOTES
[a]Arable land per male worker in Japan, Denmark, France and the United Kingdom; agricultural land per male worker in Germany and the United States.
[b]Yujiro Hayami and Vernon W. Ruttan, *Agricultural Development: An International Perspective* (Baltimore: Johns Hopkins Press, 1971). Land per worker (W7); Power per worker (W9).
[c]Adolph Weber, 'Productivity Growth in German Agriculture: 1850 to 1970' (St. Paul: University of Minnesota Department of Agricultural and Applied Economics, Staff Paper P73–1, August 1973), p. 24. Land per worker – Regressions (6) and (7): Power per worker – Regressions (4) and (5).
[d]William W. Wade, *Institutional Determinants of Technical Change and Agricultural Productivity Growth: Denmark, France and Great Britain, 1870–1965* (Minneapolis: University of Minnesota Graduate School, Ph.D. Thesis, August 1973), p. 128.
[e]William W. Wade, *Institutional Determinants*, p. 134, 136.
[f]William W. Wade, *Institutional Determinants*, p. 149.
[g]Hayami and Ruttan, *Agricultural Development*, p. 130. Land per worker (W1); Power per worker (W5).

176   *Economic Growth and Resources*

TABLE 11.6   RELATIONSHIP BETWEEN POWER[a] PER WORKER AND RELATIVE FACTOR PRICES IN SIX COUNTRIES

Country and period	Coefficients of prices of		Coefficient of determination	Standard error of estimate	Degrees of freedom
	Land relative to labour	Machinery relative to labour			
	(P_A/P_L)	(P_M/P_L)	(R^2)	(S)	
Japan (1880–1960)[b]	−0.665* (0.261)	−0.299 (0.685)	0.262	0.219	14
Germany (1880–1913)[c]	−0.238* (0.070)	−0.607* (0.020)	0.978	0.069	31
(1950–1968)	−0.234 (0.329)	−1.358* (0.207)	0.979	0.213	15
Denmark (1910–1965)[d]	1.494† (1.010)	−3.180* (0.861)	0.830	0.370	9
France (1870–1965)[e]	1.704*† (0.880)	−0.705 (0.614)	0.160	0.810	17
(1920–1965)	−0.443 (0.976)	−2.460* (0.715)	0.550	0.705	7
United Kingdom (1870–1965)[f]	−1.120* (0.295)	−1.090* (0.527)	0.810	0.075	17
United States (1880–1960)[g]	−1.279* (0.475)	−0.920* (0.266)	0.827	0.187	14

*Significant at P = 0.05 (one-tail test)
†Inconsistent with simple induced innovation hypothesis

NOTES
[a]Horsepower per male worker except in Germany where machinery investment per worker was employed.
[b]Yujiro Hayami and Vernon W. Ruttan, *Agricultural Development: An International Perspective* (Baltimore: Johns Hopkins Press, 1971). Land per worker (W7); Power per worker (W9).
[c]Adolph Weber, 'Productivity Growth in German Agriculture: 1850 to 1970' (St. Paul: University of Minnesota Department of Agricultural and Applied Economics, Staff Paper P73–1, August 1973), p. 24. Land per worker – Regressions (6) and (7); Power per worker – Regressions (5).
[d]William W. Wade, *Institutional Determinants of Technical Change and Agricultural Productivity Growth: Denmark, France and Great Britain, 1870–1965* (Minneapolis: University of Minnesota Graduate School, Ph.D. Thesis, August 1973), p. 128.
[e]William W. Wade, *Institutional Determinants*, p. 134, 136.
[f]William W. Wade, *Institutional Determinants*, p. 149.
[g]Hayami and Ruttan, *Agricultural Development*, p. 130. Land per worker (W1); Power per worker (W5).

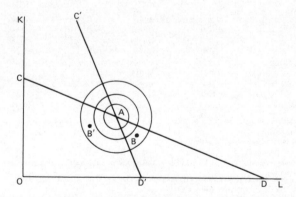

Fig. 11.5 Sampling and selection of new input–output coefficients

labour and of machinery relative to labour was confirmed in all cases except for Denmark and for France before 1920. Where the test was run for both an early and a late period the results tended to be weakest for the early period. This may simply reflect the relatively weak inducement for mechanisation in an environment characterised by very low wage rates.

The tests reported in this section that were conducted within the framework of the Hayami–Ruttan model are clearly consistent with the induced innovation hypothesis but they do not represent an adequate test of the hypothesis. The tests do not permit us to determine (a) whether the historical changes in factor use reflect the response of farmers to the rising economic value of land in relation to the price of fertiliser or to the increasing cost of labour compared to the cost of machinery along an unchanging, neo-classical production function, or (b) whether the production function available to farmers in the six countries has itself shifted to the left as a result of scientific and technical efforts by scientists, engineers and investors in response to changing factor price relationships. The magnitude of the changes in factor prices, and in factor use, strongly suggest that the induced innovation hypothesis has been involved.

In the next section we present a simple two-factor test of the induced innovation hypothesis developed by Binswanger, using the same data employed in this section.

The Binswanger two-factor test

Binswanger has suggested a simple two-factor test to overcome the limitations in the Hayami–Ruttan test. The basic task in designing a test for induced innovation is, as noted above, to divide any changes in the labour/land ratio over time, or any cross-sectional differences between countries at a particular time, into (a) a component that results from ordinary price substitution and (b) a component that is the result of technical change.

The Binswanger two-factor test proceeds in two steps. First, the *necessary elasticity of substitution* to explain the observed factor ratio differences by factor price ratio differences is computed. If these exceed the econometrically estimated elasticities of substitution by a sufficiently large margin, the hypothesis of neutral technical change can be rejected. The argument on which the two-factor test is based and the methodology used to estimate the pairwise elasticities of substitution, are summarised in Binswanger and Ruttan (1978, Chapter 3).

The results of the time series and cross-section tests conducted by Binswanger, shown in Tables 11.7 and 11.8, indicate that four different paths of technological development can be distinguished: (i) In 1880 the United States was on the same production function as France, Germany and the United Kingdom. After 1880 agricultural technology in the United States was strongly labour-saving. (ii) Continental Europe experienced neutral technical change, or possibly even labour-using technical change until the 1960s. After

TABLE 11.7   NECESSARY ELASTICITY OF SUBSTITUTION TO EXPLAIN
DIFFERENCES IN LAND–LABOUR RATIO BY PRICE RATIO
DIFFERENCES: THE CROSS-SECTION TEST

Item	1880	1930	1960	1970
US vs. other countries				
Japan	2.08*	1.35*	1.95*	3.12*
Great Britain	0.29	1.47*	2.50*	2.70*
France	0.87	1.96*	5.79*	4.13*
Germany	0.80	1.16	2.49*	4.00*
Japan vs. Europe				
Great Britain	7.01*	1.21	1.24	2.04*
France	3.26*	0.92	0.79	1.39*
Germany	4.13*	1.29	1.00	1.28
Great Britain vs. Continental Europe				
France	a*	2.47*	a*	17.12*
Germany	a*	0.98*	1.71*	5.72*
Continental Europe				
France vs. Germany	0.46	0.38	0.50	2.02*

NOTE Critical value to reject hypothesis of equal technology is 1.34, that is, twice the
value of σ for equiproportional changes in P_A and P_L.

$$\sigma_N = \frac{(A/L)_i - (A/L)_j}{(P_L/P_A)_j - (P_L/P_A)_i} \times \sqrt{\frac{(P_L/P_A)_i(P_L/P_A)_j}{(A/L)_i(A/L)_j}}$$

a*Denotes cases where the country with the higher land/labour ratio also has the higher
land/price ratio. Such behaviour is possible only if the country with the higher land/labour
ratio employs a more land-intensive technology, i.e. the hypothesis of equal technology is
rejected. No common isoquant maps can be constructed through points P and Q in
Figure 3-1.
*The paths of the two different countries differ significantly in land/labour intensity.

the 1960s France and Denmark began to experience labour-saving technical
change. (iii) The United Kingdom experienced neutral technical change until
1930. After 1930 it began to experience strong labour-saving technical change,
but its technology remains much more labour-intensive than US agricultural
technology. (iv) Japan started from an extremely labour-intensive position. Its
path of technological development since 1880 has been either neutral or,
particularly in recent years, slightly labour-saving.

The Binswanger tests are clearly consistent with the induced innovation
hypothesis. Yet there are some observations, based on the two-factor test, that
are not consistent with the simple version of the hypothesis. For example, the
United States followed a more labour-saving path with respect to its initial
land/labour ratio than did the four European countries despite the fact that in
the United States the rise in the price of labour relative to that of land was less
rapid than in Europe.

TABLE 11.8   NECESSARY ELASTICITY OF SUBSTITUTION TO EXPLAIN DIFFERENCES IN LAND–LABOUR RATIO BY PRICE EFFECTS: THE TIME-SERIES TEST

Time period	United States	Great Britain	France	Germany	Denmark	Japan[a] Land-price basis	Japan[a] Land-rent basis
1880–1930	1.03	0.16	0.20	0.04	b	–	–
1890–1930	–	–	–	–	–	c*	0.33
1890–1910	–	–	–	–	–	c*	0.33
1910–1930	–	–	–	–	–	1.09	0.34
1930–1960	16.5*	c*	0.90	0.70	0.70	c*	–
1960–1970	d*	9.43*	c*	0.74	c*	0.40	–

NOTE The critical ratio to reject the hypothesis of neutral technical change is $\sigma = 1.34$.

$$\sigma_N = \frac{\text{Percentage change in land/labour ratio between two periods}}{\text{Percentage change of labour price/land price ratio}}$$

with geometric means as a basis for the two percentage changes, that is,

$$\sigma_N = \frac{(A/L)_{i+1} - (A/L)_i}{(P_L/P_A)_i - (P_L/P_A)_{i+1}} \times \sqrt{\frac{(P_L/P_A)_{i+1}(P_L/P_A)_i}{(A/L)_{i+1}(AL)_i}}$$

where i = 1880, 1930, 1960, 1970.

a Data for 1890–1930 are taken from Table 3.10 and data for 1930–1960 from Table 3.1.
b Land/labour ratio declined very slightly, but price declined as well.
c Price ratio and land/labour ratio rose, which implies labour-saving technical change. (No common isoquant map can be constructed through P and Q in Figure 3.1 in this case.)
d No price change: technical change labour-saving.
*Significantly labour-saving.

There are several factors that may account for the less than complete consistency between the implications of the induced innovation hypothesis and the observed differences in factor price and factor use ratios. One is, of course, that there are fundamental biases in innovation possibilities. A second is the impact of borrowing – of technology transfer – from countries with different factor/price ratios. This may be particularly important for the countries with extreme differences in factor/price and use ratios such as Japan and the United States. If a country starts the process of modernisation from an extremely labour-intensive position, as Japan did in the 1870s and 1880s, or as some developing countries are doing today, the only technologies that are available to be transferred from other countries will be more labour-saving than would be induced by its own factor endowments and price ratios. Similarly, if a country starts the process of modernisation from an extremely labour-intensive position, as in the United States in the post-Civil War period, it is likely that the technologies which it borrows will be more land-saving than would be induced by its own factor endowments and price ratios. We are not, at this stage, able to provide quantitative estimates of the effects of fundamental and transfer biases.

The Binswanger many-factor test

In spite of its formal rigour a basic limitation of the two-factor test, even in comparison with the less rigorous tests of the Hayami–Ruttan type, is that a many-factor production process was treated as if it were a two-factor process. The test neglected the influence of prices other than land and labour on the land/labour ratio. In this section we present the results of a many-factor test designed by Binswanger (1974a, 1974b and 1978, Chapter 7).

The many-factor test is based on directly measured biases in the direction of technical change on the use of individual factors, rather than on factor ratios, for the United States agricultural sector from 1912 to 1968. Five factors were included in the measurement of bias-land, labour, machinery, fertiliser and other inputs. Land was, however, omitted from the test of the induced innovation hypothesis because agricultural land prices are determined by factors that are largely endogenous to the agricultural sector.

The rationale for the many-factor test can be summarised as follows. Suppose that innovation possibilities are neutral and that factor prices are exogenous to the agricultural sector. Factor-saving bias would be inversely related to the direction of change in the factor price. Furthermore, turning points in factor price trends should be followed after a lag, by corresponding changes in the direction of bias. If, on the other hand, innovation possibilities are not neutral then it is possible that a factor-using bias may be associated with a rise in the price of the corresponding factor. Such an occurrence can be used to test for the presence of a fundamental bias in innovation possibilities. Induced innovation may either offset or reinforce such a fundamental bias. But in the case of a factor-saving shift in prices, an acceleration of the price rise should, after some years, result in a decrease in the rate of factor-using bias.

The many-factor test developed by Binswanger involves partitioning the observed changes in factor shares into a component due to ordinary factor substitution and a component due to bias in the direction of technical change. This was accomplished in two steps: (a) a translog production function was used to estimate elasticity of substitution parameters from an independent sample; (b) the parameters were used to adjust the time-series factor share changes to obtain the part that was caused by technical change alone. A formal statement of the above argument has been developed by Binswanger (1974a, 1978).

The price-corrected factor shares are presented along with the actual shares and the factor prices in Table 11.9. The indices of bias for each input as computed from the price-corrected factor shares, are shown in Figure 11.6. Technical change exhibited a very strong fertiliser-using bias over the entire period. There was also a strong machinery-using bias and, after 1948, a strong labour-saving bias.

Ruttan et al.: *Induced Innovation in Agriculture*

TABLE 11.9   PRICE-CORRECTED SHARES (S$_i$), ACTUAL FACTOR SHARES AND FACTOR PRICES
USED IN COMPUTING (S$'_1$): UNITED STATES AGRICULTURE, 1912–68

	Year	Land	Labour	Machinery	Fertiliser	Other	Index of[a] input prices with respect to agricultural output prices
A. Price-corrected factor	1912	21.0	38.3	10.9	1.9	28.0	
shares S$'_i$. Model I	1916	21.2	36.7	11.6	1.8	28.7	
estimates	1920	19.6	39.3	9.3	2.1	29.7	
	1924	20.0	39.7	10.3	2.2	27.8	
	1928	18.1	41.4	10.4	2.7	27.4	
	1932	18.8	40.3	14.3	2.7	24.0	
	1936	18.9	32.5	16.3	3.0	29.3	
	1940	16.8	34.3	17.6	3.9	27.5	
	1944	16.5	38.4	16.1	4.8	24.2	
	1948	17.1	37.2	13.9	5.1	26.7	
	1952	16.5	29.8	19.7	5.7	28.3	
	1956	16.3	30.6	23.1	6.5	23.4	
	1960	17.1	27.2	23.4	6.1	26.1	
	1964	17.8	25.8	22.4	6.7	27.3	
	1968	19.1	25.3	23.1	7.2	25.3	
B. Actual factor shares S$_i$	1912	21.0	38.3	10.9	1.9	28.0	
	1916	21.6	36.5	11.6	1.9	28.4	
	1920	17.3	40.5	10.1	2.0	30.1	
	1924	19.7	38.5	10.3	1.7	29.7	
	1928	15.9	40.9	10.2	1.9	31.1	
	1932	18.6	37.6	12.6	1.6	29.7	
	1936	14.9	34.7	14.5	2.2	33.7	
	1940	12.0	35.3	15.1	2.3	35.2	
	1944	8.5	39.5	14.0	2.3	35.6	
	1948	9.4	37.7	12.2	2.4	38.3	
	1952	9.8	29.7	17.5	3.0	40.0	
	1956	11.5	27.4	20.1	3.3	37.8	
	1960	15.6	21.3	19.8	2.9	40.4	
	1964	17.5	18.3	18.5	3.3	42.3	
	1968	20.4	15.8	19.1	3.6	41.1	
C. Factor prices relative to	1912	100.0	100.0	100.0	100.0	100.0	100.0
agricultural aggregate	1916	105.2	99.2	102.1	98.1	96.4	107.7
input prices 1912 = 100	1920	81.1	107.1	83.5	88.0	107.8	97.4
	1924	99.2	112.1	93.1	77.6	88.8	120.0
	1928	79.7	117.2	97.7	68.4	90.4	131.5
	1932	97.8	118.4	140.7	78.2	61.7	164.5
	1936	59.5	97.2	162.1	85.4	95.0	116.7
	1940	49.6	101.7	164.1	58.8	91.0	176.0
	1944	32.2	107.4	120.7	31.1	104.7	202.3
	1948	34.0	115.5	105.6	23.5	103.9	214.5
	1952	39.6	119.0	130.6	23.2	93.1	230.6
	1956	48.2	134.8	140.0	21.8	75.9	302.7
	1960	71.6	141.6	155.0	17.7	68.0	355.1
	1964	82.9	149.6	159.9	15.5	66.4	407.9
	1968	100.8	160.7	154.2	12.2	58.8	477.2

The machinery case is particularly interesting (Figure 11.7). The change in
the machinery share for the period as a whole is entirely due to bias. The bias
alone would have moved the machinery share from 10.9 per cent in 1912 to
23.1 per cent in 1968. The actual machinery share rose only to 19.1 per cent. A
striking feature of the bias and the price movements is the sequence of turning
points. From 1916 to 1920 machinery prices fell. A substantial machinery-
using bias began in 1920. After 1920 the machinery price index rose slowly. By
1928 it had returned to its 1912 level. It continued to rise more rapidly until
about 1940. By 1940 the bias changed from a machinery-using to a
machinery-saving direction until 1948. From 1940 to 1948 machinery prices

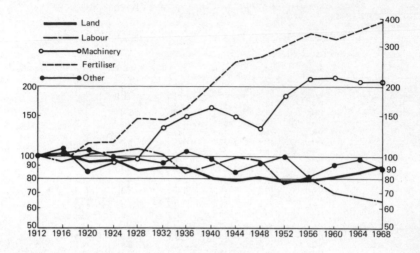

Fig. 11.6 Indices of bias on technical change

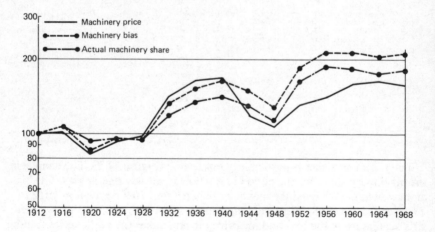

Fig. 11.7 Machinery bias, actual machinery share, and price of machinery inputs in relation to cost of all agricultural inputs

declined and eight years later another period of rapid machinery-using technical change began. In 1948 the machinery price index rose again from 1948 to 1960. In 1956, eight years after prices began to rise the machinery-using bias disappeared and technical change turned neutral.

The above sequence of turning points is fully consistent with the induced innovation hypothesis. Indeed, the price responsiveness of the machinery biases is quite remarkable. Evenson (1968) documented a five- to eight-year lag between the initiation of a research effort and the beginning of a productivity impact from the research output in US agriculture. A lag much shorter than eight years would be consistent with the choice-of-technique rather than the induced innovation hypothesis.

The results of the many-factor test support a conclusion that in United States agriculture the biases in technical change affecting machinery, fertiliser and labour use have been very responsive to changes in factor prices. In general, the direction of the biases has responded to changes in factor prices with a lag of eight years or longer. The lags have, however, tended to become shorter over time. Furthermore, in the case of machinery, fertiliser and labour the biases in the share changes due to changes in factor prices were large and greatly exceeded the changes that could be explained by simple substitution effects. It is also clear, from the machinery case, that innovation possibilities have not always been neutral. But even in the case of machinery, changes in factor prices have at times partially offset and at other times have reinforced the exogenous bias in innovation possibilities.

IV. CONCLUSION

The single most important conclusion that emerges out of the several tests of the induced technical change hypothesis is the powerful role of economic forces in inducing technical change. In view of the great differences in the physical, cultural and economic environments in the historical cases against which the tests were conducted and the different methodologies employed in the tests, this conclusion must be regarded as remarkably robust.

One clear implication of the tests of the theory of induced innovation is to reinforce the significance of the neo-classical concern with efficiency in resource allocation as central to the process of economic development. The effectiveness with which research resources have been allocated to release the constraints on growth imposed by resource endowments has been strongly influenced by the efficiency of market mechanisms in interpreting the factor price implications of relative resource endowments.

The pervasive role of economic forces in research resource allocation places a major burden on the efficiency of the pricing system. Our analysis suggests that if price relationships are distorted either through market imperfections or public intervention in market processes, the innovative behaviour will be biased. As long as the economics of technical change was cast primarily in terms of the choice of technology – to the selection by the individual firm or the agricultural producer of the 'appropriate technology' from the shelf of available technology – it was easy to assume that the effects of errors in judgement at the firm level or the effects of biases resulting from public policy could be corrected in a relatively short time. The lags that have been observed in the relationships between change in factor prices and the production impact resulting from induced innovation suggest that the effects of distorted incentives will not be confined to the short-run bias in the choice of technology but will also have an impact on the technology that becomes available five to ten years later.

We do not suggest that technical change is entirely endogenous to the economic systems. There exists in science and technology an exogenous thrust toward the accumulation of knowledge. The possibilities of technology transfer also tend to bias the possibilities that become available to countries that are lagging in their own development of capacity to invent technologies adapted to their resource and cultural endowments.

The possibility of bias in both the exogenous thrust of science and technology and in technology-transfer possibilities suggest that developing nations should place a high priority on effective institutionalisation of public sector agricultural research. Innovation in mechanical technology has been much more responsive than biological technology to the inducement mechanisms that bear on the private sector. Failure to balance the effectiveness of the private sector in responding to inducements for advance in mechanical technology (and in those areas of biological and chemical technology where advances can be embodied in proprietary products) with institutional innovations capable of an equally effective response to inducements for advance in biological technology, will lead to bias in the productivity path. This bias will be particularly inconsistent with the factor endowments of the more labour-intensive, less developed countries. The labour force explosion anticipated in the rural areas of the less developed countries in the 1970s implies that failure to design agricultural technologies consistent with factor endowments will be very costly.

A second effect of the induced innovation tests is to reveal a major gap in our knowledge. The induced innovation model, as pointed out earlier, represents an extension of the neo-classical theory of the firm. Yet much of agricultural research, particularly the research leading to advances in biological technology, has been conducted in public sector research laboratories and experimental stations. Innovative behaviour in the public sector has largely been ignored, not only in the literature on the theory of induced innovation, but in the economics generally. We have no received theory of induced institutional innovation!

An attempt has been made in Hayami and Ruttan (1971, pp. 53–63); in Hayami (1965, Chapters 3 and 6), and in Binswanger and Ruttan (1978, Chapters 12 and 13) to draw on the history of the development of agricultural research institutions in the United States, Japan and Western Europe to suggest how economic forces have induced public sector agricultural research institutions to allocate resources to research in a manner consistent with the patterns of resource allocation suggested by the induced innovation model.

Efforts by society to internalise the benefits of innovative activity represent a major source of demand for institutional innovation. In agriculture the small size of farm firm, the difficulty of maintaining proprietary control, and product homogeneity make it difficult to capture the gains and unprofitable to bear the costs of research leading to advances in biological technology. The results of research in biological technology, when embodied in new plant varieties or new cultural practices, can be copied or reproduced by other firms. Furthermore, the benefits of rapid diffusion of agricultural technology tend to be quickly transmitted from producers to consumers through lower product prices.

The socialisation of much of agricultural research, particularly the research leading to advances in biological technology, represents an example of a public sector institutional innovation designed to realise for society the potential gains from advances in agricultural technology. This institutional innovation originated in Germany, with the establishment of the Saxon agricultural experiment at Möckern in 1852. The German model of socialised agricultural research was transplanted to the United States and Japan in the latter half of the nineteenth century where it evolved along quite different patterns in response to the enormous differences in resource and cultural endowments in the two countries.

One common element in both the United States and the Japanese agricultural research system was the evolution of a dual federal-state or national-prefectural system. The decentralisation of both administration and funding of the state and prefectural systems has facilitated a dialectic interaction between farmers (or their representatives), and research scientists and administrators and has resulted in simulation of the behaviour suggested by the induced innovation model. Farmers have been induced, by shifts in relative factor prices, to search for technical alternatives which save the increasingly scarce factors of production. Perceptive scientists and science administrators have responded by making available new technical possibilities and new inputs that have enabled farmers to profitably substitute the increasingly abundant factor for increasingly scarce factors. Successful scientists and science administrators are encouraged through increased support for their research, to intensify their efforts to eliminate the constraints on production which have the highest economic payoff.

The pattern of dialectic interaction between agricultural producers, research institutions and the public decision-making bodies is likely to be most effective when farmers are organised into politically effective local and regional farm 'burcaux' or farmers' associations. The response of the public sector research and extension programmes to farmers' needs are likely to be greatest when the administration and funding of the agricultural research systems is highly decentralised. In an environment in which effective farmer organisations, a political system which views agricultural research as an investment in local or regional economic growth, and a mission- or client-oriented experiment station system tend to reinforce each other, it is not unrealistic to expect that research resource allocation and the pattern of productivity growth will appear consistent with that complied by the induced innovation model.

Neither the process of induced innovation, nor its significance in releasing the constraints on growth imposed by relatively inelastic resource endowments, are confined to the agricultural sector. It would seem particularly important for example, rigorously to test the induced innovation model against the history of trends and shifts in the relative prices of alternative energy resources (Solow, 1974). The sensitivity of technical change in energy production and utilisation, and trends in the lags in such response need to be identified. It is perhaps even more important to consider the institutional innovations that will be necessary if factor and product markets are effectively to translate the impact of changing energy endowments into incentives to invent new sources of energy and/or energy-conserving technology. Such incentives are clearly operative in some areas. In agriculture, for example, the rise in energy prices has induced a rather substantial shift in research resources into efforts to identify and develop more efficient organic and biological sources of plant nutrition as a substitute for the more energy-intensive chemical sources.

The technical and institutional response to the rising demand for amenity resources is a second area where considerable insight might be opened up by a series of systematic tests of the induced innovation hypothesis (Ruttan, 1971; Smith, 1974). In the higher income industrial societies the income elasticity of demand for commodities and services related to sustenance is low, and declining, while the income elasticity of demand for the more effective disposal of residuals and for environmental amenities is high and continues to rise. It seems reasonable to hypothesise that the continuing environmental crisis reflects a lag in technical and institutional innovation in the treatment of residuals and in the supply of environmental amenities.

The environmental stress resulting from pollution and congestion is not simply a by-product of the autonomous thrust of technical change. The system of legal and economic institutions that govern the use of common property resources has not yet fully responded to (a) the rising demand for capacity to receive and assimilate the residuals from commodity production and consumption and (b) the shift to the right in the demand for resource amenities associated with high and rising incomes in the developed countries. The effect of the undervaluation of common property environmental resources has been to induce a pattern of technical change that has widened the opportunities for substitution of the non-priced services of natural resources of those that are exchanged in ordinary commodity markets. The environmental stress now being experienced would have occurred more slowly in an environment in which the direction of technological efforts was not itself responsive to the distortions in the pricing of both conventional factor inputs and in environmental services (Smith and Krutilla, 1977; Ruttan, 1971).

Society has in the past been successful in the design of institutional innovation in response to market failure. We have already referred to the socialisation of agricultural research as a response by society to realise the potential gains from advances in agricultural technology. The modernisation of land tenure relationships, including the elimination of the commons and the shift from share tenure to lease tenure and owner-operator cultivation in much of western agriculture was in large part a result of an effort to achieve a system of property rights that would permit individual farmers to internalise part of the gains from innovative activity. There is clearly a rising demand for institutional innovations leading to greater precision in the definition of property rights in environmental resources, the organisation of private firms or public authorities with appropriate incentive to manage environmental sub-systems, and the use of market or market-like systems to direct the production and use of the commodity and service inputs and output of such systems.

In conclusion we would like to stress that the demonstration that economic forces have exerted a pervasive impact on the direction of technical change should not be taken to imply that the generation of either technical or institutional change can be left to an 'invisible hand' that directs technology along an 'efficient' path induced by either 'original' resource endowments or by the growth of demand. Development of capacity for the production of new knowledge leading to technical and institutional change is itself a product of institutional innovation. The way in which resource endowments and final demand express themselves in factor/factor and factor/product price ratios is strongly influenced by the efficiency of market processes, by the responsiveness of political institutions, and by the existing structure of income distribution. Neither the economic nor political institutions which characterise modern industrial economies occurred naturally. They are human artifacts. Their improvement depends on the generation and application of new knowledge in the economic and behavioural sciences and related professions.

REFERENCES

Syed Ahmad, 'On the Theory of Induced Innovation', *Economic Journal*, 76 (1966), 344–57.
Hans P. Binswanger, 'A Micro Economic Approach to Induced Innovation', *Economic Journal*, 84 (December 1974a), 940–58.
Hans P. Binswanger, 'The Measurement of Technical Change Biases with Many Factors of Production', *American Economic Review*, 64 (December 1974b), 964–76.
Hans P. Binswanger, 'Measuring the Impact of Economic Factors on the Direction of Technical Change', in *Resource Allocation and Productivity in National and International Agricultural Research*, (ed.) Thomas Arndt, Dana Dalrymple and Vernon Ruttan (Minneapolis: University of Minnesota Press, 1977), pp. 526–50.
Hans P. Binswanger and Vernon W. Ruttan, *Induced Innovation: Technology, Institutions and Development* (Baltimore: Johns Hopkins University Press, 1978).

Paul A. David, *Technical Choice, Innovation and Economic Growth: Essays on American and British Experience in the Nineteenth Century* (Cambridge: Cambridge University Press, 1975).

E. M. Drandakis and E. S. Phelps, 'A Model of Induced Innovation, Growth and Distribution', *The Economic Journal*, 76 (1966), 823–40.

Robert E. Evenson, *The Contribution of Agricultural Research and Extension to Agricultural Production* (PhD dissertation, University of Chicago, 1968).

Robert E. Evenson and Yoav Kislev, *Agricultural Research and Productivity* (New Haven: Yale University Press, 1975), 140–55.

William Fellner, 'Two Propositions in the Theory of Induced Innovations', *Economic Journal*, 71 (June 1961), 305–8.

William Fellner, 'Empirical Support for the Theory of Induced Innovation', *Quarterly Journal of Economics*, 85 (1971), 580–604.

Zvi Griliches, 'Hybrid Corn: An Exploration of the Economics of Technological Change', *Econometrica*, 25 (October 1957), 501–22.

Zvi Griliches, 'Agriculture: Productivity and Technology', *International Encyclopedia of the Social Sciences*, Vol. I (New York: Macmillan and Free Press, 1968), 241–5.

Yujiro Hayami (with Masakatsu Akino, Masahiko Shintani and Saburo Yamada) *A Century of Agricultural Growth in Japan* (Minneapolis and Tokyo: University of Minnesota Press and University of Tokyo Press, 1975).

Yujiro Hayami and Vernon W. Ruttan, 'Factor Prices and Technical Change in Agricultural Development: The United States and Japan, 1880–1960', *Journal of Political Economy*, 78 (September/October 1970), 1115–41.

Yujiro Hayami and Vernon W. Ruttan, *Agricultural Development: An International Perspective* (Baltimore: Johns Hopkins University Press, 1971).

John R. Hicks, *The Theory of Wages* (London: Macmillan, 1964; original edition, 1932).

Alain de Janvry, 'A Socioeconomic Model of Induced Innovation for Argentine Agricultural Development', *Quarterly Journal of Economics*, 87:3 (August 1973), 410–35.

Dale W. Jorgenson and Lawrence J. Lau, *Duality and Differentiability in Production* (Cambridge, Harvard Institute of Economic Research, Discussion Paper 308, July 1973).

Charles Kennedy, 'Induced Bias in Innovation and the Theory of Distribution', *The Economic Journal*, 74 (1964), 541–7.

R. E. Lucas, Jr., 'Tests of a Capital-Theoretic Model of Technological Change', *Review of Economic Studies*, 34 (1967), 175–80.

Richard R. Nelson and Sidney G. Winter, 'Toward An Evolutionary Theory of Economic Capabilities', *American Economic Review*, 63 (1973), 440–9.

Richard R. Nelson and Sidney G. Winter, 'Neoclassical vs. Evolutionary Theories of Economic Growth: Critique and Prospectus', *Economic Journal*, 84 (1974), 886–905.

Richard R. Nelson and Sidney G. Winter, 'Factor Price Changes and Substitution in an Evolutionary Model', *The Bell Journal of Economics*, Vol. 6, No. 2 (Autumn 1975).

Richard R. Nelson and Sidney G. Winter, 'In Search of Useful Theory of Innovation', *Research Policy*, 6 (1977), 36–76.

Richard R. Nelson, Sidney G. Winter and Herbert L. Schuette, 'Technical Change in an Evolutionary Model', *Quarterly Journal of Economics*, 40 (1976), 90–118.

William D. Nordhaus, 'The Optimal Rate and Direction of Technical Change', in *Essays in the Theory of Optimal Economic Growth*, ed. Karl Shell (Cambridge: Massachusetts Institute of Technology Press, 1967).

William D. Nordhaus, 'Some Skeptical Thoughts on the Theory of Induced Innovation', *The Quarterly Journal of Economics*, 87 (1973), 209–19.

Vernon W. Ruttan, 'Technology and the Environment', *American Journal of Agricultural Economics*, 53 (December 1971), 707–17.

W. E. G. Salter, *Productivity and Technical Change* (Cambridge, England: Cambridge University Press, 1960).

Paul A. Samuelson, 'A Theory of Induced Innovation along Kennedy–Weizacher Lines', *Review of Economics and Statistics*, 47 (1965).

A. K. Sen, 'The Choice of Agricultural Techniques in Underdeveloped Countries', *Economic Development and Cultural Change*, 7 (1959), 279–85.

A. K Sen, *Choice of Techniques* (Oxford: Basil Blackwell, 1962).

V. Kerry Smith, *Technical Change, Relative Prices, and Environmental Resource Evaluation* (Baltimore: Johns Hopkins University Press, 1974).

V. Kerry Smith and John V. Krutilla, 'The Economics of Natural Resource Scarcity: An Interpretive Introduction' (Washington, Resources for the Future, 1977, mimeo).

Jacob Schmookler, *Invention and Economic Growth* (Cambridge: Harvard University Press, 1966).

Jacob Schmookler, *Patents, Invention and Economic Growth: Data and Selected Essays* (Cambridge: Harvard University Press, 1972).

Robert M. Solow, 'The Economics of Resources or the Resources of Economics', *American Economic Review*, 64 (May 1974), 1–14.

William W. Wade, *Institutional Determinants of Technical Change and Productivity Growth: Denmark, France and Great Britain, 1880–1965* (PhD Dissertation, University of Minnesota Press, 1973).

Henry Y. Wan, Jr., *Economic Growth* (New York: Harcourt, Brace, Javanovich, 1971).

Adolph Weber, *Productivity of German Agriculture: 1850 to 1970* (St. Paul, University of Minnesota, Department of Agricultural and Applied Economics Staff Paper 73-1, August 1973).

Saburo Yamada and Vernon W. Ruttan, 'International Comparisons of Productivity in Agriculture', Paper presented at the National Bureau of Economic Research Conference on Research in Income and Wealth, Williamsburg, Virginia, 13–14 November, 1975.

12 The Impact of Agricultural Price Policies on Demand and Supply, Incomes, and Imports; an Experimental Model for South Asia[1]

Marc Osterrieth, Eric Verreydt and Jean Waelbroeck
BRUSSELS

I. INTRODUCTION

Though agricultural production has increased substantially in developing countries, much of the increase has been absorbed by population growth. Further, production per head has risen very slowly and has lagged behind consumption, while imports have increased. A number of recent studies have suggested that these trends will continue and that net imports of foodgrains by developing countries will approximately double between 1973–4 and 1985. This projected increase in imports would pose serious balance of payments problems for many developing countries, including some of the poorest.[2]

The methodology used in making these projections is, however, very crude. The projection forecasts are extrapolations from trends. Projections of demand are built up by applying income elasticities observed over time to GNP projections. These forecasts are then marginally adjusted on the basis of special knowledge about conditions in different countries. While knowledge of investment and price policies plays a role in guiding the adjustments, these variables do not appear explicitly in the equations of the projection model itself. The failure to use prices is especially a cause for concern because it may be indicative of policy-thinking which is wrong, together with difficulties in specifying adequate equations. For example, much of the literature on the food gap implicitly reflects a view of the world in which demand and supply are independent of prices and in which supply can be increased only by massive programmes of government investment. If such programmes are not undertaken, then it is held that countries may witness an intractable rise in food imports which will absorb available foreign exchange and choke off the prospects for self-sustained growth in the future.

The view taken in the present paper is that what policy-makers most need to understand is the trade-off between food imports and agricultural prices.

[1]We wish to express our gratitude for the research support received from the Economic Analysis and Projections Department of the IBRD, which made this study possible.
[2]See e.g. FAO (1974), Sandra Hadler (1976) and IFPRI (1976).

Estimates of this trade-off should be the chief basis for government decisions to import food and agricultural products or to accept the unpleasant political and social consequences of an increase in agricultural prices. Knowledge of this trade-off should also be one of the factors in decisions to step up the public funds allocated to irrigation, rural electrification, agricultural research and other efforts to speed up the rate of growth of agricultural output.

In this paper we describe a projection model which takes explicit account of the relation between prices and the agricultural balance of trade. The model is simple enough to be used for projections of supply and demand in whole regions of the developing world or for the developing world as a whole. To illustrate the applicability of the approach, the model is used to assess the impact of prices on the agricultural balance of trade of South Asia.[1]

II. EQUATIONS FOR DEMAND AND SAVING

It is desirable to use a specification of demand in which the figure derived from adding consumption of different goods and saving is consistent with disposable income. We also felt, given the poor quality of data in many developing countries, that it was desirable to use a robust specification in which fairly strong conditions were imposed on the coefficients estimated. An attractive specification from both these points of view is the Extended Linear Expenditure System (ELES) devised by C. Lluch (1973), which expands R. Stone's Linear Expenditures System to an intertemporal framework. The specification is

$$p_i q_i = p_i c_i + b_i (y - \Sigma p_i c_i) \tag{1}$$

$$s = b_s (y - \Sigma p_j c_j) \tag{2}$$

where q_i = consumption per head of good i, p_i its price, y income per head, s saving, c_i and b_i are constants, and i and $j = 1 \ldots n$ are indices characterising n goods. The c_i are often referred to as 'committed expenditures,' a term reflecting a popular interpretation of these coefficients as minimal subsistence expenditures. The expression $(y - \Sigma p_j c_j)$ is then referred to as the supernumerary income, i.e. the margin between income and the cost of committed expenditures. The b_i are marginal budget shares.

Using these interpretations, expression (1) explains expenditures as a linear function of price and supernumerary income, while (2) asserts that saving is a constant fraction of supernumerary income. It can also readily be checked that if $b_s + \Sigma b_i = 1$, then $\Sigma p_i q_i + s = y$, meaning that the system is additive. In addition, it can be shown that the system is homogeneous of degree zero in prices and income and satisfies the Slutzky integrability conditions.

C. Lluch, A. Powell and R. Williams (1975) have obtained time-series estimates of the ELES for 27 countries, including 7 developing countries (Korea, Thailand, The Philippines, Taiwan, Jamaica, Panama and Puerto

[1]As defined in this paper, South Asia includes India, Pakistan, Bangladesh and Sri Lanka.

Rico). The study was based on national income expenditures data, so that agricultural products were valued at the prices paid by consumers and not the prices received by farmers. This is a drawback from the point of view of modelling, as the figure obtained is not directly comparable to agricultural production data, which are valued in national accounts at farm-gate prices.

Lluch, Powell and Williams have also made extensive investigations of food demand on the basis of consumer budget cross-section data. An important finding confirmed that spending patterns differ substantially between town and country, with the marginal budget share for food being higher in rural areas than in cities. This situation reflects both differences in patterns of living and the lesser availability of manufactured goods outside the cities. J. Mellor (1976, p. 166) provides similar evidence for India, based on his approval of the data available.

Another significant finding – which also confirmed previous research – was that the estimated coefficients depend on income per head: committed expenditures rise with income; the marginal budget share of food declines as income rises. The finding means that the estimated ELES functions must be considered as local approximations of a more complex, underlying demand system and should not be used for projections much beyond the range of incomes observed in the sample period.

Estimated equations

To test the feasibility of applying the ELES to a broad group of countries, we built up data on consumption of agricultural and non-agricultural products and of saving for 27 developing countries. (The construction of the data is described in an appendix which is available on request.) It is important to note that consumption of agricultural products is described using farm-gate rather than retail prices, so that the agricultural consumption series can be compared directly to data on agricultural production.

The ELES imposes a strong structure on the data, and its application to regularly growing series might give a high R^2 and significant coefficients, even though the specification is not appropriate. We used the Durbin–Watson statistic as a heuristic test for misspecification to help determine whether the estimates were acceptable. The results led to our rejecting the estimates for two countries which have undergone major social and political upheaval – Bangladesh and Peru – as well as for all black African countries except Kenya and Nigeria. The difficulties experienced with the latter countries may be due to the low quality of the statistical data available.

Findings based on the successful estimates exhibited the same patterns as those noted in the earlier applications of the ELES and of the Linear Expenditure System, in particular the tendency for committed expenditures to rise with income and for the marginal budget share of food to fall as income increases.

For the model described in this paper, we needed ELES demand systems for both rural and urban populations. These systems were constructed in two stages. First we built up an ELES demand system for South Asia by averaging the coefficients obtained for India, Pakistan and Sri Lanka, using population weights to compute the averages. The coefficients for the rural and urban ELES were then obtained from that system by imposing three conditions:

(1) At base-year prices, food consumption per head should be the same according to the ELES obtained for the region as a whole and according to the rural and urban expenditures systems.
(2) The ratio of supernumerary to total income should be the same in the base year according to the regional and the rural and urban expenditures systems.
(3) Marginal budget shares should be the same in the urban, rural and regional demand systems.

It is important to examine the price and income elasticities of demand implied by the equations. The income elasticity of demand for agricultural products is equal to 0.53 in the base year, the price elasticity −0.52. Both figures are in line with other quantitative studies of demand in low-income countries (see, e.g. J. Mellor (1966), Chapter 4). The major study of consumer demand in developing countries – by R. Weiskoff (1971) – actually arrived at substantially higher income and price elasticities – 1.1 and −0.87 respectively.

The reader should note that the price elasticities defined above describe the response of consumers to increased agricultural prices where their income and the prices of other goods are held constant. In the model we have constructed, an increase in agricultural prices is assumed to increase the income of farmers, and the elasticity concept as usually defined in demand theory is therefore not considered to be meaningful. When the impact of agricultural price changes on the income of farmers is taken into account in the calculations, the price elasticity of demand for food is equal to −0.24.

III. THE AGRICULTURAL PRODUCTION FUNCTION

The agricultural production function used in the model explains production as a function of changes in the physical inputs of irrigated and unirrigated land, fertilisers and labour.

Study of the response of crops to inputs has a long history. The classic book of E. Heady and J. Dillon (1961) provides an excellent synthesis of this type of research. In another path-breaking study, U. Lele and J. Mellor (1964) developed, on the basis of available evidence, a foodgrains production function for India, which they used to analyse the sources of growth of production of foodgrains in that country. More recently there have been attempts to estimate the relation between inputs and aggregate production in agriculture.[1]

[1] The studies we know are those of the MOIRA group H. Linneman (1975); the SARU group (1976); and A. Strout (1975).

Our own approach to the problem was inspired by the work of A. Strout (1975), who estimated a cross-section production function over two periods from data for 16 regions. Strout's specification is

$$x_a/t_c = \alpha + \beta(t_i/t_c) + \gamma f/t_c + \delta(f/t_c)^2 \tag{3}$$

where x_a is agricultural production, t_c the land under cultivation (multicropped land being counted only once), t_i the irrigated land, and f the input of fertilisers expressed in terms of plant nutrients.

As irrigated land is included in the land under cultivation, its marginal productivity is $(\alpha + \beta)$. The magnitude of the coefficients implies that irrigated land is four times more productive than unirrigated land. This finding reflects the impact of a controlled supply of water both on yields and on increasing the number of crops which can be grown in a single year.

Strout's estimates of yields after the application of fertiliser are on the whole consistent with other cross-section estimates (see e.g. P. Timmer (1976)). However, they exceed by some 50 per cent the results indicated by field tests (see e.g. the results quoted by Timmer (1974)). This discrepancy probably results from the fact that in cross-section data, fertiliser use is positively correlated with the know-how of farmers and the natural fertility of the land, so that regression estimates of these yields are biased upward.

The last term in equation (3) tries to capture diminishing returns in fertiliser use, a tendency confirmed by field tests and by regression estimates. Again, experience in individual developing countries is less encouraging than is indicated by the regressions based on cross-section data which includes both developing and developed countries. According to Timmer (1975) and J. Mellor and R. Herdt (1964), this discrepancy may reflect basic differences in growing conditions in temperate and tropical climates. What is certainly true is that new growing techniques and improved seeds are required if heavier doses of fertilisers are to be effective. Caution is therefore needed in using regression estimates of fertiliser yields.

An obvious omission from the specification above is labour, for which Strout was unable to estimate reasonable coefficients. As development proceeds, the increase in human and physical capital per agricultural worker more than compensates for the migration of labour out of that sector. Intensity of cultivation therefore rises while labour input declines. Furthermore, at the latest stages of development, production tends to be concentrated on the most fertile lands, because marginal land cannot be exploited economically at the prevailing high wages.

The lack of good econometric estimates of the marginal productivity of labour in agriculture does not mean, however, that this variable is zero. The majority of development economists today reject the once prevalent view that an unproductive labour surplus exists in agriculture. A classical summation of the reasons for this view is to be found in T. Schultz (1964). Using the wage rate in agriculture as an indicator of the marginal productivity of labour, Lele and Mellor (1964) estimated that the marginal productivity of labour in agriculture is 40 per cent of its average productivity. This figure is very close to the result obtained by H. Chenery (1970) for developing economies. He tried to explain the economic performance of a sample of developing countries in terms of key growth factors (labour, force, rate of saving, ratios of capital inflow and exports to GNP, and labour). His estimates imply an elasticity of 0.4 for GNP with respect to the labour force, about half the coefficient found for developing countries, but still definitely not zero.

Estimated equations

The agricultural production function of our model is based on the specification proposed by Strout. We applied it to data for 78 countries developed by B. Choe of the World Bank, who participated in the estimation of the function presented below. While Strout's own data were aggregated over regions and covered developed as well as developing countries, Choe's data distinguished individual countries and covered the developing world only. Further, to minimise distortions due to weather, Choe's time-series were aggregated into three periods: 1965–7, 1968–70 and 1971–4, yielding four observations per country.

Not surprisingly, the correlation coefficient of 0.542 obtained by Choe was substantially poorer than that reported by Strout – 0.964. Aggregation of countries into regions improves the fit, because the intercountry differences in fertility which account for much of the regression residuals tend to average out when the data is averaged over regions. The inclusion of developed countries in Strout's data 'stretched his sample' and improved the correlation coefficient. What is notable, however, is that the order of magnitude of coefficients is the same in both estimates, and the coefficients are quite significant in both. The major difference is the larger value of the coefficient, in the estimate that does not include data for developed countries. It reflects the diminishing marginal productivity of fertilisers. This result is understandable in view of the remarks made above about the differences in growing conditions in tropical and temperate climates.

It was decided to introduce labour into the equation used in our model so that the contribution of labour to agricultural output could be reflected. The variable we introduced is the difference between actual labour input and the labour input which would normally correspond to a country's level of development. This 'normal labour supply' is calculated using a function of the type used by H. Chenery and M. Syrquin in their recent book on patterns of economic growth (1975). The relation we obtained was the basis for calculating the 'normal labour supply' in agriculture for each year in the base case simulation. The levels arrived at were then made exogenous, so that the 'normal labour supply' was identical in each simulation of the model. The coefficient of the $(1_a - 1_a^*)$ term implies that the marginal productivity of agricultural labour equalled 40 per cent of its average productivity in 1975.

Finally, we wanted a production function which would reproduce the 1961–75 experience. For this purpose a constant term was introduced into the equation, and coefficients other than labour were adjusted proportionately to ensure that the function was capable of predicting exactly 1961 and 1975 production levels.[1]

The production function obtained is given in the appendix to this paper.

IV. THE RESPONSE OF AGRICULTURAL INPUTS

It is useful to distinguish between the short- and the long-run responses of inputs to changes in agricultural prices. In the short run, prices can affect the amount of land put into production or the number of crops to be harvested. More careful husbandry offers latitude for increasing output by raising labour inputs. Farmers may use more or less fertilisers.

In the long run changes in prices can affect capital and labour supply. Through their influence on incomes, prices can affect incentives to migrate from agriculture to other sectors. The ability and willingness of farmers to improve and extend their land also depends on the level of their incomes.

Specification of the fertiliser input function

The short-run responses of inputs of labour and land to price changes are hard to study in quantitative terms because of an absence of data. With some exceptions, such as Argentina, the amount of land under cultivation in developing countries is not affected sharply, and the data necessary for accurately measuring short-run changes are not available. Weather also affects the responses in terms of the feasibility and extent of multicropping and the area of land which can be harvested.

There is even less data on short-run changes in labour inputs. The chief sources of information on the agricultural labour force are censuses, but these are useful only in mapping out long-term trends.

Fertilisers are the only input for which it is possible to observe short-run fluctuations. Not surprisingly, therefore, numerous studies of the response of fertiliser demand to prices are available. An excellent survey of these has been done by P. Timmer, who concluded that the short-run elasticity of demand for fertilisers in response to prices is around -0.5, whereas the long-run elasticity is as high as -1.5 to -2.0. In our model, the price response of fertiliser demand is assumed equal to -1.0.

The function used in the model also reflects long-run factors which influence demand for fertilisers. One of these is the increase in cultivated and irrigated areas. The coefficients assume that fertiliser input per unit of output on

---

[1]The proportional adjustment of the estimated coefficients also allows for differences between the domestic prices used in the model to value production, and the somewhat arbitrary prices used by both Strout and Choe to evaluate output.

irrigated and unirrigated land is equal in any given year.[1] Fertiliser input coefficients are also markedly influenced by trends in the development of new fertilisers which provide intensive high yields and the improved understanding by farmers of the role of fertilisers in increasing output. A coefficient for the trends was chosen that assumes that demand for fertilisers will grow by 80 per cent over the next 10 years if prices do not change, the situation predicted by the forecasts of specialists for the agriculture of South Asia (see e.g. the forecast for India by W. Hendrix (1975)).

The long-run response of the labour force: background and specification

Many studies, the most important of which are those of Colin Clarke (1940), Simon Kuznets (1971) and H. C. Chenery (1975), have identified and measured the long-run relation between GNP per head and the share of the labour force in agriculture. Their work has put in quantitative focus the massive urban migration of workers which is a part of the growth process. It is generally accepted that economic incentives are the main force behind this movement. The best known statement of this idea is that of J. Harris and M. Todaro (1970), which has inspired a great deal of work on individual countries. Recently Linneman *et al.* (1975) and Y. Mundlak (1976) have estimated, using cross-sections of countries, functions which explicitly link rural–urban migrations to income differentials, as well as to other variables.

Our model's equations are based on the estimates of Mundlak. We have adjusted his multiplicative constant to match migration between 1960 and 1970 to observed data. The specification used is given in the appendix to this paper.

The long-run response of capital and land: background and specification

Changes in agricultural prices affect both the incentive to increase agricultural output and the ability of farmers to purchase required equipment and materials. By influencing rural purchasing power, prices affect the ability of local authorities to finance investments in local infrastructure, which play an important role in facilitating increases in production. Prices probably influence even the decisions of the central government by making clearer the profitability of investment projects.

We do not know of any studies specifying agricultural investment equations for developing countries, and it is doubtful that it will be possible to estimate good functions for this aggregate. This is in part due to lack of data. The first broad set of data on agricultural investment in the developing world was published in the *World Tables*, but the series do not go back beyond 1967 and are too short for estimations except in country cross-sections. The national

---

[1]This implies that *per hectare* input is four times as high on irrigated as on unirrigated land.

accounting series are heavily influenced by large public investment projects in irrigation and rural electrification and do not give a good measure of the efforts of farmers to improve and extend their farms. Many of the farmers' efforts involve their own labour and local materials. The only 'statistically visible' component – purchases of tractors and agricultural implements – probably represents only a fraction of actual total investment in developing countries.

In the absence of good econometric data, we decided to adopt a crude but it is hoped sensible representation of the response. It is based on four assumptions:

(a) In the central variant of the model, irrigated and non-irrigated areas were assumed to grow at rates corresponding to the projections for India made by Hendrix (1975).

(b) The coefficients of the investment-response function assumed that investment by farmers accounts for 80 per cent and 40 per cent of the increases in non-irrigated and irrigated areas respectively. They allow for government investment in land reclamation, extension of government canals and the contribution of rural electrification to the spread of tubewell irrigation.

(c) The extension of the cultivated area due to private efforts is assumed to be proportional to the savings of farmers, as predicted by the appropriate ELES function.

(d) The extension due to government efforts was assumed to be exogenous. In the base case solution it increases at the rate projected for India for Hendrix for the increase in total cultivated and irrigated areas.

V. RESULTS OF MODEL SIMULATIONS

As 1974 was the last year for which we had complete data, the model was used to simulate the period 1974–84. Simulations were made as though the period 1974–84 were entirely in the future, so that any changes, e.g. in economic policies, would have come into force in 1975. The results are therefore to be taken as indicators of the impact of policies pursued over a decade, rather than as a calculation of goals which are achievable by 1984. Table 12.1 provides a summary of the main results of the simulations.

The base case results

The base case projection of the model, which assumed unchanged domestic agricultural prices, indicates a sharp deterioration in the agricultural trade balance.

A direct comparison with the results of other studies is not possible. The $5.3 billion deterioration predicted by our model covers all agricultural products, whereas other studies have focused on foodgrains only. However, our model does seem to give more pessimistic projections than do other studies. At 1974 prices, the predicted increase in the deficit is equivalent to 29 million tons of grains, roughly double the deterioration foreseen by other studies.

The discrepancy undoubtedly results in part from the inclusion in our study of all agricultural products and not just foodgrains. We suspect, however, that a more important reason is our use of a demand function which is responsive to prices, instead of the regressions of food demand on income used by others. The relative price of agricultural products had risen during the sample period (though there was a sharp fall in 1975). Price-sensitive demand functions such as ours tend, then, to yield higher income elasticities than do straight regressions of consumption on income.

The base case simulation implies that the gap between urban and rural incomes will widen, whereas in the past the ratio between the two has been roughly constant. This reflects the assumption that agricultural prices will cease to rise as compared with urban incomes. It can be calculated that agricultural products will account for a fifth of the increase of per capita consumer spending over the coming decade.

It is interesting to distinguish between the contribution to output resulting from extending the cultivated area and from higher per hectare applications of fertilisers. Increases in cultivated areas would account for 53 per cent of the increase in output, greater use of fertilisers for the balance. Diminishing returns for fertiliser use would set in as follows: the marginal yield of fertilisers would drop from the equivalent of 15.6 kilograms of foodgrains per kilogram of plant nutrients in 1974 to 14.1 kilograms in 1984.

The model's response to population growth and to growth of the urban sector

We ran two simulations to test the sensitivity of the agricultural trade gap to the rate of growth of population and of the urban sector. They indicated that the gap is not very sensitive to the kind of reduction in population growth which may be hoped for in the next decade. A 0.3 per cent drop in the rate of population growth would reduce the trade gap by $0.9 billion. This decline would result entirely from a decrease in consumption. The agricultural labour force would grow more slowly than before, and this would have a negative impact on output. That impact, however, would be entirely offset by an increase in per capita saving and investment by farmers which would occur as a result of faster growth of their per capita incomes.

Given a 1 per cent acceleration in the rate of growth of output of the non-agricultural sector, a $2.0 billion increase in the agricultural trade deficit would result. The ratio of urban to rural incomes would rise by 21 per cent as compared with 8 per cent in the base case, but that change would have only a small impact on migration out of agriculture.

It appears that the migration function used in the model is not very sensitive to income disparities.

The model's response to prices

The trade gap would respond strongly to a 1 per cent per annum increase in the ratio of agricultural to non-agricultural prices. Consumption would drop by

200 *Economic Growth and Resources*

$1.1 billion, production increase by $2.4 billion. As a result, the trade gap would fall by more than half.

The increase in farm incomes would then outstrip that of urban workers with farmers benefiting from the increase in output generated by the price increase as well as from that increase itself. The rate of growth of their nominal incomes would be 1.5 per cent higher than in the base case. In real terms – allowing for the higher price of food which they consume – the improvement would be 1.4 per cent.

It is interesting to calculate the supply response of the net sales of farmers – the much debated net supply response of subsistence agriculture (see e.g. J. Behrman (1968)). Higher prices would lead to a 1.7 per cent increase in the food consumption of farmers, because of the impact on their incomes, while, as a result of reduced migration, farm population would exceed by 0.5 per cent the figure derived in the base case. Hence slightly more than half of the 4.2 per cent increase in agricultural output would be retained on the farm, to be consumed there.

An 'accelerated growth' solution

As a final test of the model, we simulated economic growth in South Asia using assumptions which implied a substantial improvement in economic trends in that area. The assumptions were:

(a) A 2 per cent increase in the rate of growth of non-agricultural output. This could be achieved without any increase in the investment rate by reducing the incremental capital/output ratio to the level achieved in many other developing countries.
(b) A 1.6 per cent per year increase in agricultural prices to maintain rural incomes in balance with urban incomes and to keep the agricultural trade gap from growing to unmanageable proportions.
(c) A gradual drop in the rate of population growth to a level in 1984 which would be 0.3 per cent lower than that assumed in the base case.
(d) Increases of 30 per cent in both the government's and farmers' activities to extend cultivated and irrigated areas. For government this could be achieved by better upkeep of canals and drainage and by stepping up the spread of rural electrification. The investments of farmers could be promoted by improving the rural credit network and similar measures.

The model suggests that, given these assumptions, there would be a balanced increase of rural and urban incomes, with per capita rates of growth of 3.3 per cent and 3.5 per cent per year respectively. These gains would tend to accelerate over the period. What is interesting is that the agricultural trade gap would remain manageable: it would increase by $1.3 billion, equivalent to 7 million tons of foodgrains.

TABLE 12.1   MAIN RESULTS OF THE SIMULATIONS[a]

	Base year 1974	Base case 1984	Low population growth 1984	High urban growth 1984	Agricultural price increase 1984	Growth take off 1984
Growth rate: agricultural prices	–	0.000	0.000	0.000	0.010	0.0160
Growth rate: non-agricultural output	–	0.052	0.052	0.062	0.052	0.0720
Population growth rate	–	0.026	0.023	0.026	0.026	0.0245
Fertiliser consumption (mil. tons NPK)	3.69	6.58 6.0	6.60 6.0	6.58 6.0	7.40 7.2	8.43 9.0
Net arable land (millions ha)	228.10	243.30 0.6	243.40 0.6	243.30 0.6	244.60 0.7	251.50 1.0
Net irrigated land (millions ha)	53.20	71.10 2.9	71.20 2.9	71.20 2.9	21.90 3.1	80.20 4.2
Agricultural labour force (mil. workers)	198.40	237.80 1.8	230.80 1.5	237.10 1.8	238.70 1.9	234.60 1.7
Rural–urban migration (mil. workers)	1.37	1.94 3.5	1.83 2.9	2.05 4.1	1.78 2.7	1.81 2.8
Agricultural production (bil. 1974 $)	43.00	53.80 2.3	53.80 2.3	53.90 2.3	56.10 2.7	59.80 3.3
Per cap. income, farm pop. (1974 $)	84.60	87.50 0.3	90.20 0.6	87.60 0.4	101.50 1.8	117.40 3.3
Per cap. income, urban pop. (1974 $)	150.90	169.60 1.2	175.80 1.5	187.30 2.2	170.70 1.2	212.90 3.5
Urban labour force (mil. workers)	101.20	149.50 4.0	144.20 3.6	150.20 4.0	148.50 3.9	146.40 3.7
Per cap. consumption, agric. prod., farm pop. (1974 $)	51.60	52.40 0.2	53.20 0.2	52.50 0.2	53.30 0.2	55.50 0.7
Per cap. consumption, agric. prod., urban pop. (1974 $)	70.60	75.90 0.7	77.70 1.0	81.00 1.4	71.60 0.1	79.20 1.1
Per cap. saving farm pop. (1974 $)	10.10	10.60 0.5	11.10 0.9	10.70 0.5	12.50 2.2	14.90 3.9
Total consumption, agric. prod., (bil. $)	43.60	59.70 3.2	58.90 3.1	61.70 3.5	58.60 3.0	61.70 3.5
Agric. imports (bil. 1974 $)	0.58	5.92	5.06	7.86	2.48	1.90

[a] In each column, the first number indicates the level reached by the variable in the given year, the second its 1974–84 rate of growth.

Equations (Notations on these equations follow below.)

Consumption, saving of farmers and personal incomes

$$q_a = \frac{1.062}{p_a} \{n_a[34.04p_a + 0.269(y_a - 34.04p_a + 3.58p_o)]$$
$$+ n_o[40.92p_a + 0.269(y_a - 40.92p_a - 15.1p_o)]\}$$
$$s_a = 0.186[y_a - 34.04p_a + 3.58p_o]$$
$$y_a = (p_ax_a - p_ff)/n_a$$
$$y_o = 36399(1.052)^t/n_o$$

Production function

$$x_a = 15,484 + 3.256f + 44.050t_c^{-1} + 121.0t_i^{-1} - 0.012(f^2/t_c^{-1})$$
$$+ 81.26(l_a - 1_a^*)$$
$$1_a^* = 0.015\, l_ae[1.79661ny - 0.1924(1ny)^2]$$
$$y = [n_ay_a + n_oy_o]/[n_a + n_o]$$

Agricultural input response

$$f = (p_a/p_f)(9.347(t_c - t_i) + 35.027t_i)(1 + 0.055t)(0.307\, \ln((y_o - 0.9y_a)/y_a)$$
$$+ 0.571\, \ln(l_o/l_a) + 9.867\, \ln(1 + n))$$
$$l_m = 0.0082\, l_ae$$
$$l_a = (1 + n)l_a^{-1} - l_m$$
$$n_a = 2.51\, l_a$$
$$1 = 299(1 + n)^t$$
$$l_o = 1 - l_a$$
$$n_o = 2.51\, l_o$$
$$t_c = 0.00022s_an_a + 0.25844(1.0057)^{t-1} + t_c^{-1}$$
$$t_i = 0.00013s_an_a + 0.29928(1.029)^{t-1} + t_i^{-1}$$

Agricultural import gap

$$m_a = q_a - x_a$$

Notations

Endogenous variables:

f   Fertiliser consumption, thousands tons NPK
l_a Labour force in agriculture, millions workers
l_a^* Labour force equation, 'normal level' predicted by patterns of growth equation, millions workers
l_o Labour force, non-agricultural sector, millions workers
l_m Number of workers migrating from rural to urban areas, millions workers
l   Labour force, millions workers
m_a Net imports of agricultural products, millions 1974 dollars
n_a Rural population, millions persons
n_o Urban population, millions persons
q_a Consumption of agricultural products, millions 1974 dollars
s_a Savings of farmers, 1974 dollars
t_c Net cultivated area, millions hectares
t_i Net irrigated area, millions hectares
x_a Agricultural production, millions 1974 dollars
y   Average income per head in South Asia, 1974 dollars
y_a Income per head in agriculture in South Asia, 1974 dollars
y_o Income per head in non-agricultural sector in South Asia, 1974 dollars

Exogenous variables:

n   Rate of growth of the population and of the labour force
p_a Agricultural prices
p_o Prices of non-agricultural products
p_f Prices of fertilisers

REFERENCES

Behrman, Jere R., *Supply Response in Traditional Agriculture: A Case Study of Four Major Annual Crops in Thailand in 1937–63* (Amsterdam, North-Holland, 1968).
Blakeslee, Leroy L., Earl O. Heady and Charles F. Framingham, *World Food Production, Demand, and Trade* (Iowa State University Press, 1973).
Chenery, Hollis B. and Hazel Elkington, 'A Uniform Analysis of Development Patterns', Discussion Draft, July 1970.
Chenery, Hollis B. and Moises Syrquin, *Patterns of Development, 1950–1970* (Oxford University Press, 1975).
Clarke, Colin, *The Conditions of Economic Progress* (Second edition 1951, Third edition 1957) (Macmillan, 1940).
Choe, Boem, Marc Osterrieth and Jean Waelbroeck, 'Agricultural Prospects of Developing Countries', Discussion Draft (forthcoming in *Proceedings of the Fourth Conference on Global Modeling*, International Institute for Applied Systems, Vienna), 1976.

Food and Agriculture Organisation, *Assessment of the World Food Situation, Present and Future* (Rome, 1974).

Hadler, Sandra, 'Developing Countries Foodgrains Projections for 1985', IBRD Working Paper, 1976.

Harris, J. R. and M. P. Todaro, 'Migration, Unemployment, and Development: A Two Sector Analysis', *American Economic Review*, 60 (1970), 126–42.

Heady, Earl Q. and John L. Dillon, *Agricultural Production Functions* (Iowa State University Press, 1961).

Hendrix, William E., 'Foodgrain Supply and Demand Situation and Prospects for Eleven Asian Nations', World Bank Agricultural and Rural Development Department Working Paper, 1975.

Herdt, Robert W. and John Mellon, 'The Contrasting Response of Rice to Nitrogen: India and the United States', *Journal of Farm Economics*, XLV (1964), 150–60.

Hoogh, Jan De, Michiel De Keyzer, Hans Linneman and H. D. J. Van Heemst, 'Food for a Growing World Population', in Gerhart Bruckman (ed.), *Moira: Food and Agriculture Model, Proceedings of the Third IIASA Conference on Global Modeling*, September 22–25, 1975, International Institute for Applied Systems Analysis, Vienna, 1977.

IFPRI, 'Meeting Food Needs in the Developing World', Research Report No. 1, Washington, DC, 1976.

Kuznets, Simon, *Economic Growth of Nations: Total Output and Production Structure* (Cambridge, Bellknap Press of Harvard University, 1971).

Lele, Uma and John W. Mellor, 'Estimates of Changes and Causes of Changes in Foodgrains Production, India 1949–50 to 1960–61', *Cornell International Development Bulletin 2* (Cornell University, Ithaca, 1964).

Linneman, Hans, 'Food for a Doubling World Population Project', Discussion Draft, 1975.

Lluch, Constantino, 'The Extended Linear Expenditures System', *European Economic Review* (April 1973), 21–32.

Lluch, Constantino, Alan Powell and Ross Williams, 'Household Demand and Savings in Economic Development: Applications of Linear Demand Systems', Discussion Draft, 1975.

Mellor, John W., *The Economics of Agricultural Development* (Cornell University Press, 1966).

Mellor, John W., Uma Lele, Debra Biamante and Arthur Goldsmith, 'Estimates of Foodgrains Production and Marketing from Input Estimates, India, 1949–50 to 1973–74, and Projections to 1983–84', Occasional Paper No. 83, Cornell University – USAID Employment and Income Distribution Project, Department of Agricultural Economics, Cornell University, 1975.

Mellor, John W., 'The Economics of Growth', *A Strategy for India and the Developing World*, Twentieth Century Fund Study (Cornell University Press, 1976).

Mundlak, Yair, 'Migration In and Out of Agriculture – Empirical Analysis Based on Country Data', Discussion Draft, International Fund Policy Research Institute, Washington, DC, 1976.

Strout, Alan, 'World Agricultural Potential, Evidence from the Recent Past', Discussion Draft, 1975.

Schultz, Theodoro W., *Transforming Traditional Agriculture* (New Haven Yale University Press, 1964).

Systems Analysis Research Unit, 'Systems Analysis Research Unit Model (SARUM)', Discussion Draft 1976.

Timmer, Peter, 'The Demand for Fertilizers in Developing Countries', Stanford Rice Project Working Paper No. 5, 1974.

Timmer, Peter, 'The Political Economy of Rice in Asia, Lessons and Implications', Discussion Draft, 1975.

Timmer, Peter, 'Fertilizers and Food Policy in Developing Countries', Discussion Draft, 1976.

Weisskoff, Richard, 'Demand Elasticities for a Developing Economy, An International Comparison of Consumption Patterns', in Hollis B. Chenery (ed.), *Studies in Developing Planning* (Harvard University Press, 1971).

Index

Entries in the Index in bold type under the names of participants in the Conference indicate their Papers.